Pocket-Watch Slide Rules

Peter M. Hopp, C. Eng. M.B.C.S.

Copyright © Peter M. Hopp C.Eng. M.B.C.S., 2011

All rights reserved. Including under all international and Pan American Copyright Conventions. No part of this publication may be displayed, reproduced, or transmitted in any form or by any means, electronic, mechanical, including the internet, photocopying, recording or any other storage and retrieval system now known or to be invented, except by a reviewer who wishes to quote brief passages in connection with a review written for inclusion in a magazine, newspaper or broadcast.

ISBN: 978-1-931626-31-6

Published by
Astragal Press
An Imprint of Finney Company
8075 215th Street West
Lakeville, Minnesota 55044

www.finneyco.com
www.astragalpress.com

Table of Contents

Pocket-Watch Slide Rules	I
Acknowledgments	1
Preface	2
Introduction	3
Definition of a Pocket-Watch Slide Rule	3
Historical Review	4
Patents	5
Pre-Boucher Calculating Rules	8
Pocket-Watch Slide Rule Patents Post Boucher	10
Other Pocket-Watch Calculators	14
Summary	15
Pocket-Watch Slide Rules of the World	16
Manufacturers	16
Families of Pocket-Watch Calculators	19
The Boucher Calculator	20
Introduction	20
The Patent	20
Implementations	22
Manufacturers	23
Calculigraphe	29
Introduction	29
Other Retailers of 'Standard' Calculigraphes	32
Other Versions of Calculigraphes	34
Summary	36
Meyrat & Perdrizet Pocket-Watch Calculators	40
Introduction	40
Types of Calculator	40
Lord's Pocket-Watch Calculator	42
Introduction	42
Lord's Patents	42
Types of Lord's Pocket-Watch Calculators	43
Summary	48
Keuffel and Esser (K&E) Pocket-Watch Calculators	49
Introduction	49
K&E Catalogues	49
Early K&E Pocket-Watch Devices	51
K&E Patents	51
Sperry / K&E Pocket-Watch Slide Rules	52
Summary	56
'Scientific Publishing' Pocket-Watch Calculator	57
Introduction	57
History	57

Pocket-Watch Type Calculators	57
The 'Mechanical Engineer' (ME) Calculator	58
Other SPC Pocket-Watch Calculators	60
Summary	63
Fowler's Pocket-Watch Calculators	64
Introduction	64
Fowler's Patents	64
Fowler's Design Changes	66
Serial Numbering	67
Calculator Types	67
Fowler as Manufacturer	84
Halden's Calculex	86
Introduction	86
Calculex Type Patents	86
Calculex Developments	89
Calculex Variants	92
Evolution of the Calculex and Numbers Made	94
Other Calculexes	96
The 'Desk' Model Calculex	97
Gebr. Wichmann's Pocket-Watch Calculators	100
Introduction	100
Wichmann Catalogues	100
Fact or Fantasy - Gebr. Wichmann Calculexes	101
Molter Pocket-Watch Calculators	104
Introduction	104
History	104
Summary	105
Schacht Und Westerich's Pocket-Watch Calculators	106
Introduction	106
Types of Calculator	106
Russian Pocket-Watch Calculators	109
Introduction	109
Types of Calculators	109
Russian Calculex	111
Other Pocket-Watch Calculators	112
Introduction	112
Breitling	112
John Davis & Son	112
Dyson	112
Frappant A.G., Berlin, Germany	113
Heckendorf, Berlin, Germany	113
Lancashire Optical Manufacturing Co. Ltd.	113
Ollech & Wajs GEC Slide Rule	114
H. Reiss GmBH.	114
Rechen-Max Calculex Look-alike	114
Selectron Model A	115
Selectron Model B	115

Unattributable Pocket-Watch Calculators	116
Introduction	116
Unattributable Calculigraphe-like Device	116
Unattributable Watch-Pocket Device	117
Unattributable Calculator	117
Undiscovered Pocket-Watch Calculators	118
Introduction	118
Watch Slide Rules	120
Introduction	120
Patents	120
Early Watch Slide Rules	122
Watch Slide Rules	124
Breitling	124
Seiko and TAG Heuer	124
Pocket Cash Registers	125
Pocket-Watch Exposure Meters	127
Watch Pocket Calculators	129
The Graphoplex Roplex	129
Key Chain Calculator	129
The Small Calculator	130
The Supermathic	130
The Calculimetre	130
Glossary	131
Notes on Makers of Pocket-Watch Rules	133
Makers & Retailers of Pocket-Watch Rules - Alphabetical	134
Unknown Makers	158
Appendix 1	159
Instructions for the Calculigraphe	159
Instructions for Russian Pocket-Watch Slide Rules	160
Instructions for the Calculigraphe A.F.	162
Appendix 2	164
Bibliography	166
Late Additions	167
Manlove Alliott & Co Limited	167

Figures and Tables

Figure 1.1:	International Currency Watch	8
Figure 1.2:	A Drawing from Lefevre's Patent	9
Figure 2.1:	Thomas Mudd's Patent of 1888	10
Figure 2.2:	Front Dial Shown on Wilkinson & Gibson's Patent	10
Figure 2.3:	Wilson's Patent, 1903	11
Figure 2.4:	E.A. Sperry's Patent, 1904	11
Figure 2.5:	Hinks Patent, 1904	11
Figure 2.6:	Oelschlager's Patent, 1909	11
Figure 2.7:	Watts' Patent, 1912	12
Figure 2.8:	Brunton's Patent, 1913	12
Figure 2.9:	Eastwood's Patent, 1917	12
Figure 2.10:	Zénith Patent, 1918	13
Figure 2.11:	The Brotherton Patent, 1921	13
Figure 2.12a:	Robinson's Patent, 1926	13
Figure 2.12b:	Robinson's Patent, 1926	13
Figure 2.13:	Scale for Robinson's Calculator	13
Figure 3.1:	Moko Lightning Calculator	14
Figure 3.2:	Unknown Pocket-Watch Adding Machine	14
Figure 3.3:	Other Pocket-Watch Devices for Various Uses	14
Figure 4.1:	Boucher's Pocket-Watch Calculator	20
Figure 4.2:	Very Early Boucher Calculator with the "AB" Signature, Made in France	21
Figure 4.3:	Early Boucher Calculator with the "AB" Signature, and Different Scale Layout	21
Figure 4.4:	Early Boucher Calculator with the "AB" Signature, on Metal Face in its Case	22
Figure 4.5:	Boucher's Calculator - Desk Version	22
Figure 4.6:	Boucher's Desk Calculator and on its Wooden Stand	23
Figure 4.7:	Flyer for Boucher's Calculator from the 1898 Stanley Catalogue	24
Figure 4.8:	From the 1931 Stanley Catalogue Illustrating the Two Versions	25
Figure 4.9:	Boucher's Calculator by Stanley (Back and Front)	25
Figure 4.10:	Boucher's Calculator by Stanley with Additional Rev Counter on the Back Face	25
Figure 4.11:	Boucher's Calculator from Manloves	26
Figure 4.12:	Boucher's Calculator from Manlove, Alliott & Fryer	26
Figure 4.13:	Nouveau Calculigraphe from H. Morin, 1910	27
Figure 4.14:	1907 Army and Navy Stores Catalogue	27
Figure 4.15:	Boucher's Calculator by K&E from Cajori, 1909	28
Figure 4.16:	Boucher's Calculator from Queen	28
Figure 5.1:	H-C Thin Calculigraphe	29
Figure 5.2:	F-C Calculigraphe	31
Figure 5.3:	1894 Single Dial FC Calculigraphe	31
Figure 5.4:	1902 Halden Catalogue	32
Figure 5.5:	French H-C Calculigraphe with Address for L. Fischer	33
Figure 5.6:	Callculigraphe pour Reports de Bourse	33
Figure 5.7:	A-F Calculigraphe - Swiss	34
Figure 5.8:	A-F Calculigraphe - Fabrique en France	34
Figure 5.9:	Pedos S.A. Instructions for the A-F Calculigraphe	35
Figure 5.10:	F-C Logo	37
Figure 5.11:	H-C Logo	37

Figure 5.12:	Showing Side Views of 'fat' and 'thin' Calculigraphe, and Internal View of 'thin' Calculigraphe	37
Figure 6.1:	M&P Type 1 With Watch Movement Inc. Second Hand	40
Figure 6.2:	M&P Type 1 Showing the Watch Movement	40
Figure 6.3:	M&P Type 2 Calculator Without Watch Movement	40
Figure 6.4a:	M&P Rear of Type 2 Calculator	41
Figure 6.4b:	M&P Calculator	41
Figure 6.5:	A Section from the 1899 M&P Instruction Book	41
Figure 7.1:	Front View of Lord's Desk Calculator from Patent 22,210	42
Figure 7.2:	Rear View of Lord's Desk Calculator from Patent 22,210	42
Figure 7.3:	Desk Calculator Made by Elliott Bros.	43
Figure 7.4:	Pocket-Watch Calculator from Patent 7,081	43
Figure 7.5:	Type 1 Lord's Calculator from Elliott Bros.	43
Figure 7.6:	Type 1 Lord's Calculators from W. Waddington and R. Waddington of Coventry, and J. Casartelli & Son of Machester	44
Figure 7.7:	Type 2 Lord's Calculator, Unknown Maker	45
Figure 7.8:	Type 2 Lord's Calculator, Unknown Maker (2)	45
Figure 7.9:	Type 2 Lords Calculator from W.Wilson, London, Front and the Blank Rear.	46
Figure 7.10:	Type 3 Lord's Calculator from W. Wilson, London, Front and Rear Faces.	46
Figure 7.11:	Type 4 Lord's Calculator from W. Wilson, London, Front and Rear Faces.	47
Figure 8.1:	1895 K&E Catalogue	49
Figure 8.2:	Text Cut from 1903 K&E Catalogue	50
Figure 8.3:	Illustration of K&E 4016 and 4017 Early Calculators from 1906 Catalogue	50
Figure 8.4:	Illustration of K&E 4017 and 4018 Early Calculators and Charpentier 4020 from the 1909 Catalogue	51
Figure 8.5:	K&E Boucher from Cajori	51
Figure 8.6:	Boucher and Instructions from K&E	51
Figure 8.7:	E.A. Sperry 1904 Patent	52
Figure 8.8:	G. Lange 1907 Patent	52
Figure 8.9:	E.A. Sperry 1928 Patent	52
Figure 8.10:	Early Sperry Calculator	53
Figure 8.11:	Sperry 1904 Patent Calculator	53
Figure 8.12:	Type 3c Calculator	54
Figure 8.13:	Sperry 1911 Patent Calculator	54
Figure 8.14:	Sperry 'Patent Applied for' Type 4a Calculator	54
Figure 8.15:	Sperry 'Patent Applied for' Type 4a Example 2	55
Figure 9.1	SPC 'Mechanical Engineer' Calculators Various	58
Figure 9.2:	Single Scale ME	58
Figure 9.3:	ME Marked 'Swiss Make' on Dial	59
Figure 9.4:	1901 SP Advert	59
Figure 9.5:	1909 SP Advert	59
Figure 9.6:	1913 SP Advert for the 1910 Patent Calculator	60
Figure 9.7:	Fowler's Patent Calculator by SPC	60
Figure 9.8:	Fowler's Patent Calculator	60
Figure 9.9:	Scientific Publishing Type O (The Patent Pocket Calculator)	61
Figure 9.10:	Scientific Publishing Textile Calculator	61
Figure 9.11:	Scientific Publishing Type T Textile Calculator	62
Figure 9.12:	Type T Textile Calculator with Yellow Lens and Showing Mechanism	62
Figure 9.13:	Fowler & Co Type M Textile Calculator	62

Figure 9.14:	ME Marked 'Swiss' on the Axle	63
Figure 10.1:	Fowler Patent 5,528	64
Figure 10.2:	Fowler Patent 20,416	65
Figure 10.3:	Fowler Patent 3,638	65
Figure 10.4:	Fowler Patent 15,990	65
Figure 10.5:	Fowler Patent 215,648	66
Figure 10.6:	Fowler Calculator Logo	66
Figure 10.7:	Construction of Early Calculators	66
Figure 10.8:	Cast and Pressed Steel Cases	67
Figure 10.9:	Fowler Spanner	67
Figure 10.10:	Fowler Calculator	67
Figure 10.11:	Fowler Calculator (Later Version) Type R	68
Figure 10.12:	Type H, RX and R Fowler Calculators	68
Figure 10.13:	Fowler Type A Calculator	69
Figure 10.14:	Fowler Type B Textile Calculator Various	69
Figure 10.15:	Fowler Type E1 Textile Calculator	70
Figure 10.16:	Fowler Type E1 Textile Calculator, Different Mechanism	70
Figure 10.17:	Type H Textile Calculator (Early)	71
Figure 10.18:	Type H Textile Calculator (Later Version)	71
Figure 10.19:	Type H from the Fowler Leaflet	71
Figure 10.20:	Fowler Type M Textile Calculator	72
Figure 10.21:	Fowler Type O Calculator	72
Figure 10.22:	Fowler Type T Textile Calculator	72
Figure 10.23:	Fowler Textile Conversion Calculator	73
Figure 10.24:	Fowler Short Scale Textile Calculator (Early)	73
Figure 10.25:	Fowler Short Scale Textile Calculator (Mid)	73
Figure 10.26:	Fowler Short Scale Textile Calculator (Late)	73
Figure 10.27:	Fowler Long Scale Textile Calculator (Pick Finding)	74
Figure 10.28:	Fowler Long Scale Textile Calculator	74
Figure 10.29:	Fowler Magnum Textile Calculator	74
Figure 10.30:	Fowler Textile Calculator (Type 2)	75
Figure 10.31:	Fowler Universal Calculator	75
Figure 10.32:	Fowler 'Twelve-Ten' Calculator (Bakelite Back)	76
Figure 10.33:	Fowler 'Twelve-Ten' Calculator (Anodised Back)	76
Figure 10.34:	Fowler 'Twelve-Ten' Calculator (Rexine Back)	76
Figure 10.35:	Fowler 'Magnum' Long Scale Calculator	77
Figure 10.36:	Fowler Jubilee 'Magnum' Extra Long Scale Calculator	77
Figure 10.37:	Fowler Long Nautical Calculator	77
Figure 10.38:	Fowler Artillery Calculator (Early)	78
Figure 10.39:	Fowler Artillery Calculator (Later)	78
Figure 10.40:	Fowler Type R from the Advertising Leaflet	78
Figure 10.41:	Fowler Long Scale Type RX	79
Figure 10.42:	Fowler Type RX from the Advertising Leaflet	79
Figure 10.43:	Variant with Type Marking on the Axle	79
Figure 10.44:	Fowler Long Scale Calculator (Early)	79
Figure 10.45:	Fowler Long Scale Calculator (Late)	80
Figure 10.46:	Fowler Long Scale Calculator (Variant)	80
Figure 10.47:	Fowler Long Scale Calculator (Variant 2)	80
Figure 10.48:	Fowler Circular Slide Rule / Fowler's Calculator	81
Figure 10.49:	Fowler Circular Slide Rule / Junior Calculator	81
Figure 10.50:	Fowler Kearns Machine Type Computer	81
Figure 10.51:	Fowler Mackay Paper & Board Calculator	82
Figure 10.52:	Fowler Mackay Paper & Board (Variant)	82
Figure 10.53:	Fowler Bakelite Backs	83

Figure 10.54:	Fowler Bakelite Case	83
Figure 10.55:	Harold Fowler and unknown assistant assembling calculators in the workshop at Oakleigh about 1917	84
Figure 10.56:	Parts for the construction of a Long Scale Calculator, with a completed example, probably taken at the Station Works in around 1929.	85
Figure 10.57:	Cutting head of the machine used for marking out the steel die for a calculator scale, c1929	85
Figure 11.1:	Taken from Wilson Patent	87
Figure 11.2:	A Wilson Calculex	87
Figure 11.3:	H.T. Hinks Patent Calculator	88
Figure 11.4:	All Figures from H.R. Watts US Patent of 1912	88
Figure 11.5:	Halden Type 1 Calculex	91
Figure 11.6:	Halden Type 2 Calculex	91
Figure 11.7:	Halden Type 3 Calculex	92
Figure 11.8:	Variant Type 2 Calculex	92
Figure 11.9:	Variant Type 3 (3a) Calculex	92
Figure 11.10:	Another Variation of the Type 3 (3b) Calculex	92
Figure 11.11:	1915 Halden Catalogue Adverts	93
Figure 11.12:	1925 Halden Catalogue Adverts	93
Figure 11.13:	Halden Calculex Manufacture	96
Figure 11.14:	Yellow Calculex ex Dietzgen	96
Figure 11.15:	Both Sides of a Desk Model Calculex	97
Figure 11.16:	Details of a Desk Calclex,	97
Figure 11.17:	Desk Calculex in its Case	98
Figure 11.18:	Halden Calculex Handbooks	98
Figure 11.19:	Advert from 1931 Dietzgen Catalogue (with a note that the cursor is amber coloured)	99
Figure 11.20:	Early Single-Screw Calculex in Plastic Pill-box Case	99
Figure 12.1:	1910 Gebr. Wichmann Catalogue	100
Figure 12.2:	1920 Gebr. Wichmann Catalogue	101
Figure 12.3:	1939 Gebr. Wichmann Catalogue	101
Figure 12.4:	Wichmann 'Calculex'	102
Figure 12.5:	Labelling on Wichmann 'Calculex'	103
Figure 12.6:	Undated Wichmann Advertising Flyer	103
Figure 13.1:	First Page of Molter's Instructions	104
Figure 13.2:	Molter Calculator Made for Maskin a.b.	104
Figure 13.3:	Pocket-Watch, Unmarked	105
Figure 13.4:	A. Leitz Version of the Molter Calculator	105
Figure 14.1:	Schacht U. Westerich (Molter) 'Very Early' Calculator	106
Figure 14.2:	Schacht U. Westerich (Molter) 'Later' Calculator	106
Figure 14.3:	Schacht U. Westerich (Molter) 'Later' Calculator II	107
Figure 14.4:	Schacht U. Westerich (Molter) 'Later' Calculator Variant	107
Figure 14.5:	Schacht U. Westerich (Molter) 'Pocket-Watch' Calculator	108
Figure 14.6:	S u. W. System Thomas 'Rechenuhr' 1923	108
Figure 14.7:	S u. W 8406 1925	108
Figure 15.1:	Russian 'Matsku' Calculator	109
Figure 15.2:	Russian 'Matsku' Calculator Variant	109
Figure 15.3:	Russian 'Sunrise' Calculator	110
Figure 15.4:	Russian KL-1 Calculator	110
Figure 15.5:	Early Russian Calculator	110
Figure 15.6:	Russian 'Heart' Calculator	111
Figure 15.7:	Unknown Russian Calculex Look-alike	111
Figure 15.8:	Unknown Russian Calculex Look-alike	111

Figure 16.1:	Breitling Stopwatch	112
Figure 16.2:	John Davis Mechanical Engineer Calculator	112
Figure 16.3:	Dyson Calculator	112
Figure 16.4:	Frappant A.G. Advertisement	113
Figure 16.5:	Heckendorf Advertisement	113
Figure 16.6:	Robinson Calculator	113
Figure 16.7:	Reiss 1925 Catalogue	114
Figure 16.8:	H. Reiss (Molter) Calculator	114
Figure 16.9:	Rechen-Max Calculex Look-alike	114
Figure 16.10:	Selectron Timer Model A	115
Figure 16.11:	Selectron Timer Model B	115
Figure 17.1:	Unattributable Calculigraphe-like Device	116
Figure 17.2:	Unattributable Watch-Pocket Device	117
Figure 17.3:	Unattributable Calculator	117
Figure 18.1:	Snippet from 1880 Calculigraphe Instructions	118
Figure 18.2:	Snippet 2 from 1880 Calculigraphe Instructions	118
Figure 18.3:	Snippet 1902 Halden Catalogue	119
Figure 18.4:	Snippet 1903 K&E Catalogue	119
Figure 18.5:	Snippet 1916 Thornton Catalogue	119
Figure 18.6:	Snippet 1895 K&E Catalogue	119
Figure 18.7:	Marking for a K&E Type 4B	119
Figure 18.8:	Marking for a K&E Type 5	119
Figure 19.1:	Homis Watch Co. Patent	120
Figure 19.2:	Walter Moser CH 204,559 Patent	121
Figure 19.3:	Mimo Patent	121
Figure 19.4:	Breitling Patent	121
Figure 19.5:	Details from Wittgenstein's Patent	122
Figure 19.6:	Early Breitling Chronomat Advert	122
Figure 19.7:	Early MIMO Loga	122
Figure 19.8:	Early Breitling Chronomat	122
Figure 19.9:	Early Juvenia Arithmo	123
Figure 19.10:	Early Breitling Navitimer	123
Figure 19.11:	Breitling Watch Slide Rules	124
Figure 19.12:	Watch Slide Rules from Seiko (Either Side) and Heuer	124
Figure 19.13:	Seiko Slide Rule Watch, Early and Late Selectron Watch Slide Rules	124
Figure 19.14:	Ventura 'Design on Time' Slide Rule Watch	124
Figure 20.1:	The American Pocket Cash Register	125
Figure 20.2:	Pocket Register by C. Sebastian	125
Figure 20.3:	The Lafond Cash Register	125
Figure 20.4:	Ken + Add Machine	126
Figure 21.1:	Watkins Bee Pocket-Watch Exposure Meters	127
Figure 21.2:	Watkins Bee Pocket-Watch Exposure Meters 2	127
Figure 21.3:	Watkins Bee Pocket-Watch Exposure Meters 3	128
Figure 21.4:	Wynne and Other Makers Pocket-Watch Exposure Meters	128
Figure 22.1:	Graphoplex Roplex	129
Figure 22.2:	Key-chain Calculator	129
Figure 22.3:	The 'Small' Calculator	130
Figure 22.4:	The Supermathic Calculator	130
Figure 22.5:	The 'Calculimetre' Calculator	130
Figure 1a:	Manloves	136
Figure 1b:	Manlove Alliott & Fryer	136

Tables:

Table 1	Pocket-Watch Slide Rule Patents	5
Table 2	Pocket-Watch Slide Rules: Major Manufacturers and Retailers	18
Table 3	Catalogue of Calculigraphe Markings	38
Table 4	RKO/PMH K&E Pocket-Watch Chronology	56
Table 5	Fowler Pocket-Watch Slide Rule Patents	64
Table 6	Fowler – Serials of Bakelite Backed Examples	82
Table 7	Calculex Type Slide Rule Patents	87
Table 8	Adverts for Calculex Devices	89
Table 9	Calculex Specifications	95
Table 10	Calculex Sales Estimates	95
Table 11	Molter Pocket-Watch Slide Rule Types	105
Table 12	Fowler Models	141
Table 13	K&E Models	146

Acknowledgments

The slide rule collecting fraternity has been their normal generous selves in providing me with loads of germane information, I thank them immensely.

This book would not have been possible without the generosity of Conrad Schure. Conrad made available a vast amount of information and images from his splendid collection – thank you Conrad!

Also deserving of special mention is Dave Green in Australia. Dave very kindly made available to me his collection of about 350 images of pocket-watch and other interesting slide rules which brought to light a number of 'new' designs as well as variants of existing known ones – thanks Dave!

Many others have also contributed. In particular Harold Bailey Jnr., and his son Tim who did the photography, Bert Bolton and Cyril Catt for the original Moko pictures; Colin Barnes, Jim Bready, Victor Burness, Richard Cook, Thomas Frank, Ray Hems, John Hunt Snr., Heinz Joss, Ms's. Annegret Kehrbaum, Nina Senger-Martens and Mr. Holgar Klaen of the Forschungsinstitut für Diskrete Mathematik (Arithmeum) in Bonn, Gunther Kugel, Klaus Kühn, Rod Lovett, (and his excellent web-site) Tom Martin, Thomas Munsterman, Bob Otnes, David Rance, David Rees, David Riches, Willy Robrecht, Hans Peter Schaub, Georg Schreiber, IJzebrand Schuitema, Pierre Vander Meulen, and Francis Wells amongst the many others who let me have details of pocket-watch calculators and data from their collections, and also the late John Knott and Herman van Herweijnen. All have been particularly generous with examples, images and ephemera relating to the companies, also encouragement. For these mere thanks is indeed small recompense, but thanks anyway! The French Linealis Forum of slide rule collectors hosted by Daniel Toussaint, and the translation provided by Sigismond Kmiecik was incredibly helpful in resolving some of the continuing discussion on French slide rule manufacturers. Finally I must thank the Oughtred Society for giving me full access to the 1998 Readers Survey which provided many useful contacts that have helped with a wealth of detail.

On the production side, my thanks to Roy Williams and Colin Barnes for proof reading, also my daughter Suzanne continues as a stalwart supporter and all-round hero. Once again she has been my ever faithful proof-reader and commentator on good English, and this time also designer of ideas for the covers – thank you Suzanne.

My wife Carol continues to put up with this all engrossing hobby and the strange directions it has taken me with amazing support and good humor; she truly is again the unsung hero!

Preface

My book "*Slide Rules, Their History Models and Makers*" [1]; includes very little on the particularly attractive genre of pocket-watch and wrist-watch slide rules and calculators, one of the earliest designs and a most entertaining and varied area of slide rule collecting.

A surprisingly large number of makers apparently made these devices. Not all are known in detail or accurately documented and an even larger number of retailers advertised and may have ultimately sold them. Sadly much of the information and evidence relating to these makers and manufacturers, as well as the retailers, has probably disappeared for ever. However sometimes it takes a book such as this to catalyze a 'flood' of new information from which hopefully we can complete a bit more of the picture. Most of the slide rule manufacturing countries had at least one indigenous manufacturer of pocket-watch slide rules, some of these devices then appeared in a variety of guises from a number of local and international retailers in other countries. This makes them all the more interesting to research.

This book sets out to document what we do know about pocket-watch and watch slide rules, and to raise awareness of the interesting variants and differences that can be found in this delightful class of rules. They would make a varied collection in their own right. It also raises questions about a number of devices that were advertised but have never been seen – yet? There are also surprisingly few un-attributable devices, but finding a home for these would be a delightful result.

Once again I am interested in gaining more information on the subject. Should any reader have new, additional or corrected information, I would be delighted to hear from you...

Introduction

The pocket-watch slide rule is my favorite slide rule type. It is not the most accurate; the honor for greatest accuracy must go to the large grid-iron types such as Thacher, Loga and other similar devices, or indeed the larger cylindrical calculators such as the Fuller. However the pocket-watch types are such nice examples of the high-quality mechanical engineering world, capable of reasonable accuracy and with a smooth and silky 'feel' to them – like a well oiled watch – and with 'adequate' accuracy, which makes them my undoubted favorite.

Not very much has been written on these devices previously. There have been a few articles on individual designs and some of the makers, this has led to some misunderstandings, not least due to the different nuances of the languages spoken on the two sides of the Atlantic, and undoubtedly there will be some disagreement with my choice of the taxonomy of the genre. No matter, it is one man's interpretation.

It was only while researching the topic that I came to realize that the history of the type was surprisingly old and their manufacture was wide spread. We will have a historical look at the device, and their manufacture in different countries. We will also briefly look at a number of examples of other pocket-watch calculators such as light meters and pocket cash registers, and then finally discuss some possible anomalous devices which might be better described as watch-pocket slide rules.

Definition of a Pocket-Watch Slide Rule

My definition of a pocket-watch slide rule is very simple. The device has to look like a pocket-watch. Size is not important, if required, it can go into a bigger pocket! A pocket-watch slide rule must have at least one 'stem winder', 'crown' or 'key', (the knob on the top) but more than one does not disqualify it. Equally it should have a 'loop' for a watch chain, but that is not absolutely essential, and this is often the first thing that gets lost. It should also have its scales covered in a 'crystal' which can be glass or plastic. It can be (and often is) double sided, a feature I am not aware of in a proper pocket-watch. The case can be metal or, rarely, it can be plastic. It can be made and or sold in any country of the world. In other words, I am trying to spread my net as wide as possible to cover a wide population of types, and some devices which may be better described as watch-pocket are included, but even here we may have to draw the line somewhere, but more about that later.

Nevertheless, having had the discussion with many collectors, there are enough devices which might not count to be able to add a section on anomalous devices; all eventualities should be covered!

What to call these devices presents a small problem. Even though they are slide rules, most manufactures called them calculators, which with the passage of time may cause confusion. Therefore they have been called whatever their manufactures called them.

Historical Review

The history of the genre starts with some educated guesswork beginning with the patent data that we have found. There are examples of pocket-watch slide rule dating back to the middle or late 19th century, but not all are covered by an extant patent. These are covered within the following 'Historical' section to create a foundation before studying the pocket-watch designs themselves which were undoubtedly aimed at the higher and more expensive end of the slide rule market, and possibly created to give a calculating equivalent of a fine pocket-watch.

It is quite difficult to get a real chronological perspective on the earliest designs. The earliest patent for a pocket-watch type device is probably German, dated early in the mid-nineteenth century. We have a picture of the device which was apparently patented, though we have not actually been able to find a patent or an example. The purist may argue that the device described is not a true pocket-watch slide rule - it is however a pocket-watch calculator, which is near enough. There is then an unexplained gap to the first patented devices where we have examples

The seminal patent is A.E.M. Boucher's 1876 patent in France; the patent for the same device in the United Kingdom is by H.E. Newton (a London patent agent) for A. Boucher's pocket-watch calculator. This was followed in quick succession by a number of 'Boucher' type calculators, though there does not appear to have been patents for Boucher's calculator in any of the other European countries who were equally capable of making the device, for example, Germany; nor was it patented in the USA. There were many 'manufacturers' and retailers who sold pocket-watch slide rules as 'Boucher's type', however which were makers and who simply sold is not so certain. The first American (U.S.A.) patent we can find is Elmer Sperry's patent of 1903, almost 30 years after Boucher.[1]

The list of patents that follow is surprisingly short. There are less than 50, and they cover a period of less than 60 years from 1871 to 1928. This is an average of less than one patent per year which gives us a first indication that the devices are rare and unusual. One might have thought that a calculating device based on the ubiquitous pocket-watch would have been much more common than it was. This does not mean that there are no more – just that they have yet to be found! Patent data is one of the best ways of achieving a historical view, and Patents as a specific subject are covered in further detail later and specifically for some of the makers within their chapters. Otherwise our historical view has to come from maker's catalogues and what we can find from actual examples of the devices themselves.

No pocket-watch slide rule design survived in manufacture to the end of the slide rule period. The Russian types were probably the last to have been designed and manufactured in the late 1950's and 60's, and Fowler and Halden calculators were probably the last to be on regular sale. Simple expense probably meant that they became poor value as rectilinear and circular rules became ever better value having benefited from manufacturing improvements.

---

[1] "Elmer A. Sperry and His Calculator" Bob Otnes in Journal of the Oughtred Society, Vol. 6, No 2, Fall 1997 Pg 19.

HISTORICAL REVIEW

Patents

Listing relevant patents chronologically gives a first view as to how the design of pocket-watch slide rules evolved. Studying the patent specifications and the complexity of some of the designs allows us to guess that quite a high proportion may never have been made, either because they could never have been made cost effectively, or else because they just would not work reliably. Research into the pocket-watch patents started about 20 years ago, this list has been considerably enlarged during subsequent research, and hopefully yet more relevant patents may be unearthed. The search so far has raised a number of 'mysteries' which might never be resolved, for example, which was the true original Calculex patent.

Pocket-Watch Slide Rule Patents		
Date	Patent No.	Patent Information
c1850	GER??	German patent for International Currency watch - earliest? Note that no references have been found to any other earlier pocket-watch designs.
1871	UK 1,665	Henri Lefevre – no example known
1876	FR N° 114,520	Titre: Cercle à calcul; Inventeur: Boucher; Descriptif: Brevet de 15 ans, 13 septembre; Boucher, représenté par Armengaud ainé, Paris, rue Saint-Sébastien, 45,- Cercle à calcul remplaçant la règle à calcul ordinaire,
1876	UK 4,310	H.E. Newton, A.E.M. Boucher's patent in the UK
1880	FR N° 139,898	Titre: Règle à calcul circulaire; Inventeur: Meyrat et Perdrizet; Descriptif: Règle à calcul circulaire,- Meyrat et Perdrizet. Earliest Instructions 1884?
1888	UK 10,311	Thomas Mudd patent - no examples known.
1892	UK 22,210	Lawrence Lord – Lord's first patent – large circular slide rule with handles, not a pocket-watch design.
1893	UK 10,617	G.F. Wynne's patent for a pocket-watch exposure meter.
1894	UK 25,000	A. Watkins first patent for a pocket-watch type exposure meter
1898	USA 602,918	Charles Sebastian received his patent for this pocket-watch cash register.
1898	UK 3,628	A. Watkins patent for another pocket-watch type of exposure meter
1899	UK Prov. Pat. 17,306	F.A. Wilkinson & C.C. Gibson, British designers of a very complicated pocket-watch design specifically for UK £.s.d. No example, or a full patent, is known.
1899	UK 2,195	George Lafond for his pocket-watch cash register
1899	CH 19,395	George Lafond for his pocket-watch cash register
1900	USA 657,916	R.W. Connant, Patent for the 'Small' calculator – not a true pocket-watch calculator
1900	USA 661,096	F.A. Wilkinson & C.C. Gibson, US patent for the very complicated pocket-watch design, see above.

1902	UK 27,822	A. Watson for 'Bee' type exposure meter following earlier designs
1903	UK 7,081	Ernest Lord – pocket-watch calculators which were made by several manufacturers.
1903	UK 14,533	Edward Wilson – It is believed that this is actually the Calculex patent, passed to Halden at some time.
1904	USA 773,235	Elmer Sperry's original patent pocket-watch calculator, a device with a single crown
1904	UK Prov. Pat. 19,061	H.T. Hinks, UK Provisional patent see above. No full patent has been found.
1904	UK 22,359	UK Patent for Elmer Sperry's patent pocket-watch calculator.
1907	USA 845,463	H.T. Hinks, a slide rule with electrical and normal scales in pocket-watch format. It is not believed to have been ever made, see above.
1909	UK 11,029	Wilhelm Oelschlager, a Hungarian engineer with a patent for a tape rule with loop, scales on the side, it was probably never made.
1909	USA 933,605	A. Watkins, one of his many US patents for exposure meters which generally mirror an equivalent UK patent.
1909	CH 46,796	George Lafond for his pocket-watch cash register
1910	UK 5,528	W.H. Fowler's first patent pocket-watch slide rule, the Improved Circular Slide Rule with the single milled knob on the back
c1910	UK n/a	Halden's supposed patent date for the Calculex – quoted by Halden. It has never been separately identified and may actually be a reference to Wilson's 1903 patent, see above.
1911	USA 1,012,660	George Lange patent for improvements to Sperry's patent 773,235, the recognizable concentric nuts.
1912	USA 1,017,719	H.R. Watts. Another device that is instantly recognizable as a Halden Calculex, see also Edward Wilson 1903.
1913	USA 1,056,775	D.W. Brunton, Circular slide rule with a watch loop and glass face – not a true pocket-watch rule.
1913	UK 20,416	Fowler patent which covers a method of reducing the expense of the design and improvements to enable the radial shafts (which replaced the milled knob) to be better fitted.
1914	UK 3,638	First of two patents by Fowler for improvements in the design by using a variety of patented anti-backlash mechanisms.
1914	UK 15,990	Fowler's second design improvements patent which is unusual in that it is for a design of circular slide rule that uses a ring to rotate the pointer as his first patent.
1917	UK 13,488/17	Application number for Harrison and Frank Brotherton.
1917	UK 17,665/17	Application number for William Eastwood.
1917	UK 120,980	William Eastwood – was probably never made.
1917	UK 134,833	Fabriques des Montres, Zénith of Switzerland, not made.
1919	USA 1,322,770	US Patent for William Eastwood – was probably never made despite being patented in the UK and USA.

HISTORICAL REVIEW

1921	UK 167,843	Harrison and Frank Brotherton – probably never made.
1924	UK 215,648	Fowler's last patent for further design improvements, this time for radial shafts and the methods of applying controlled fiction.
1926	UK 11,919/26	Application number for Frederick Robinson.
1926	UK 256,903	Frederick Robinson – made, not sure by whom.
1928	USA 1,671,616	Elmer Sperry, yet another improvement to his 1904 patent slide rule, this has one crown and two clutch buttons.
1937	CH 189,447	Oisier Szymanski, Homis watch Co. First slide rule bezel patent.
1939	CH 204,559	W. Moser, perhaps the earliest patent for a slide rule bezel on a watch or clock.
1940	CH 216,602	Graff & Cie. Fabrique MIMO, MIMO Loga non chronograph watch with slide rule bezel
1940	CH 217,012	Adrien Schweitzer, (Breitling) patent for chronograph slide rule watch.
1943	CH 536,000	G. Wittgenstein, slide rule bezel on a wrist watch.
1948	USA 2,435,705	G. Wittgenstein, slide rule bezel on a wrist watch, the same as CH 536,000.
1992	CH 680,330A	Swiss patent for slide rule bezels for calculating fuel consumption on wrist watch.

Pre-Boucher Calculating Rules

The initial study of pre-Boucher calculators and its attendant research followed a presentation on pocket-watch slide rules with an accompanying paper presented at the International Meeting of Slide Rule Collectors in Switzerland in 1998. In the 12 years since then, several rich veins of research have at least managed to correct some of the earlier misunderstandings, but have not managed to find any further examples of relevant pre-Boucher rules.

We can make the not unreasonable assumption (at least until any new information to the contrary may emerge) that the first real production pocket-watch calculator or slide rule was a result of the 1876 design of Alexandre Emile Boucher of Le Havre, initially patented in France and shortly after covered by a UK Patent in the name of H.E. Newton, a very well known British Patent Agent. This can be recognized as the truly seminal design of pocket-watch slide rule, many followed his ideas afterward. We can speculate what might have happened before that, and we can study what we know after that date.

Calculators in pocket-watch format which carried out other calculating functions must have been available at about the same time as Boucher's patent, however we have not managed to find any which can be accurately dated. However, while investigating relevant patents, a number of patents which appear to refer to pocket-watch rules were found which required further study.

An 'International Currency Watch', a calculator in pocket-watch format, is described and illustrated in a book on unusual patents [2] where it is speculated that this could have been made as early as 1870 or 1880, and '...was invented by a Rhenian[2] station-master... and was used by many banks and money exchange offices'. The device was illustrated, see Figure 1.1. The implication is that many were produced however there is no information relating to a specific patent, and no examples have not seen or heard of.

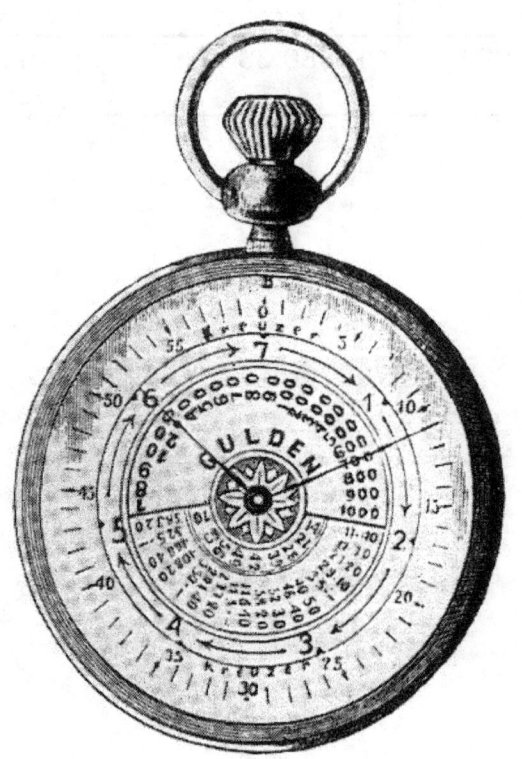

Right in the middle of the speculated dates for this device is Boucher's patent date, and as no examples or patents have been found with an earlier date, and if this watch is truly the earliest patent, then there are actually very few years in which when we can find relevant 'pre-Boucher' patents.

Figure 1.1: International Currency Watch

---

2 This term is very confusing as Rhenian usually refers to **The Confederation of the Rhine, 1806-1813**. In 1806, the HOLY ROMAN EMPIRE was dissolved; Emperor FRANZ II. Gave up the crown and assumed the title Emperor of Austria instead. The southern and western German territories joined the CONFEDERATION OF THE RHINE. The Rhenian Confederation avoided the label 'German' and pursued a pro-French policy. In 1807 the Rhenian confederation expanded north- and eastward, uniting all German states except Prussia, Austria, Holstein-Lauenburg (Danish) and a stretch of territory in the north west on the left bank of the Rhine, annexed by France. When Germany was liberated in 1813, German borders were redrawn again, and many of the statelets that had formed the Rhenian Confederation disappeared from the map. The International Currency Watch could thus be very much earlier in date.

One other example calculator has been found within the time span for the International Currency watch discussed above is by Henri Lefevre of Oxford Street, London. He was the only person around that date to be awarded an apparently relevant patent. Patent No 1,665, applied for 24 June 1871, sealed 26 September 1871; precedes Boucher's patent and would appear to cover a two-sided pocket-watch device, see left. However, the patent detail shows this actually to be a type of calculating board that uses the theory of similar triangles in performing calculations. The confusion comes from the device having two hands on each side which are geared so that one moves at twice the rate of the other. It was not a pocket-watch slide rule, and it is doubtful that it was ever made.

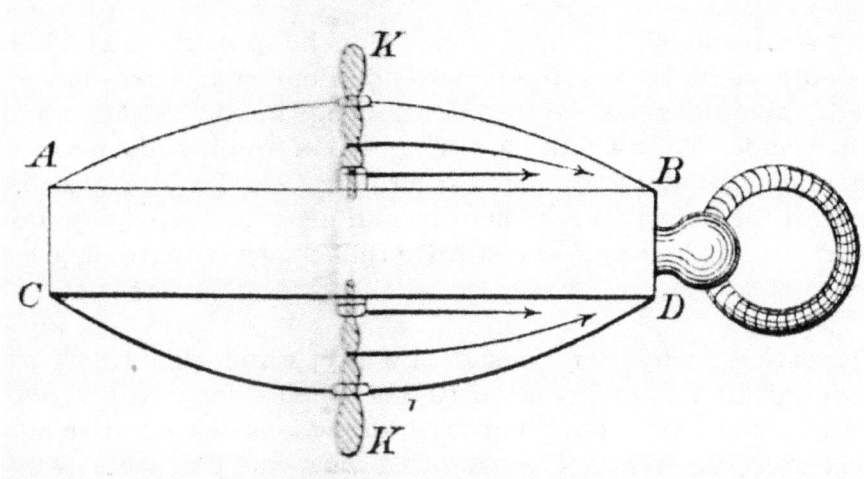

Figure 1.2: A drawing from Lefevre's patent

Pocket-Watch Slide Rule Patents Post Boucher

Once Boucher's patent had been awarded in France and England, it seems as if the floodgates opened and there was a concentrated effort to create new and exciting designs of pocket-watch slide rule. The work involved in producing an effective pocket-watch slide rule design, and then to match it with the capability of making them was such as to render them specialized and expensive items. It has also meant that there were designs and the attendant patents on these designs, where we have not found a maker. We can guess that there are any number of reasons for this situation, including complexity, expense and the sheer lack of appropriate capability.

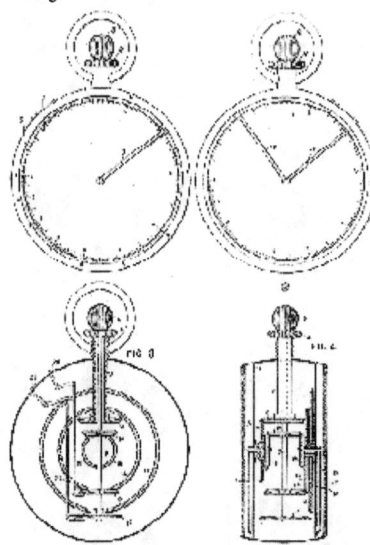

Figure 2.1: Thomas Mudd's patent of 1888

In the chronological listing of post-Boucher pocket-watch slide rule patents which follows, the majority of them were never manufactured. This presents an agreeable challenge to find examples that were made. They will be rare. There are a number of patents for unusual calculators, including several for Calculex look-alikes, which, with the benefit of hindsight, would need further explanation or exploration, as it seems very strange that they were actually ever granted.

The earliest patent for a design of pocket-watch slide rule where we can find no maker is No 10,311, applied for 16 July 1888, accepted 1 June 1889 from Thomas Mudd, who is described as an Engineer from Hartlepool. His patent shows a very clever device (Figure 2.1) with scales on two sides and a sophisticated mechanism to work them.

There is one crown and a 'nut' (similar to early K&E designs) as well as two push-buttons which work several of the scales on each side, and two pointers on one side and a single pointer on the other. Mudd's major claim is to make a slide rule '... applicable for the pocket'.

Mudd's extremely complicated design uses a number of bevel and circular spur gears, as well as having the moving elements worked by the push buttons. It would have been expensive to make, and it is doubtful if anyone made it.

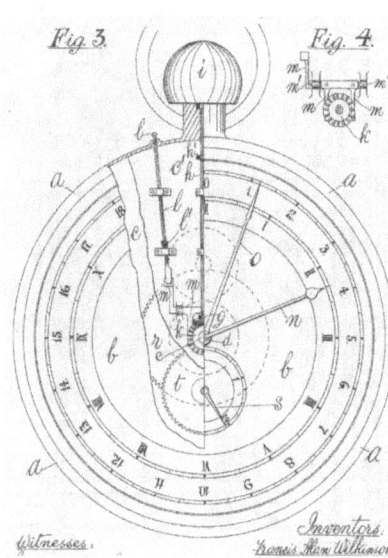

Figure 2.2: Front dial shown on Wilkinson & Gibson's patent

Another pocket-watch design comes from F.A. Wilkinson of Manchester and C.C. Gibson of London, this for a pocket-watch slide rule design also of some sophistication (Figure 2.2). This carries both a provisional British patent (17,306/1899) and a full US patent (661,096/1900).

The main patent claim for this device is to specialize in UK £.s.d. calculations. Why then would it have a US Patent? It uses a very complicated mechanism including a type of differential-gear to make it work. No examples are known, and it is doubtful that it was ever made.

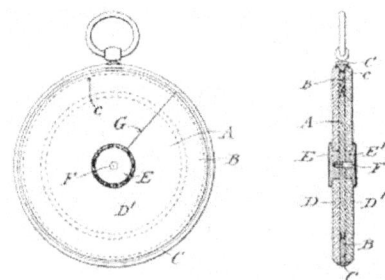

Figure 2.3: Wilson's patent, 1903

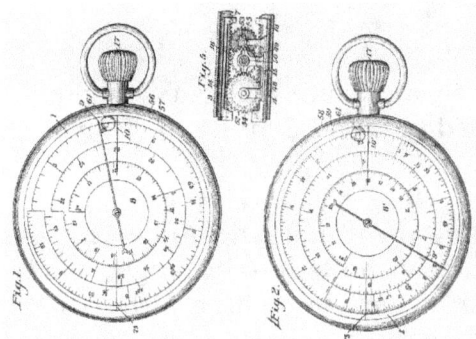

Figure 2.4: E.A. Sperry's patent, 1904

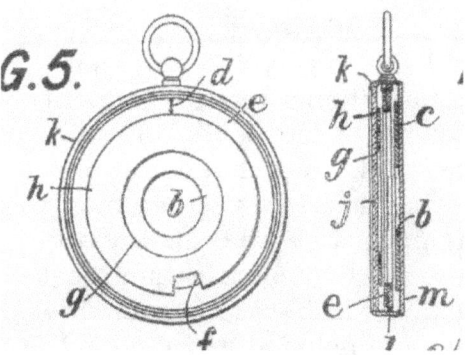

Figure 2.5: Hinks patent, 1904

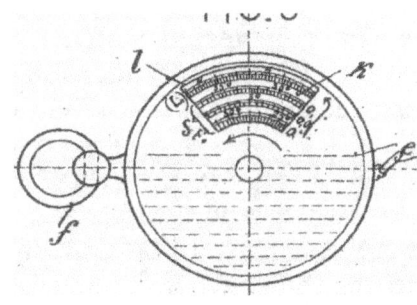

Figure 2.6: Oelschlager's patent, 1909

On studying the patent drawings, this becomes immediately recognizable as Halden's Calculex, which is known as a very popular and long lasting watch-pocket device. Nowhere in the patent, or indeed elsewhere, are any clues given as to what relationship there may have been between Wilson and Halden. Wilson does not specify any scales; the patent covers only the physical implementation. The details on the patent allow us to reliably speculate that Calculex devices with the single screw holding the 'centre nut' are an early version (see picture), and ones which have more than one screw, a logical design improvement, are later devices. It is however odd that the patent shows a thin ring and beveled glass, which is characteristic of a later Calculex device. See the chapter on the Calculex. And then, delightfully, it was found that a 'Wilson' device was actually made and an example is in a collection. See later.

Elmer Ambrose Sperry of the United States applied for and was awarded UK patent No 22,359 respectively on 17th October and 17th Nov 1904 which describes a very complex pocket-watch calculator. This mirrors the American patent No 773,235 of similar date, a version of which was made by K&E, but does not actually look like the patent, see Figure 2.4. Note that this is a normal looking pocket-watch device with a single crown. A later patent from George Lange resulted in a device with the more familiar concentric nuts instead of the single crown. There were in fact three K&E devices with two different patent dates, and the third claiming to be pre patent: 'Patent Appd. For'. This and other Sperry patents are further discussed in the chapter on K&E slide rules.

Yet another 'mystery design' with both provisional British patent (19,061/1904) and a full US patent (845,463/1904) is from Harold Thornthwaite Hinks of Chester in England. This too has apparent similarities with Wilson's Calculex patent as shown in the diagram at left, Figure 2.5. The patent claims a specialization in electrical calculations; however the multitude of alternative dials shown in the patent included a normal calculating capability. What, if any, relationship there was to Wilson's patent is not known, and there does not appear to have been a full patent awarded in the UK. It is very possible that it was not granted as being in direct conflict with the Wilson patent.

William Oelschlager, in 1909, had UK patent 11,029 awarded for what at first sight also appears to have been a pocket-watch device (Figure 2.6). Closer study shows that this device with its loop (but no winder!) is actually a measuring tape which drives calculating scales visible through the side plates of the tape holder and is probably not even pocket-able.

POCKET-WATCH SLIDE RULES

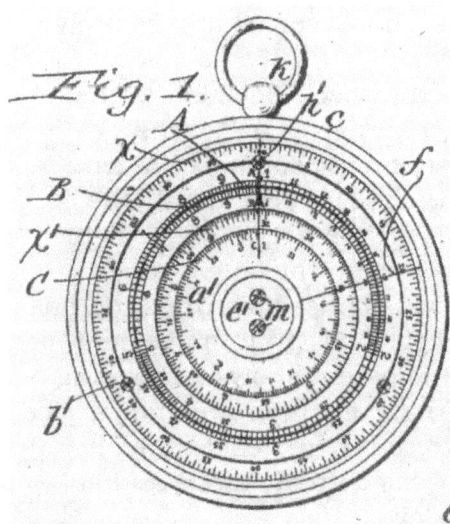

Figure 2.7: Watts' patent, 1912

An American 'Calculex' look-alike patent No. 1,017,719 was awarded to Herbert Richard Watts, another Englishman from the county of Chester, in 1912. This is so clearly similar to the UK Calculex, down to a single screw in one side of the device and the double screws in the other, as well as the shape of the 'Thumb Nuts' the rotatable glasses and so on, that it is hard to understand how it could be awarded when the Wilson patent already existed and Calculex devices were being manufactured (Figure 2.7).

As it was only granted in the USA makes this more understandable, however this topic will be explored in more detail later.

Another apparent pocket-watch slide rule is covered by US Patent No 1,056,775 awarded to David Brunton of Denver Colorado, in 1913 (Figure 2.8).

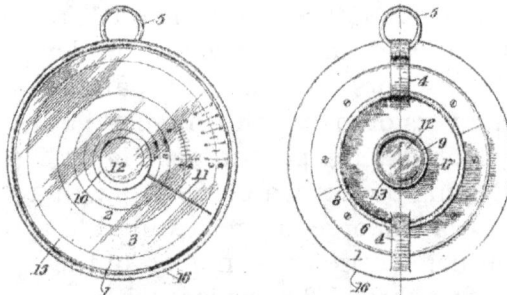

Figure 2.8: Brunton's patent, 1913

Brunton also at first sight had patented a Calculex look-alike. Further study shows it to be single sided with rotatable glass covered scales, but with a rather more complex geared actuating mechanism – not a true pocket-watch device. Again, no examples have been found, another case of a well intentioned patent which was never manufactured.

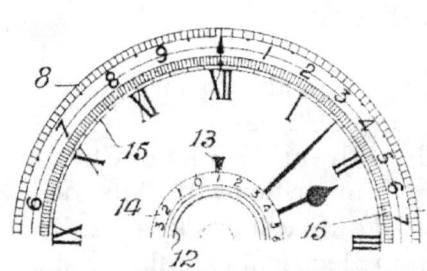

Figure 2.9: Eastwood's patent, 1917

William Eastwood's patent 120,980 applied for on 29th Nov 1917, and awarded 29th Nov 1918, is very different as it covers the ideas associated with an additional rotating element, a bezel, applied to 'watches'. It does not discriminate between wrist and pocket-watches, but uses pocket-watch illustrations (Figure 2.9). While this design feature has been used on many wrist-watch designs, there do not appear to have been any pocket-watch design that uses a bezel to rotate one logarithmic scale against a fixed logarithmic scale either within the instrument or externally. Further embellishments are included in the patent, such as magnifiers, separate pointers etc.

There is an American patent No. 1,322,770 for a 'watch type slide rule design' also in the name of W. Eastwood dated 1919. This is the equivalent of the 1917 UK patent, and even with both UK and USA patents it is not believed that the device was ever manufactured in either country.

UK Patent No 134,833 from Fabriques des Montres, Zénith, of Switzerland, (watchmakers) was applied for on 30 Oct 1919, awarded 29 April 1920. It has a Swiss convention date of 5 Nov 1918. This is most interesting. As it describes a number of features that have been seen in other devices, but not all incorporated into a single complex device as described in the patent, (Figure 2.10). It includes rotating scales 'b' and 'd' (as used in Lord's and M&P calculators), button clutches 's' and 't' (as in the Calculigraphe) and a cursor which is a transparent 'finger' 'd°' (used in the Schacht u. Westerich / Molter calculator). It is a two-sided device though the patent diagram only shows the logarithmic scales on one side.

POCKET-WATCH SLIDE RULE PATENTS POST BOUCHER

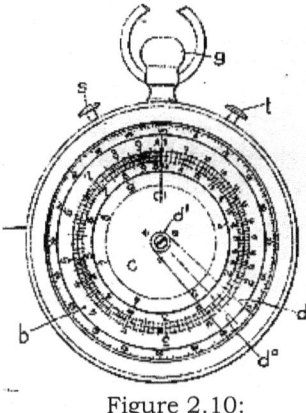

Figure 2.10: Zénith patent, 1918

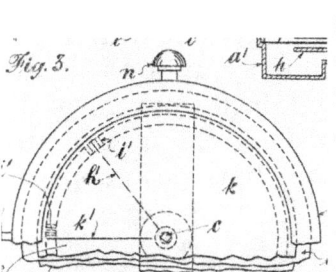

Figure 2.11: The Brotherton Patent, 1921

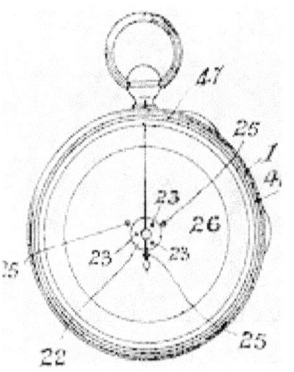

Figure 2.12a: Robinson's patent, 1926

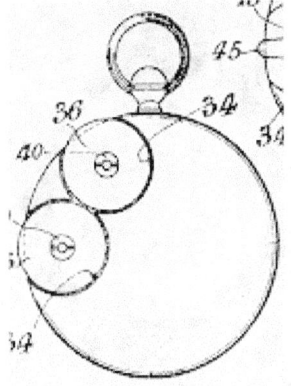

Figure 2.12b: Robinson's patent, 1926

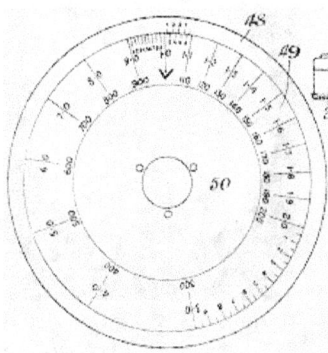

Figure 2.13: Scale for Robinson's calculator

As with most of the other sophisticated designs patented, no device incorporating all these features appears to have ever been made anywhere, let alone in the UK where the patent was awarded.

The brothers Harrison and Frank Brotherton had patent No 167,843 applied for 17th May 1920, accepted 17th Aug 1921. This was for a pocket-watch device where two pointers could be moved either together or individually against a log scale for calculating purposes. This was very much a watch-based implementation of Oughtred's original '...opening compasses' design. No examples of the design have been found on any manufactured calculator – See Figure 2.11.

Another fascinating patent for a pocket-watch slide rule is No. 256,903 from Frederick Robinson in conjunction with the Lancashire Optical Manufacturing Company Limited, both of Manchester, applied for 7th May 1926, and awarded 19th August 1926. It shows an unusual and very complex device – See Figure 2.12.

The patent makes great play of the ability to operate the calculator with one hand, the thumb and fingers being able to work the movements of scale and pointer by means of the toothed wheels, which protrude through the side of the case. An alternative lever operating system (45 in Figure 2.12) is also given. An example which uses the toothed wheels is known; see later, though not one which uses the levers.

A very simple scale is also included on Robinson's patent as shown in Figure 2.13. No further information is given and the benefits of such a scale with the vernier markings can only be speculated. The patent says that the space '50' (Figure 2.13) can be '...provided with data to which it may be necessary for the calculator to frequently refer'.

Happily, well after the patent was first discovered, we then find that it was made, and an example is described later.

Amongst other apparently relevant patents is one from Major Francis James Anderson, of Waterford, Ireland, with Patent 22,762 applied for late in 1903 and awarded in February 1904. This proves to be a complicated disc calculator with spiral scales and not a pocket-watch device at all.

This exploration of a number of patents gives us a good idea of many of the design ideas that were actually included, or could be included, in any of the pocket-watch slide rules that went on to be manufactured. A part of any on-going confusion relates to the definition of pocket-watch or watch-pocket, as we shall see.

POCKET-WATCH SLIDE RULES

Other Pocket-Watch Calculators

The pocket-watch calculators listed in this section are both relevant and interesting, as well as a prompt for more information. They also illustrate pocket-watch devices other than slide rule type calculators, i.e. a different form of pocket-watch calculator and the pocket-watch makers' art. Many different types are described on the internet, for example.[3] These all really do look like a pocket-watch and are calculators of various sorts,

Figure 3.1:
Moko Lightning Calculator

Moko Lightning Calculator

Whether Moko is a trade name or the name of a company is not known. Figure 3.1 shows the device that was made in Germany, it is not known when. It is a very simple form of multiplication table with a rotating 'cursor' carrying the multiplier up to x15 that allows products to be easily ascertained from the multiplicand, from 2 to 24 on one side and 25 to 48 on the other. The mechanism could easily have been applied to a Boucher style calculator.

Unknown Pocket-Watch Adding Machine

This is a simple form of circular adding machine from an unknown Swiss maker, discovered in a watch auction. Exactly how it works is not known, however it is entirely relevant to this section of the book, as the quality of the workmanship is such that they could have made other calculators or pocket-watch style slide rules.

Figure 3.2: Unknown pocket-watch adding machine

Other Pocket-Watch Calculators

The first of these devices (Figure 3.3) may be a type of artillery 'flash-and-bang' timer; the second is some form of aperture calculator. The two devices are from unknown makers who would have been capable of making any pocket-watch slide rule.

They are included here to show that there were many different forms and types of calculation as well as measuring instrument in pocket-watch format, these together with the pocket-watch slide rules make an interesting area of collection in any case.

Figure 3.3: Other pocket-watch devices for various uses

---

3   For example the web site http://www.icollector.com/Clock-Curiosity-Museum-Puidoux-Switzerland- which shows many examples

Summary

It is too early to draw any conclusions, however a number of questions are raised where the answers could either clarify what we know or start new avenues of research. For example:

- Does anyone happen to have a calculator of any of the types covered by a patent where no examples are known, for example, Mudd, Eastwood, Zenith, or Brotherton calculators?
- Does anyone have any information which show what (if any) was the relationship between Wilson and Halden, or indeed Watts and Hincks and Halden?
- Are any other pocket-watch calculator patents known, whether the device may have been made or not?
- Who made the International Currency Calculator, and did they make any other type of calculator or slide rule?
- Who made the Moko, and did they make any other calculators or slide rules?
- What more might be known of the unknown maker devices illustrated at the end of this chapter?

Pocket-Watch Slide Rules of the World

Manufacturers

Most of the countries of the industrial world where slide rules were manufactured appear to have had a company who produced at least one design of pocket-watch slide rule. The notable exception is Japan, but even here we may yet hear of a Japanese pocket-watch slide rule or calculator. We do know that they produced numerous designs of wrist-watch slide rules; covered briefly in a later chapter. It should be noted that wrist watch slide rules are very different. They are effectively a circular slide rule with one logarithmic scale mounted on a separate rotating bezel. This is not the same as a pocket-watch example with the mechanical 'works' that drive hands and/or scales.

One of the major difficulties in giving an accurate view of the world's pocket-watch slide rule manufacturers is that who actually manufactured, and who only sold other manufacturers designs, is not well documented, and in all probability will never be completely resolved. The information available to date is presented in the ensuing discussion of the various 'manufacturers' and 'families' we have identified. Looking at each country in turn:

United Kingdom

The United Kingdom was extremely well served with pocket-watch calculator manufacturers many of whom exported as well as producing models which were sold under their own as well as other badges. The premier manufacturer in terms of sheer quantity and ubiquity was English: Fowler and Co. of Manchester. The UK also had Stanley, the various Lords' makers, and then other companies such as Manloves, Elliotts and others who may have made (they had the capability, or certainly Elliotts did) but may just have been retailers of self branded calculators, and of course Joseph Halden who made one of the most common watch-pocket devices.

Germany

Germany undoubtedly had the fine engineering capability that was well able to produce the mechanisms that were required for this type of device, and there are a number of German slide rule companies who still provoke debate as to whether they were makers in a 'cottage industry' style of working, or manufacturers or whether they were simply retailers. The chronology of the German pocket-watch slide rule 'makers' is not so certain. We have Molter, (who is possibly the leader of the German pocket-watch slide rule industry) Reiss, Schacht und Westerich and Wichmann (probably the earliest) as four immediate candidates for continuing the debate for some considerable time yet.

Switzerland

For centuries Switzerland has been the pre-eminent maker of fine watch and clock mechanisms which were entirely relevant to making pocket-watch slide rules. In terms of actual makers, or even names that could possibly have made such devices, the list is somewhat limited. We only have Pedos of Rehan who made a Calculigraphe AF. Then we have the marking 'Swiss' on a number of ME calculators produced by the Scientific Publishing Company, but whose root can not be defined. There is not either an extensive or definitive list of makers and their pocket-watch slide rule products.

France

France does not immediately strike one as an obvious center of fine engineering – there may well be a howl of opprobrium following that statement! However it is probably wrong, as we do know that all the early designs from Boucher were made in France, and they are splendid and sophisticated pocket-watch devices. Then we have Morin who made a Boucher calculator, Henri Chatelain (and his followers who made the Calculigraphe) and continue to this date making opisometers, pedometers and other delicate mechanical devices. The M&P is yet another fine pocket-watch calculator, and is the only device in the genre with its integrated timepiece. So France has to be the manufacturer of at least two of the pre-eminent devices for the calculating fraternity, Boucher and M&P, as well as one of the work-horses, Calculigraphe.

Russia (USSR)

The USSR was most certainly a major manufacturing country, or perhaps the Soviet Union as it was then, is better described as a collection of countries. The centralization of control produces an intriguing commonality of design wearing a variety of maker's names that implies choice, but is not. During the Soviet period rules were made to state standards and the only significant variations were in the logos used to identify the factory of origin. The Russian KL-1 'Sunrise' types are a common design produced with different names across a number of makers in a number of towns and regions – perhaps we will get a better or more accurate view of this country's manufacturing capability following publication of this book.

America (U.S.A.)

Despite the multitude of slide rule makers in the USA, there are not a large number of pocket-watch slide rule manufacturers. Keuffel & Esser are the only American company who manufactured these devices, starting over a quarter of a century after Europe. Dietzgen, in all probability was only a retailer, as were a number of other American companies who sold foreign devices 'badged' with an American name (e.g. Queen, Leitz) or indeed proudly sold the Calculex.

Others

There must have been other manufacturers of pocket-watch type calculators which we have yet to identify. For example, we know that possibly the earliest known device was supposedly made in Bavaria in 1850 by an unknown maker. We also know of the MOKO Lightning Calculator and other types of pocket-watch calculator, which are not a pocket-watch slide rule, but are a type of pocket-watch calculator, also made by unknown makers and we are not sure when or by who. Hopefully this book will catalyze new information on makers.

| Pocket-Watch Slide Rules: Major Makers & Retailers ||||||
Country	Maker	Type	Made or Sold	Date
UK	W.H. Fowler	Numerous types	Made	1898 - 1975
	Scientific Publishing	Various types	Made & Sold	1898 - 1910
	Casartelli	Lord's Calculator	Sold?	?
	J. Davis	Mech Eng	Sold?	c1900
	Dyson?			
	J. Halden	Calculex	Made	1910 - ?
		Desk Calculex	Made	1910 - ?
	W.F. Stanley	Boucher	Made?	1895?
	Manlove, Alliott & Fryer	Boucher	Sold?	1895?
	J.F. Steward	Boucher	Sold?	1895?
	Elliott Bros.	Lord's Calculator	Made?	1910?
	'Manloves'	Boucher	Sold	?
	Army and Navy	Calculigraphe	Sold	1906
	Waddington R&W	Lord's Calculator	Made?	?
	W.Wilson	Lord's Calculator	Made?	?
	E. Wilson	Wilson calculator (Calculex)	Made	1903?
Germany	Frappant	System Thomas	Made/sold	1923
	Heckendorf	S u. W	Sold?	1925
	MOKO	Lightning Calculator	Made	?
	Molter	various	Made/sold?	1921
	Reiss	S u. W	Made/sold?	1925
	Schacht u. Westerich	Non-Boucher	Made?	?
	Gebr. Wichmann	S u. W.	Sold	c1938/9
		Calculex	Sold	c1900 - 1910
	Unknown	Currency Calculator	Made?	c1850?
United States	Keuffel & Esser	Sperry calculator	Made	c1903
		K&E Calculator	Made	1908 - 19
	Dietzgen & Co.	Boucher (card dial)	Sold?	1902 - 1936
		Boucher (metal dial)	Sold?	1904 - 1931
		Calculex	Sold	Sole US agent.
	Queen	Calculigraphe	Sold only?	
France	Henri Chatelain	Calculigraphe H-C	Made?	1875?
	Unknown	Calculigraphe F-C	Sold?	
	Pedos S.A. (?)	Calculigraphe A-F	Sold?	
	M&P	Cercle a Calcul	Made?	
	H. Morin	Boucher & Calculigraphe	Made	1880?
Soviet Unio	Sunrise	KL-1	Made?	1950/60
	Matsku		Made?	1950/60
	Heart		Made?	1950/60
Swiss	Renan -J-B	Calculigraphe A-F	Sold?	?

Table of Pocket-Watch Manufacturers and Retailers.

Families of Pocket-Watch Calculators

There are only a small number of 'families' of pocket–watch calculators, it is not the same situation as with rectilinear slide rules where there are multitudes of different scale layouts, makers and retailers. These families are the designs that were either:

- made by more than one manufacturer, e.g. Boucher
- or were sold by more than one retailer, e.g. Calculex
- or can be found in more than one style e.g. Lords
- or where a particular manufacture had more than one design of pocket-watch slide available, e.g. K&E, S. u. W.
- or was common in one country e.g. Russian.

As it is not certain when some companies started to manufacture, we can list these families 'almost chronologically' as follows:

- 1876: The Boucher Calculator – the seminal design
- 1878: Calculigraphe – the first and almost simultaneous off-shoot of the Boucher
- 1880: Meyrat & Perdrizet Pocket-Watch Calculators, another early French design
- 1892; 1903: Lord's Calculator – has early patents and many variants
- 1895; 1906: Keuffel & Esser calculators – the only American manufacturer
- 1898: Scientific Publishing calculators – the root of the Fowler brand
- 1898; 1914: The Fowler family of calculators
- 1903; 1908: Wilson/Halden's Calculex – an early and iconic watch pocket design
- 1910: Wichmann calculators – possibly the earliest German producer
- 1921: Molter – maybe the founding and seminal German manufacturer
- 1925: Schacht und Westerich calculators – another German maker or retailer
- 1950: Russian calculators – unique single design sold by many retailers
- Other makers or retailers:
  - Davis < 1910
  - Reiss c1925
  - Robinson c1926
  - Breitling   }
  - O&W   } 1960?
  - Selectron   }
  - Frappant c?
  - Heckendorf c?

The following chapters are in the order shown above, however Fowler follows Scientific Publishing their root and not as expected from their dates. Halden takes its position from the Wilson patent rather than any perceived wisdom as to when they might have produced the earliest Calculex.

Where two dates are quoted they are either a founding date and then a date for a major change, or a date when the particular company may have first started selling pocket-watch slide rules, and then later made the devices themselves.

My selection is made on the basis of today's information and open to debate. New information could well change the basis for the above selection. The hope, as always, is that discussion will bring about new information!

The Boucher Calculator

Introduction

It has been established from the patent information that the Boucher Calculator is the seminal design in pocket-watch slide rules. A number of manufacturers claimed to have made variants of the calculator, many more retailers sold them. It is illuminating to study Boucher's original patent and to compare it with a number of 'Boucher' designs from other manufacturers which were sold over the next 50 years. There is considerable commonality across all designs, particularly with the scale layouts, attesting to the excellence of Boucher's original ideas.

The Patent

Alexandre Emile Marie Boucher submitted his patent Breveté, no. 114,520, in France, on the 13th September 1876. Boucher's English patent specification No. 4310 was originally submitted on 7th November 1876 by Henry Edward Newton, patent attorney in London, on behalf of Boucher, 'Agent Administrateur de la Société des Forges et Chantiers de la Méditerranée of Paris, France', and granted on 1st May 1877[4]. The patent described two variants of calculator shown here in Figure 4.1 and Figure 4.4. In view of the prominence of Newton's name on the British patent, it is interesting that it was always known as the Boucher Calculator and not the Newton, presumably because it was also patented in France under his own name at the same time.

Little is know of Boucher. The description from the patent makes him an official of a foundry and shipyard. What other relationship there may have been between him and Newton or Manlove (see p. 26) is also unclear, probably none other than as with many other patents submitted by a Patent Agent on behalf of a client, or with an agent for that item in a second country. Whether it was patented elsewhere on the continent or in America is not known but unlikely as none has been found to date. The French patent is a lovely hand-written 14 page document including two double-pages of drawings which are slightly different to the UK patent. They are not good enough to copy for here. On at least one page the hand-written number can be read incorrectly, though thank heavens there is also a stamped number on the second and subsequent pages. As with many other patentees, Boucher seems to have been a one-patent wonder, what sort of a living he made from this patent is not known. Nevertheless, a number of manufacturers in France and England credit him as the source of their devices and it is interesting to note the different, but common, interpretations of his design by these makers.

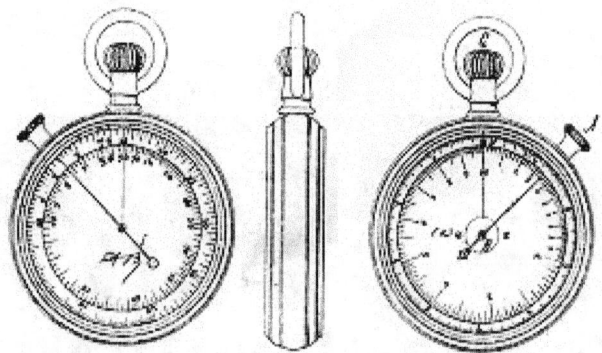

Figure 4.1: Boucher's pocket-watch calculator

The patent covers two options, one of having scales that move relative to each other (as Lord's), a second option having a single scale with index and pointer. The left-hand diagram in Figure 4.1 shows a sine and tan scale, the right-hand diagram shows a single cycle log scale with mantissa of logarithms, on an obviously double sided pocket-watch device. All the makers followed the basic pattern shown in Figure 4.1, with some interesting variation. There are two 'early' variants with an 'AB' (Alexandre Boucher?) signature, apparently made by two different companies, one being by A. Boucher of Le Havre.

---

[4] 'The Boucher Calculator' Peter Hopp in *Slide Rule Gazette*, Inaugural Issue, Autumn 2000, p58.

THE BOUCHER CALCULATOR

Figure: 4.2: Very early Boucher Calculator with the "AB" signature, made in France

These are shown Figure 4.2, one example is in the Museum of the History of Science (MHS) in Oxford, and a second is known in a private collection. Other examples have been sold on e-Bay.

The example shown in Figure 4.2 is in the MHS, they describe it as Boucher's Circular Logarithmic Calculator post 1876. It is inscribed 'Cercle à Calcul / Bté S.G.D.G.' and 'A. Boucher. 5, rue du Canal. HÂVRE.' On one side and with the script initials 'A.B.' on the other. The two faces on the instrument, one for numbers, the other with a spiral scale for Sines and Tangents. The main key turns the logarithmic scale and the smaller key the pointers on each face. Using the two pointers (one fixed) on the face shown, any interval on the scales (the outer being uniform, the inner logarithmic) may be recorded, and by the subsequent movement of the scales added to any other part of the scales, i.e. the numbers multiplied. This device looks to have paper scales; another similar model has beautiful engraved metal scales.

Due to the similarities of the scales on this example and those shown on the patent, this has been taken as the earliest design and hence shown as a 'very early' example dated within one or two years of the patent being awarded i.e. the appellation '… Bté S.G.D.G.' shows award of the patent in France. This early device and the following devices are approx. 2.0625″ (53 mm) diameter, and .5625″ (14 mm) thick.

The maker of this earliest device has not been identified. The oblate spheroid crown and the tapered shoulders on the side winder are different to the furniture found on the later models, (still signed 'AB') as is the 40° angle between crown and winder. The angle of the side winder to the crown is 60° on the later models, by my theory (Appendix 2) this alone would show that they are made by a different maker, however we can also see that the furniture is different. The crown is more diamond shaped and the side winders have a narrower more cylindrical body.

Figure: 4.3: Early Boucher Calculator with the "AB" signature, and different scale layout

While not possible to identify the earliest maker, it is possible that the maker of these later models is H. Morin of Paris. Morin catalogues from 1910 and 1914 show a confusingly labeled 'Nouveau Calculigraphe' with an 'AB' signature and the later scales on the illustrations, see later.

An 'early' (i.e. later than the device in Figure 4.2) example shown in Figure 4.3 was sold on e-Bay during 2002, it looks to have the first evolution in scales and these are recognizable as the scales that would feature on the Calculigraphe, albeit in a different font and with different labeling. The spiral Sin/Tan scale has now become 4 circular scales still with the script 'AB' on that face, while the pair of original logarithmic scales has also turned into 4 scales but with the inventor's name and a simpler address, 'A. Boucher. Hâvre.' Another example with different hands and metal faces and a splendid carrying/display case is shown in Figure 4.4.

Figure: 4.4: Early Boucher Calculator with the "AB" signature, on metal face in its case

Images Courtesy of the Conrad Schure Collection

It is not known when Boucher lived in 5, rue du Canal Hâvre, but he was living in Paris by the time of his UK patent. To me calculators carrying the complete street and town address are the earliest versions; the simpler address is shown on later versions.

A third 'early' example was offered for sale on e-Bay in 2004. This has a similar scale layout to the example in Figure 4.3, and another similar example is illustrated in Figure 4.12 as part of the Manlove, Alliott & Fryer discussion.

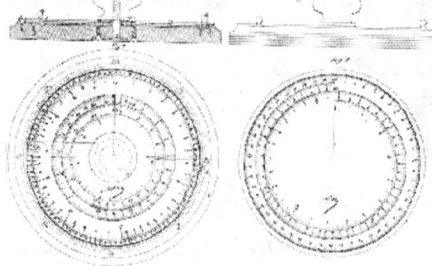

Figure: 4.5: Boucher's calculator - desk version

Comparing the three early versions is interesting as they are different with no immediately obvious evolutionary path between them. A suggestion of their evolution is made based on the MHS version being the earliest. As noted, it has the simplest scales which are similar to those described in the patent; the later versions evolve towards the suite of scales used on the Calculigraphe.

The pocket-watch variant shown in the patent is two sided with separate crowns for moving the movable scale and pointer respectively. A very simple layout of scales is described (see Figure 4.1); few makers produced a design with such a simple layout, and most had some additional scales.

The patent tries to cover all eventualities, and makes the suggestion that: 'The central part of the case may be used to receive a mariner's compass, an aneroid barometer, a thermometer, or any other useful instrument'. Elsewhere the suggestions also include '...a watch and ... building it into the round handle of a walking stick or umbrella ...' whether this was the source of inspiration for some of the later calculators which did these things can only be speculation, but it does try to be all-embracing!

Implementations

The majority of Boucher implementations have two sides, and are controlled via two crowns, all manufacturers opting for the single scale with index and pointer. There are a number of interesting variants which carry the name Calculigraphe, the best known is labeled the HC Calculigraphe is by Henri Chatelain of Paris. This would appear to be one of the earliest implementations, originally produced in 1878 (according to Cajori [3]) very soon after the original UK patent was granted. It was sold all over the world by various retailers and had a number of variants in physical form and layout as well as differences in scales. Where the Calculigraphe

Images Courtesy of the Conrad Schure Collection

Figure: 4.6: Boucher's desk calculator and on its wooden stand

uses a push-button to activate the movement of the hand, all other versions of 'Boucher's' use the second crown. All types share a common scale set which generally follows the patent, i.e. single-cycle log, mantissa, sine and tan, generally there is also a square and cube scale. These two extra scales are in all probability the main elements of the 'Improved Boucher Calculator' that were produced by a number of manufacturers. It is described in detail in the following chapter.

There is one known example of the desk version, described below and shown in Figure 4.6.

This splendid example of the calculator maker's art is approx 5″ (127mm) in diameter in a mahogany and brass frame which can be removed from the attractive turned mahogany stand which makes it sit some 6″ (152mm) above the desk. It can be used when it is off the stand, a very large pocket-watch!

The scales are slightly different to the pocket-watch example as the desk version is single sided. From the innermost reading out, the first two are trig scales, the second relating to a number of gauge marks to do with metals round the periphery of the face. The three calculating scales mirror those of the pocket-watch design. The two crowns or knobs are on the bottom half of the calculator, the one at 'six o'clock' rotates the entire face, and the second smaller crown rotates the movable cursor, which is very much in line with a number of later designs. The markings on the scale are as on the earliest pocket-watch version: 'Cercle à Calcul / Bté S.G.D.G.' and 'A. Boucher. 5, rue du Canal. Hâvre.' This gives the strong indication that these are both early examples, or at least made within the same time frame, and probably by the same maker.

The desk Boucher must be one of the rarest devices for the collector to aspire to.

Manufacturers

The unknown French maker who was responsible for the earliest examples of Boucher, those with the 'AB' signature, and the splendid desk model, obviously made a number of improvements during the period they were made in France. It is highly unlikely that it was Boucher himself, a foundry official would be unlikely to have the watch making skills that would be required, they would have been made for him. All have the very prominent spindle, though which scales are positioned on the spindle side is obviously not fixed, or perhaps it changed sides from earliest to later examples.

Many of the following companies may have been simply retailers. It is certainly true that there were numerous spurious claims of manufacturing capability amongst the slide rule fraternity. Where the claims relate to rectilinear or circular rules they could be true, the fine engineering specialization required to make a geared movement in a pocket-watch case must have been beyond many such 'manufacturers'.

Pre-eminent amongst slide rule manufacturers in the late 19th and the turn of the 20th century is W.F. Stanley, established in 1853, with a wide range of slide rules in their later catalogues including Boucher's calculator.

POCKET-WATCH SLIDE RULES

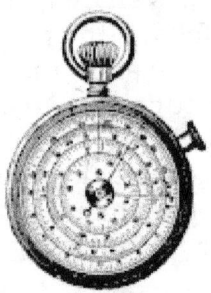

Figure: 4.7: Flyer for Boucher's calculator from the 1898 Stanley Catalogue

W.F. Stanley

Did Stanley ever make Boucher's calculator? It is not certain, and not even the documentation available clarifies the situation particularly. Looking at this available documentation we have Stanley's numerous books and catalogues. Starting with the books, we have:

W.F. Stanley, **A Descriptive Treatise on Mathematical Drawing Instruments**, 4th edition, 1873 makes no mention of slide rules at all; the only calculating device covered is his Computing Scale also (confusingly) known as a Computer.

W.F. Stanley's **Mathematical Drawing and Measuring Instruments** of 1888 (6th edition) makes no mention of Boucher's calculator in the section on slide rules though a number of slide rules (including the Fuller's) feature in both this book and Surveying and Levelling Instruments by the same author.

W.F. Stanley's **Surveying and Levelling Instruments** of 1890 may shed some light on the progress of this instrument into the UK, he quotes:

Boucher Calculator, 'the invention of M. Alex. E. M. Boucher, engineer of Paris'. (With a footnote relating to the 1876 UK Patent) '... This instrument was formerly made in France for this country [UK] in a very slovenly manner. It is now made in London of sound work and accurate centring. Manloves are the patentees' agents, but the instrument can be had of any opticians'. There follows a description of its use taken directly from the patent.

Mathematical Drawing and Measuring Instruments of 1900 mentions both versions of Boucher's calculator as documented in the 1898 catalogue.

Looking at Stanley catalogues we have:
1898 Catalogue: 2 versions of Boucher are described:
- D553, Boucher's Pocket Calculator '... latest improvements ...' and as '... my own make', but whether this means 'I made it' or 'it was made exclusively for me' we can only speculate.
- D553A, Stanley-Boucher Calculator '... gives also the number of revolutions of the log hand on centre of dial'.

A 'flyer' for the calculator was included loose in some 1898 catalogues. See Figure 4.7. Note the advertised availability of Nickel Silver, Silver and Gold cases, no examples of the latter are known. A 'Patent Stanley-Boucher Calculator' Presentation Model, with hallmarked sterling silver case, dated 1901, was recently sold at auction. They are obviously rare.

1912 Catalogue: 4 versions of Boucher described:
- K3622, Boucher's Pocket Calculator standard in 'Nickelled case' and,
- K3623, in silver case,
- K3624, Stanley-Boucher Calculator with third hand, in Nickelled case, and
- K3625, in silver case.

1924 Catalogue: only the one version of Boucher's calculator (M3622 – without the revolution counter) is mentioned. Note the change of identity number, the alpha character preceding the number identifies the catalogue, in this case an 'M' catalogue.

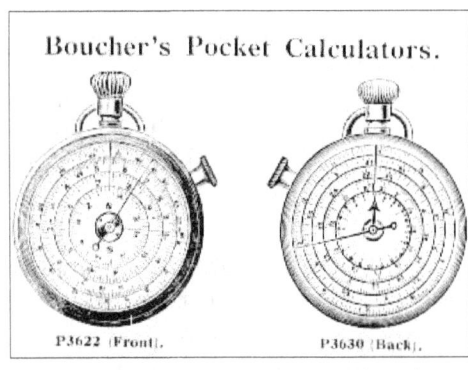

Figure 4.8: From the 1931 Stanley catalogue illustrating the two versions

1931 Catalogue: two versions shown. See Figure 4.8. These are:
- P3622, Boucher's Pocket Calculator,
- P3623, as 3622 but a presentation model in a silver case,
- P3630, Patent Stanley-Boucher Calculator, with the addtional rev-counter scale,
- P3631, as 3630 but also a presentation model in a silver case.

1958 and 1960 Stanley Catalogues: No Boucher calculators are shown.

Figure 4.9: Boucher's calculator by Stanley (back and front)

From this evidence we can therefore summarize the following scenario. Sometime prior to 1890 Stanley started selling Boucher's calculators which was made in France. About 1890 they started making these devices themselves (or they were exclusively made for Stanley). By 1898 the Stanley–Boucher with its additional 'rev-counter' was also being made. It is claimed that this was subsequently patented sometime between 1924 and 1931, but no trace has been found of this later patent. Note, Cajori shows the Stanley–Boucher as dating from 1905. Why only one version is described in the 1924 catalogue is difficult to understand, when the 1931 catalogue also has four versions including the presentation models. Sometime between 1931 and 1958 they stopped selling them, exactly when has yet to be established.

Figure 4.10: Boucher's calculator by Stanley with additional rev counter on the back face

The two versions appear to have lasted largely unchanged throughout their lives. Known examples, see Figures 4.9 & 4.10, are all very similar, and both types seem equally common (or rare).

Figure 4.9 shows the standard suite of scales:
- Front: degrees, single cycle log, two-turn √ (called n^2)
- Back: mantissa of log, three-turn ^{3}√ (called n^3)

The second crown moves the pointers, the main crown the front dial; this closely follows the Boucher patent description. A number of examples are known, they are not exceptionally rare.

The Stanley–Boucher is also fairly well known and has the same scales with the rev counter as an additional facility. An example was used to illustrate an article in 'All About Science', a monthly magazine which was published in 1973, well after Stanley ceased selling them but while slide rules were still generally available. Note, the Patent statement on the front dial, one has to assume that this refers to Boucher's original patent as no other is known.

Cajori states that Stanley manufactured Boucher's calculators, whether this can be taken as definitive is open to debate. Cajori's book was published in 1909, with Stanley's address given as Holborn rather than Great Turnstile, Holborn, where they were till 1926 which ties in with the information quoted in the earlier references. The 1898 Catalogue shows the Great Turnstile address.

Manloves, London

Manloves were a well known general engineering firm from Nottingham dating from about 1892 who produced a wide variety of civil engineering equipment and are well known as the originators of incinerating apparatus as well as some state-of-the-art engines. They were originally called Manlove, Alliott & Fryer (see below), and were originally agents for Boucher (see quote in Stanley above). How this related to Newton who was patent agent for the original application, and what business relationship existed between the parties is not known. The Boucher's calculator shown in Figure 4.11 from Manloves has the second crown and the standard suite of scales as per patent and Stanley's implementation, and was probably made by the same people but with Manloves name rather than the Stanley name. There is nothing to indicate whether the calculator was made in France or England.

Figure 4.11: Boucher's calculator from Manloves

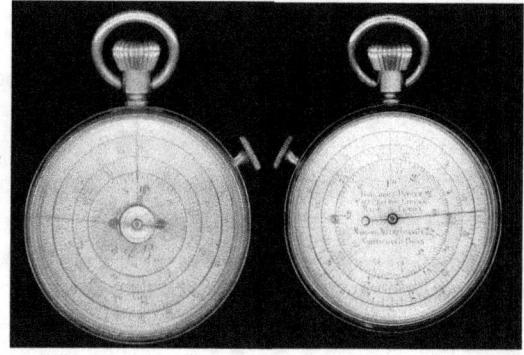

Figure 4.12: Boucher's calculator from Manlove, Alliott & Fryer

Manlove Alliott & Co Limited

Late addition, see page 167 for description with corresponding Figures 1a & 1b.

Manlove, Alliott & Fryer, Nottingham and Rouen

As previously noted, this firm was probably a predecessor to Manloves (see above). This is confirmed by the fact that the example shown in Figure 4.12 is made in France, $2\frac{1}{16}"$ (52 mm) diameter, $\frac{9}{16}"$ (14 mm) thick and is an 'early' version with the 'A.B' signature. Also the firm claims Nottingham and Rouen as working addresses. This speculation assumes that all later examples of Boucher calculator were made in England, but this could be far from the truth. Manlove, Alliott & Fryer, like the later Manloves, were a well established, forward looking and long lived engineering firm based in Nottingham who made steam engines, pumps and other civil engineering and waste disposal equipments supplied throughout the world. What the Rouen address was based on is not known or has not yet been found. Manlove, Alliott & Fryer are mentioned in Cajori as 'making Boucher's calculators', the example in Figure 4.12 is marked 'Boucher's Patent Calculating Circle Made in France' and 'Manlove, Alliott, Fryer, & Co. Nottingham & Rouen' and having an 'AB' 'Boucher' signature on the reverse which would imply that it was an early example – see other examples of early Boucher calculators.

H. Morin, Paris

Morin was a highly respected French mathematical instrument and slide rule maker who made numerous designs of slide rules in his workshops in Paris from 1880 (i.e. contemporaneously with Boucher) and up to the mid 20th century. So far catalogues from the late 19th century have not been forthcoming; however catalogues from 1910, 1914, 1925/6 and 1930 have all carried adverts for a 'Calculigraphe' first labeled 'Nouveau Calculigraphe' (1910). These are complete with an 'AB' signature and what could also be the Boucher name and address information that features on the 'early' calculators. These confusingly labeled 'Calculigraphes' appears under part number 8488, and are shown in Figure 1042 in all their catalogues. It looks to have a winder (not a clutch), and is also captioned in 1910 'd'apres la systeme A. Boucher'. In 1914 it is labeled 'Systeme Boucher', and in 1925/6 and 1930 and 1940 it is simply labeled 'Calculigraphe Boucher.'

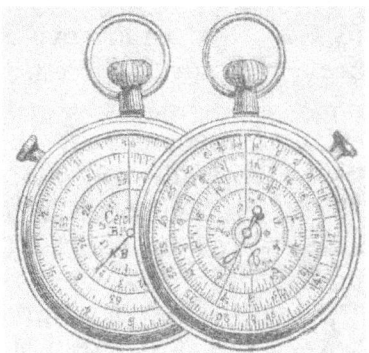

Figure 4.13: Nouveau Calculigraphe from H. Morin, c1910

At present it is difficult to explain how the Boucher calculator, patented in 1876, and what appear to be very early devices (Figures 4.3 and 4.4) could still be being sold 65 years afterward under the same illustration, albeit at steadily increasing prices of (1910) 20 FFr; (1925/6) 45 FFr, to 89 FFr in 1930. There is no price in the 1940 catalogue, and the item numbers have changed, but the diagram is the same.

However what is very obvious is that all the Morin catalogues do show what has become known as early Boucher calculators, and this could be entirely reasonable given that their involvement could have been from the earliest days, just 2 years after Boucher's patent. What remains to be found is exactly how early their involvement with Boucher was and likewise how long afterward did they continue to sell this device.

To add further confusion to the overall scenario, Morin in 1914 also advertised a true Calculigraphe, that is one with a clutch, and in this case a quite unusual specification. It is dealt with in more detail in the next chapter.

J.H. Steward

Advertised a Boucher's calculator and are also shown in Cajori and the 4th (1897) edition of Pickworth as suppliers of such devices along with W.F. Stanley. No examples are known.

Negretti & Zambra

Known from an example that appeared in a Tool Shop auction in 1998, the minuscule illustration looks to be a Calculigraphe type device, i.e. it looks to have the push-button rather than a second crown.

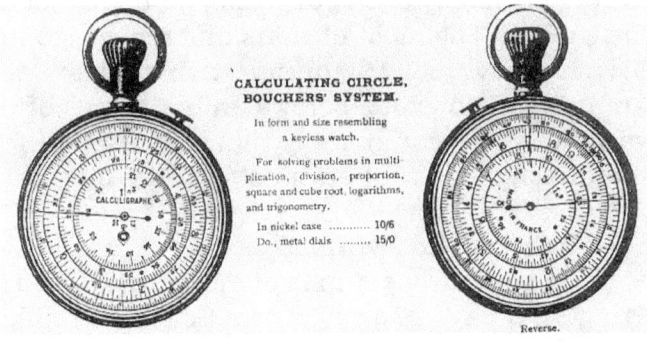

Figure 4.14: 1907 Army and Navy Stores Catalogue

POCKET-WATCH SLIDE RULES

Army & Navy Stores

Known from their 1907 Catalogue (Figure 4.14) which advertised Boucher calculators with metal and paper scales. These are the HC Calculigraphe type, and are shown as made in France, they could have been the source of many of the Calculigraphes found in England, and are competitively priced.

Dietzgen, USA

They advertised a Model 1797 'Boucher' with card dials (available between 1902 and 1936) and the Model 1797½ with silvered metal dials (available between 1904 and 1931). No examples are known, a 1910 Dietzgen catalogue shows a Calculigraphe type, complete with push-button, and marked "E.D.Co" in the same style as the mythical K&E device. The two alternatives could be the same as advertised by the Army and Navy Stores, and thus a Calculigraphe type. Dietzgen sold a number of different pocket-watch calculators at various times, but it is believed that they never manufactured.

Keuffel & Esser, USA

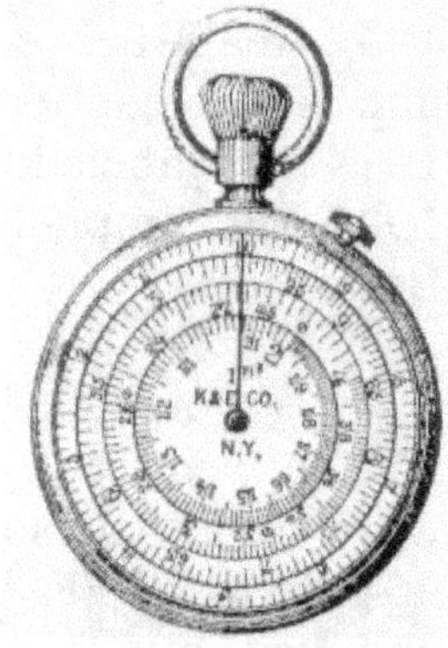

K&E were mentioned in Cajori [3] as makers of Boucher calculators, and an illustration of the K&E Boucher calculator features as Figure 12 in the book (Figure 4.15). They advertised the Model 1743½ as Boucher calculators from 1895 to 1899, and 4022 and 4024 from 1901 and the 4022-A and 4023 from 1903, through to 1906, before they started producing their own Sperry Calculator and later K&E Watch calculators from 1906 and 1909 respectively. Note that neither of these two later designs are Boucher, even though the earliest Sperry designs use two push-buttons to provide the functionality. Perhaps the Calculigraphe inspired this? It could be that the device is a bought-in Calculigraphe type device, the adjuster on the side looks more like a push-button than a second crown. Note also that the scales marked n^3 are identical with the standard H-C Calculigraphe scales. K&E calculators are covered in their own chapter later.

Figure 4.15: Boucher's calculator by K&E from Cajori, 1909

Queen, USA

The Boucher's calculator made for or sold by Queen is very obviously a Calculigraphe, albeit labelled specifically for Queen. The most obvious differences (comparing Figure 4.15 and Figure 4.16), or indeed any other Calculigraphe, are the more obvious screws on both faces of the Queen variant, which could imply that they used different scale materials, and is not obvious from the illustrations.

Figure 4.16: Boucher's calculator from Queen

Scientific Publishing

Some early editions of Pickworth[5] (6th (1900) and 7th (1901), page 83, 8th (1903) and 9th (1904) page 97,) refers to a Scientific Publishing 'Mechanical Engineer' calculator (see later chapter) incorrectly as a 'simpler and less expensive form of Boucher's calculator'. How Pickworth, who is normally extremely reliable in his commentary on slide rules, came to make such a statement relating to a single-sided pocket-watch slide rule is perhaps indicative of the generic tenor that the name 'Boucher' achieved for any 'pocket-watch type calculator', something that is further discussed in the next chapter on the Calculigraphe, which also achieved an almost interchangeable name with Boucher.

---

5   Pickworth – a series of books called 'The Slide Rule' by Charles N. Pickworth, published almost continuously between 1894 and 1962 which carried makers adverts as well as up-to-date descriptions of new slide rules allowing it to become a useful source of change information

Calculigraphe

Introduction

Cajori [3] identifies Henri Chatelain of Paris as making "... an improved form ..." of Boucher calculator in 1878. This is the Calculigraphe, which many retailers sold either as a Calculigraphe under their own name, or as the Boucher's Calculating Circle or Boucher's Calculator. It appears that 'Boucher's' or 'Calculigraphe' became interchangeable as one and the same device in a number of countries. This is confusing, however it is sometimes difficult to segregate the two devices, nevertheless we shall do just that while recognizing that in general a Calculigraphe is a separate variant of the Boucher Calculator.

The identifying feature of the Calculigraphe is the idiosyncratic method of providing control of the pointers via a push-button clutch, which enabled the crown to rotate the pointers instead of the front scales. This obviously produced a much cheaper design. A comparison of prices of a Calculigraphe, a K&E Boucher and a Stanley made Boucher at about the same period gives:

Calculigraphe from Army and Navy Catalogue (1907)	10/6d
Boucher (Stanley 1898 Catalogue)	27/6d
Stanley-Boucher (Stanley 1898 Catalogue)	45/-
K&E Boucher (Catalogue 1906)	$7 (approx. 60/-)

This is for broadly similar specification devices; the nearly 3:1 and 4½:1 price difference between Calculigraphe and Stanley devices inevitably reflects the difference in quality. However the K&E Boucher is very expensive in comparison, especially as it turns out to be a Calculigraphe. Yet it is cheap compared to the Sperry and K&E devices that followed. Calculigraphes have a decidedly 'notchy' feel to their rotation while the Stanley device is incredibly smooth in operation. A number of Calculigraphes also have been seen with stripped gears, which probably results from incorrect operation of the push-button and crown, and more fragile gears.

Figure 5.1: H-C thin Calculigraphe

Nevertheless the Calculigraphe is a surprisingly common device. The 1998 Oughtred Society survey of pocket-watch calculator ownership showed this to be the third most common design after Fowler and Halden amongst those who completed the Survey Questionnaire[6].

Further research has also shown that there are two major variants of Calculigraphe mechanism, which I have cared to call a 'fat' Calculigraphe, and a 'thin' Calculigraphe. These are respectively 20 mm (¾) and 16 mm (5/8") thick weighing respectively 97 and 75 grams. The 'fat' device is noticeably smoother in operation and a lot of the adverse comment on the functioning of the calculator is overcome in this device. We do not know whether the 'fat' and 'thin' devices were made by the same manufacturer.

Subsequent investigation has shown that the standard Calculigraphe has a large number of detail variations and was retailed by many suppliers of slide rules. Even so, it is not possible to be absolutely sure who made the device, and who purely sold them.

---
[6] 'Oughtred Society Pocket-Watch slide rule survey' in *Journal of the Oughtred Society*, Vol. 7, No. 2. Fall 1998, p17

Henri Chatelain

It is now believed that Chatelain of Paris was the originator of the design, sold as the H.C. Calculigraphe Calculating Circle, and also by other retailers under their own name, e.g. Army and Navy, Queen and probably even K&E.

An early set of instructions in French for a 'Cercle a Calcul (Calculigraphe H.C.) Système Boucher' dated August 1880 with the address 'Havre' which implies close links to Boucher himself (he was in the same town), describes three variants:

- ***Type 1***: A watch type with scales that follow the Boucher patent, and give '... average accuracy'.
- ***Type 2***: A desk type with a single dial that is in a different format allowing greater accuracy. This broad description is similar to the desk version described in Boucher's patent (Figure 4.4), no examples are known. This is a strong possibility as the Type 1 above follows the watch type described in the patent (Figure 4.1).
- ***Type 3***: A further watch type with the addition of square and cube scales. These can be seen as the 'improvements' which are advertised on the cover of most instructions for the Calculigraphe, and probably became the only variant to be sold. The instructions are for the Type 3 calculator only.

The later French manuals and known examples of English instruction books have never described the three types. This would make either Type 1 or Type 2 Calculigraphes extremely rare, and possibly only available for up to 2 years, between 1878 and 1880.

The differences on HC Calculigraphe examples examined are more detailed:
- We have the 'fat' 2″ (52.5mm) diam, ¾″ (20 mm) thick and 97 gms and 'thin' 2″ (55mm) diam, ⅝″(16mm) thick and 75.5 gms examples, with what appears a significantly different internal mechanism. See Figure 5.11 for a picture of the side views and the internals. The mechanism is incredibly 'agricultural' and it can now be seen why the thin Calculigraphe has the 'notchy' feel. My thanks to Richard Cook who was brave enough to open his example and supply a picture, I have not been brave enough to open mine or find any one else who has opened a 'fat' example!
- There are various differences in the furniture and the pointers, these are probably down to different batches
- There are numerous differences in the markings. Some 36 examples, 20 'fat' and 16 'thin', have been catalogued in the table at the end of the chapter, showing their markings. Some show 'Made in France', others do not and the logo of Chatelain (an opisometer or map-measurer, see Figure 5.10) does not always appear. There is no obvious logic between the variations; perhaps further examples will produce an answer.
- We then have a number of different makers' names. The traditional Calculigraphe has been seen as either made by 'H.C' or 'F.C.'. How 'F.C.' relates to the apparent original maker 'H.C.' we do not know.
- There are then other pocket-watch calculators bearing the 'Calculigraphe' name, such as the 'A.F.' device

The Calculigraphe is a very nice device in its own right and a worthwhile addition to any collection.

F-C Calculigraphe

There has been considerable discussion and debate about 'F-C' who made or sold one model of the Calculigraphe pocket-watch calculator. This appears identical in all respects, apart from the logo, to the H-C Calculigraphe. The significance of F-C is not known, and the logo (Figure 5.10) does not have an obvious meaning. It is an understandable assumption that F-C Calculigraphes are French the same as the H-C variety, however some items carrying the 'FC' trade mark are also known to carry the appellation 'Manufacture Francaise St Etienne', and some F-C opisometers also say 'Importe de Suisse' and an F-C opisometer has been seen marked 'made in Switzerland'. How this becomes 'FC' is not known. According to an article from 1894[7], there may be a link to Henri Chatelain. Whether this is a strong or tenuous link needs exploring further. This may simply reflect that F-C were a retail outlet, possibly of Swiss made instruments. It is possible that another known example is actually marked H-C on the back scale, which is interesting and very confusing. Interestingly Halden advertised an F-C Calculigraphe in 1902, see below.

Figure 5.2: F-C Calculigraphe

In addition to the standard double sided calculator (Figure 5.2) and the article) which the 1894 'Science' article describes, it also discusses a single sided device with a single pair of scales (Figure 5.3). The translation of the first few paragraphs of this article presents an interesting view of the history of the Calculigraphe:

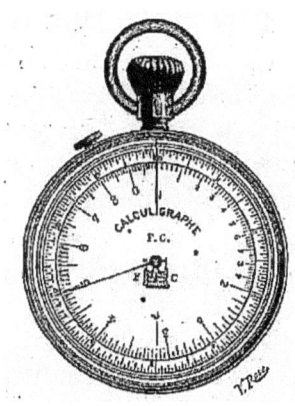

Figure 5.3: 1894 single dial F-C Calculigraphe

NEW INVENTIONS

The Calculigraphe or circle of calculation.

This little device was invented some twenty years ago by Mr. Boucher, an engineer at [Le] Havre, but manufacturing defects prevented the public from taking it up when Mr. Chatelain recently updated it again from top to bottom in order to make it a precision instrument, with safe and flawless operation. The calculigraphe, as now constructed, is effectively a new invention. Its use will soon become widespread because it provides people responsible for effecting long and careful calculations, with the use of a fast and reliable aid, and gives results of irreproachable accuracy.

The Calculigraphe is manufactured in two models. The simplest has a single dial, sufficient for all the arithmetic operations. The double sided model solves all problems of algebra, geometry, trigonometry.

The principle of this device relies on the property of logarithms, namely that the sum of the logarithms of two numbers is equal to the logarithm of their product, and conversely, if from the logarithm of a number we subtract the logarithm of another number, we get the logarithm of the quotient of dividing the former by the latter.

---

[7] La Science Illustrée Edition No 347, 21 Juillet 1894. Les Inventions Nouvelles. "Le Calculigraphe ou cercle à calcul"

So here is a view that is at variance with information available from HC Calculigraphe instruction books, but confirms that Chatelain (of whom nothing more is learned) redesigned Boucher's device and the impression given is that his devices are the FC labeled ones within the article. However this is likely to be wrong, as both Cajori and a Calculigraphe instruction book give dates of 1878 and 1880, some 14 years before this article was written.

Other Retailers of 'Standard' Calculigraphes

Halden UK

The Halden catalogue of 1902 (before they started selling the Calculex) advertised a 'Calculating Circle, Boucher System' calculator with a very obvious F-C Calculigraphe as the illustration – why is not known. The bigger mystery is that there are two models advertised, who made the 'superior English make' device at over double the price? Note they also sold the Mechanical Engineer calculator, and a desk version.

Dietzgen, USA

The Eugene Dietzgen Co. Catalogue of 1902 – 1903, 6th edition, shows and describes a Calculigraphe which is called a Boucher Calculator.

K&E, USA

K&E catalogues from 1895 through to 1899 shows a Calculigraphe which it also goes on to call a Boucher Calculator and sold as the Model 1743½. This became the Model 4022 and 4024 with card or metaled dials in 1901, to which was then added Models 4022-A and Model 4023, the latter with an extra dial, no example of which has ever been found, and could be an extremely rare device.

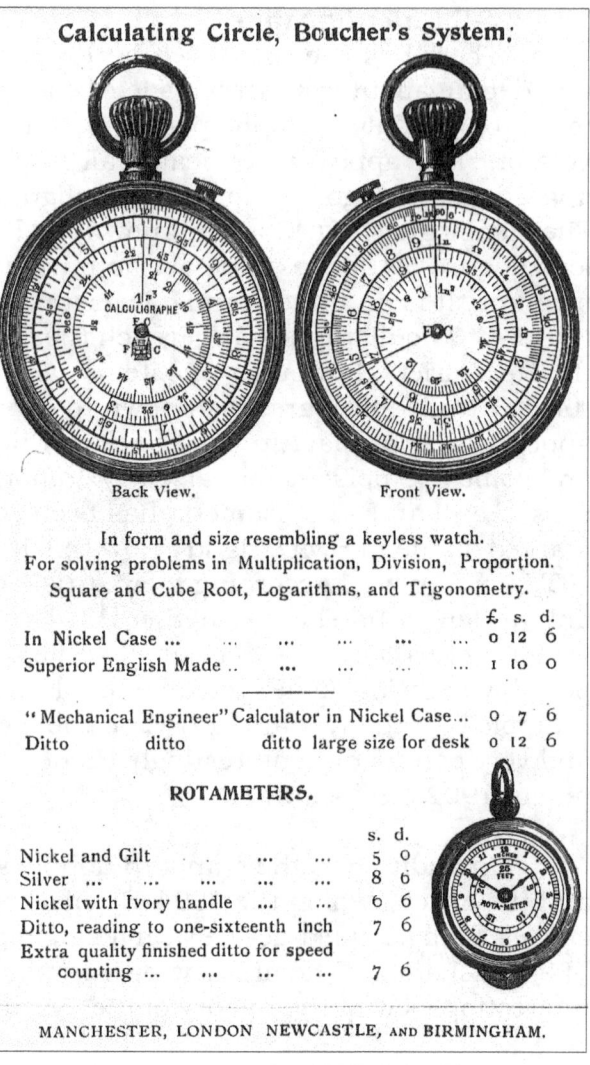

Figure 5.4: 1902 Halden catalogue

Technical Supply Company, Scranton PA, USA

Their 1913 catalogue describes a Boucher calculator that is clearly marked Calculigraphe on its face.

Queen, USA

An example of a Calculigraphe labeled Queen is illustrated in the Boucher chapter (Figure 4.16). Perhaps in the USA at least, 'Boucher' and 'Calculigraphe' had become synonymous.

L. Fischer, Paris, France

An H-C 'thin' Calculigraphe which carried a retailer's address in the same way as the Queen example: 'L. Fischer, 12. B. des Capucines Paris. Hotel' was sold on e-Bay in 2002. Whether there is any relationship to any of the other Fischer's involved with Calculigraphes is not known.

P. Berville, Paris, France

Another H-C 'thin' Calculigraphe which carried a retailer's address in the same way as the Queen and Fischer examples has been noted at a Scientific Instrument Fair, this one is labeled: 'P. Berville, 24 Chausee D'Antin, Paris'. As illustrated above there was no attempt at hiding the H.C labeling, and the practice must have been more common than was initially thought.

Figure 5.5: French H-C Calculigraphe with address for L. Fischer

Stanley's quote that they (Boucher's) could be '...had from any optician ...' should mean that there are other models of Boucher calculator to be found. Perhaps the ubiquitous Calculigraphe is what Stanley was referring to. Details of any other models are eagerly awaited!

H. Morin, Paris, France

Morin has been mentioned in the context of early Boucher calculators, however in 1910 he also advertised a 'Calculigraphe pour Reports de Bourse'. (Figure 5.6). This double sided device with simple scales was advertised under item number 9903, and illustrated in Figure number 1288.

Figure 5.6: Callculigraphe pour Reports de Bourse

The description in the catalogue can be translated and summarized as follows:

- This unit has a fixed dial and a mobile dial num ber on the scale are decreasing.
- The needle is moved by turning the crown and simultaneously pressing the button beside the pendant, [loop] the mobile dial is powered by the crown only.
- The two hands are on the fixed dial, one letter M indicating the postponement of the month and the other, the letter Q, the postponement of two weeks.
- The side of the mobile dial, has the needle for deferrals (letter R) and an index or fixed needle placed directly under the pendant (loop).

Hopefully this description might catalyse the discovery of an actual model of this particular Calculigraphe.

Secretan, Paris, France

A 1924 Secretan catalogue advertises a 'Calculigraphe Boucher' with either metal or cardboard faces. They are not illustrated to confirm whether they are a Boucher or a Calculigraphe (winder or clutch) and have been listed here due to the use of the Calculigraphe name.

Other Versions of Calculigraphes

A-F Calculigraphe

We know of an A-F Calculigraphe, and it has been rumored that others exist, however without specific information we can only assume that these are mythical devices.

Pedos S.A. Switzerland

An advertising leaflet and instructions (Figure 5.9) for the A-F Calculigraphe was produced by Pedos S.A., a Swiss firm in Renan, a municipality in the district of Courtelary in the canton of Bern in Switzerland. This is located in the French-speaking Bernese Jura. The

Figure 5.7: A-F Calculigraphe - Swiss

A-F Calculigraphe is a very different device of much higher quality. It is 2½″ (63mm) diam, ⅝″ (17mm) thick and weighs about 145 gms, and marked 'Swiss'. A variant is marked 'Fabrique en France'; who truly made them remains a mystery. The known examples (Figure 5.7 and 5.8) are marked 'Calculigraphe' and 'A. Fischer', presumably the A-F in the title of the instruction leaflet. The differences in the two examples are in the detailing. Little is known about Pedos, the firm, and nothing is known about Fischer. It can be assumed that he was responsible for the scale layout and the additional features which allow volt-drops to be calculated for power cables.

It would appear that Pedos sold the device, which was made by yet another unknown Swiss or French manufacturer. The use of the push-button may explain the continued use of the Calculigraphe name, and its inclusion in this section, or indeed he may have used what sounds like a generic name for a type of calculator.

There was a watch movement in the 1950's called Pedos, whether this is related in any way is not known, however it is possible as their catalogue/instruction leaflet shows other examples of high quality precision engineering, with the statement of regular make and guarantee.

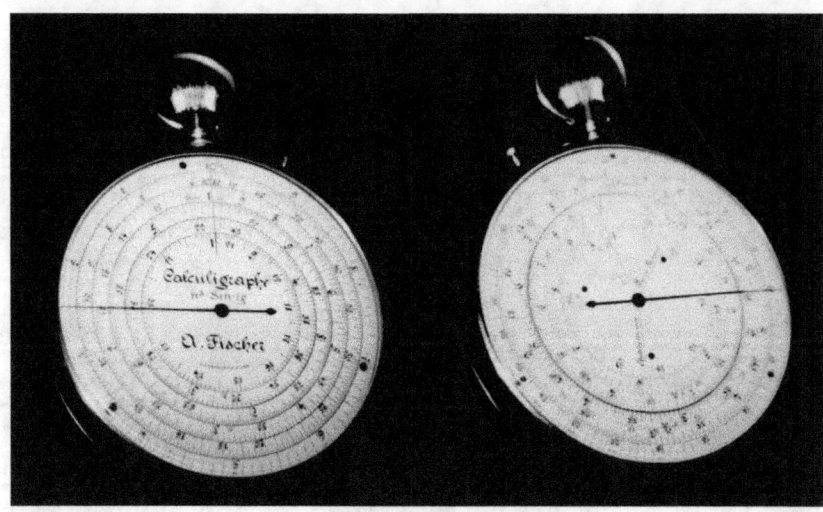

Figure 5.8: A-F Calculigraphe - Fabrique en France

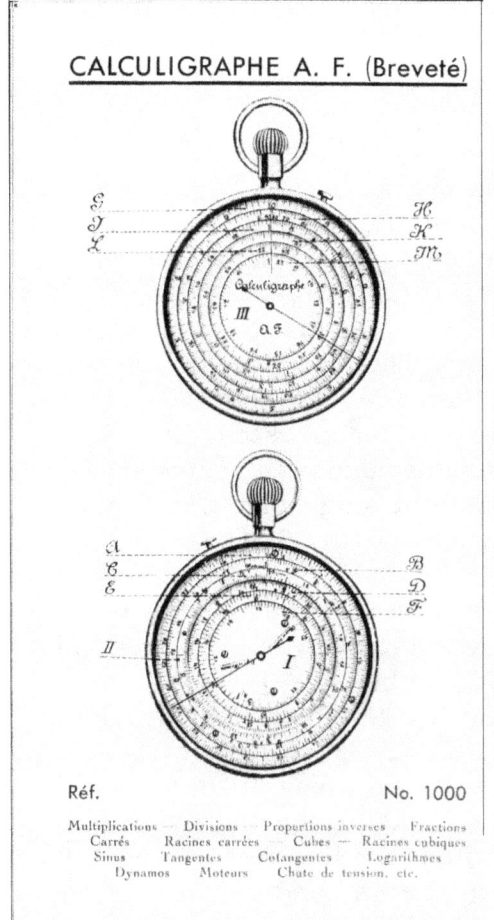

Figure 5.9: Pedos S.A. Instructions for the A-F Calculigraphe

The device operates somewhat differently to a "normal" Calculigraphe and has a very different scale layout. The front face, III on the leaflet, and that which carries the makers and type marks, and the 'Swiss' or 'France' appellation, is fixed and has six scales, from outer to inner:
- a Mantissa scale which works against the 'C' scale on the opposite side (G on leaflet)
- a Sine scale which works against the single cycle log scale that is adjacent as the third scale (H)
- single cycle log scale, anti-clockwise (J)
- scales 4, 5, and 6, three cycles of log scale, clockwise, with the breaks unusually, at 4.64 and 2.15 (K,L,M)

The rear face is in two halves, one outer fixed half (II) and a rotatable inner half (I).

Rotating the winder only turns the inner central part of the scale (I) which carries the one half of the usual C/D scales (also called C and D on the leaflet) with electrical and power gauge points, and then two square root scales working to the center (E & F). The outermost fixed scale on the back face looks to be a Tan scale (A); the next two going towards the center are a 'Motor' and 'Dynamo' ('B' & 'C') scale. Rotating the winder with the clutch button pushed in rotates the two pointers in synchronism.

There are minor detail variances in the 'Fabrique en France' marked A-F Calculigraphe, otherwise the scales and the calculator in general appear identical. A translation of the 'Summary Instructions' for the A-F Calculigraphe is included at Appendix 1.

Summary

So who actually made Boucher's and Calculigraphe calculators? The most likely scenario we can come up with is as follows:
- 1876 Boucher's patent is accepted in France and very shortly after in the same year, in England. It is not patented in either the USA or Germany.
- About the same time he has made (we are not sure by whom) the very early versions of his design (which has two winders, not one winder and one clutch as Calculigraphe) - see also Morin above.
- In approximately 1878 (Cajori) to 1880, Henri Chatelain makes the first HC Calculigraphe (from a French instruction sheet marked 'Août 1880 Havre'). This describes three versions of Calculigraphe, something that is not repeated in later French versions or the English instruction books. The common Calculigraphe we usually see is the third version described, the second is a desk model, the first has two dials but simple scales. There are no details given, but it could be that they are like the single pair of scales on the single dial FC version described in the 'Le Science' article. (Figure 5.3)
- We still do not know anything about Henri Chatelain.
- Some time before July 1894 (the date of the 'Le Science' article) FC (whoever they were) designs two versions of Calculigraphe. They are illustrated in the article. The single dial example is new; the two sided one is similar to HC Calculigraphes.
- French Intellectual Property records from January and April 1896 shows that Henri Chatelain was granted two logos. These are not the known ones, the early one uses a lower case 'hc' with serifs that may have been misread as 'fc' and this was changed in April to uppercase 'HC'. It is thus possible that HC and FC may be one and the same person, but why the different logos were maintained to date is not known.
- Manloves (not Manlove Alliott & Fryer) were agents for Boucher in London. I do not be lieve that they made Calculigraphes. They sold a Stanley version.
- Manove Alliott & Fryer certainly sold a Boucher calculator which, apart from the name is the same as one of the later 'AB' calculators
- K&E sold HC Calculigraphes; Figure 12 in Cajori is of a Calculigraphe marked K&E Co. NY. No examples are known.
- A number of other retailers (including Steward) are supposed to have made Calculigraphes (or indeed Bouchers) but no examples are known.
- In about 1902 Joseph Halden (before they made and sold their Calculex) advertised an FC Calculigraphe with a more expensive 'superior English make' version at about twice the price.
- We do not know who made the very early Boucher calculators, however various H. Morin catalogues (1910 and 1925/26) have illustrations of what could be an early Boucher with the 'AB' signature. This raises its own questions:
    - The Boucher was invented and patented in 1876, and so is it reasonable to be selling the same device in 1910 and 1925?
    - The Morin adverts for a 'Calculigraphe Boucher' which is a Boucher with winder, not a Calculigraphe with clutch button. So the terms 'Boucher' and 'Calculigraphe' become interchangeable in France as well as the USA, but not in the UK?
- Sometime prior to 1890 Stanley started selling a Boucher's calculator which was made in France. About 1890 they started making these devices themselves (or they were exclu sively made for Stanley). By 1898 the Stanley-Boucher with its additional 'rev-counter' was also being made. It is claimed that this was subsequently patented sometime between 1924 and 1931, but no trace has been found of this later patent. Note that Cajori shows the Stanley-Boucher as dating from 1905. These are very different calculators to either the original Boucher, or the Calculigraphe.

CALCULIGRAPHE

- Manloves (not Manlove Alliott & Fryer) sold a Stanley Boucher's calculator (without rev counter) at sometime.
- Manlove Alliott & Fryer sold an early Boucher's calculator at some time.
- 'FC' marked devices are relatively well known. Some items carrying the 'FC' trade mark are also known to carry the appellation 'Manufacture Francaise St Etienne', and some F-C opisometers also say 'Importe de Suisse'. How this becomes 'FC' and what the 'castle' logo has to do with the name is not known or what the relationship is also not known.
- The AF Calculigraphe is again very different. Versions marked 'Swiss made' and another marked 'Fabrique en France' are known - why the differences?
- The majority of third parties that retailed Boucher calculators sold the Calculigraphe under a variety of different 'makers' names, which is testament to its value-for-money appeal.
- There is no evidence to back up Stanley's statement that 'Boucher's calculators' were widely available unless he was talking about the Calculigraphe. This might also account for the (relatively) large number of standard Calculigraphes available to the collector.
- The Boucher Calculator and its close relative the Calculigraphe are a design of pocket-watch slide rule that is a valuable and interesting addition to any collection. That it was available from a variety of suppliers in a number of variations (some unknown other than as catalogue references) adds to the interest, and can make a major collection in its own right.

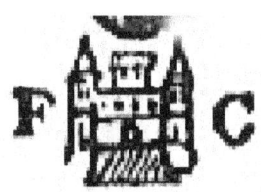

Figure 5.10: F-C Logo

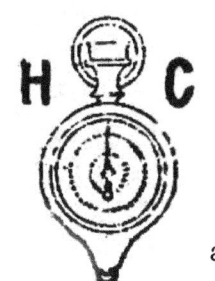

a

Figure 5.11: H-C Logo

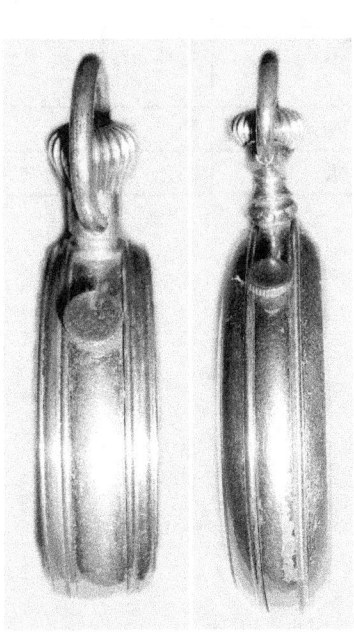

Figure 5.12: Showing side views of 'fat' and 'thin' Calculigraphe, and internal view of 'thin' Calculigraphe

Catalogue of Calculigraphe Markings

	Source	Front		Rear		Fat / Thin	UK Inst
		Text	Logo[1]	Text	Logo		
1	PMH	Calculigraphe	No	Nothing	No	Fat	
2	021279	Calculigraphe HC	Yes	Made in France	No	Fat	
3	134485	Calculigraphe	No	HC	Yes	Fat	
4	357228	Calculigraphe HC	Yes	Made in France	No	Fat	Fr.[2]
5	551843	Calculigraphe FC	FC logo	FC	No	Fat	
6	554856	Calculigraphe HC	Yes	Made in France	No	Fat	
7	722374	Calculigraphe HC Paris	No	Made in France	No	Fat	
8	871883	Calculigraphe HC	Yes	Made in France	No	Fat	
9	876871	Calculigraphe	No	Nothing	No	Fat	Y
10	972955	Calculigraphe	No	Nothing	No	Fat	
11	996442	Calculigraphe HC	Yes	Made in France	No	Fat	
12	Calc His Mus	Calculigraphe HC Paris	Yes	Made in France	No	Fat	
13	Slide rule Mus	Calculigraphe HC Paris	No	Made in France	No	Fat	Y!
14	HB	Calculigraphe HC	Yes	Made in France	No	Fat	
15	HB	Calculigraphe FC	FC logo	HC	No	Fat	
16	RKO	Calculigraphe HC Paris	No	Made in France	No	Fat	
17	Photocal.com	Calculigraphe HC Paris	No	Made in France	No	Fat	
18	Photocal.com	Calculigraphe FC[3]	FC logo	FC	No	Fat	
19	Ganymede	Calculigraphe	No	HC	Yes	Fat	Y
20	PMH pics	Calculigraphe FC	FC logo	Made in France	No	Fat	

(Table Footnotes are Separate)

---

1 The logo is the well known Opisometer for Henri Chatelain (HC) or the Castle for FC (see Figs 5.10 & 5.11)
2 The Instructions are French and dated 1880
3 Diagram from La Science Illustrée, No. 347, 21 Juillet 1894; Les Inventions nouvelles. With diagrams of FC Calculigraphe.

	Source	Front		Rear		Fat / Thin	UK Inst
		Text	Logo	Text	Logo		
1	PMH	Calculigraphe HC	Yes	Nothing	No	Thin	
2	339324	Calculigraphe HC	Yes	Nothing	No	Thin	
3	347780	Calculigraphe HC	Yes	Nothing	No	Thin	
4	382269	Calculigraphe HC	Yes	Made in France	No	Thin	
5	466408	Calculigraphe HC	Yes	Nothing	No	Thin	
6	547987	Calculigraphe HC	Yes	Nothing	No	Thin	
7	549419	Calculigraphe HC	Yes	Nothing	No	Thin	
8	TM[4]	Calculigraphe	No	HC	Yes	Thin	
9	714669	Calculigraphe HC	Yes	Nothing	No	Thin	
10	880971	Calculigraphe HC	Yes	Nothing	No	Thin	
11	957278	Calculigraphe HC	Yes	Nothing	No	Thin	Y
12	962573	Calculigraphe HC	Yes	L. Fischer etc.	No	Thin	
13	HvH	Calculigraphe HC	Yes	Nothing	No	Thin	
14	DR	Calculigraphe HC	Yes	Nothing	No	Thin	
15	RL	Calculigraphe	No	HC	Yes	Thin	
16	HB	Calculigraphe HC	Yes	Nothing	No	Thin	

Catalogue of Calculigraphe Markings

---

[4] Is a Thin Calculigraphe, but has "Fat" furniture.

Meyrat & Perdrizet Pocket-Watch Calculators

Introduction

This is probably the only genuine 'Pocket–Watch calculator', that is, one that includes a watch movement within the slide rule scales. This design was originally quoted wrongly as a possible fourth type of Lord's Calculator, because the first example seen carried no names or any other documentation. However, this is now known not to be the case. This is a 'Cercle a Calcul' made by the French firm of Meyrat & Perdrizet, of Seloncourt, Doubs in France. Very little is known of the maker, more information would be very welcome. Seloncourt, is a tiny town on the river Doubs in the far east of France. It was under the rule of Württemberg, and 10 kms. from Switzerland. It was a center of watch making in the 18th and 19th centuries. Firms located here included the Fréres Beurnier, well known and long established clock makers. This could well be the motivation for making the device here.

Figure 6.1: M&P Type 1 with watch movement inc. second hand

Types of Calculator

The M&P calculator was patented in France; about four years after Boucher patented his pocket-watch calculator. Under the title 'Règle à calcul circulaire' in 1880, the inventor is given as Meyrat et Perdrizet, the patent number is 139,898 with a description as 'Règle à calcul circulaire, – Meyrat et Perdrizet'. Other than this, little is known of M&P or who the designer was within this organization. Nevertheless they produced a delightful and unique device.

The inclusion of a watch movement within the slide rule makes this an unusual and unique true pocket-watch slide rule (Figure 6.1 here). The watch functions are controlled by the central winding and adjustment key, the slide rule functions by the two side keys at about 15° each side of the center key. I have seen illustrations of examples with and without a second hand. These are different versions as 'une petite seconde trotteuse' – a second hand – was an extra 5 Francs on the price, which was 60Fr. for an ordinary metal cased watch and 75 Fr. for a silver cased version. The model with second hand had a blued steel sweep second hand with gold hour and minute hands, the one without had blued steel hour and minute hands. A version with hinged internal black with its own crystal is also known.

Figure 6.2: M&P Type 1 showing the watch movement

For the calculating function a short pointer is attached to a rotating element on the inner edge of one of the slide rule scales, and moves independently of the scale.

A second version without the watch movement (Figure 6.3) is also known and is possibly more common. This has the same scales, but the slide rule functions are now controlled by the central key and one side key, the pointer rotates from the central axle.

Figure 6.3: M&P Type 2 calculator without watch movement

MEYRAT & PERDRIZET POCKET-WATCH CALCULATOR

Figure 6.4a: M&P rear of Type 2 Calculator

The Instructions are usually signed Meyrat & Perdrizet, Alse Beaudroit F'cant, Seloncourt, Doubs, No. 140 (a serial number). They are often dated 1899, some time after the patent date. Instructions dated 1884 have been rumored, I am not aware of how different these would be.

A description of the watch movement is as follows:

'The frosted gilt bar movement jeweled to the third, with mono metallic balance and cylinder escapement, the white enamel dial with Roman numerals, outer Arabic five minute divisions, the dial centered by two slide rule scales, one scale and a cursor adjusted by two buttons in the band, in plain metal case, 60 mm.(2⅜") diameter'.

It would also appear that M&P calculators are serial numbered. I have not been able to find enough information on this subject; however examples have been seen with numbers as disparate as No 140, 162, 327 and No 507, whose auction description is given below:

Meyrat & Perdrizet, Breveté S.G.D.G., Alse. Beaudroit Fabricant, Seloncourt (Doubs), France, No. 507, circa 1900. Unusual, nickel, large, keyless watch with centre-seconds and calculator. C. (Case) Three-body, "bassine et filets", polished. D. (Dial) White enamel with Roman numerals, outer Arabic minute and seconds ring and silvered revolving calculator scale. Blued steel "spade" hands. M. (Movement) 18''', gilt brass, cylinder escapement, plain brass three-arm balance, flat balance spring. Diam. 60 mm. (2⅜")

The short-hand parts of the description cover Case, Movement and Dial, however the '507' appears to be a serial number, a similar three-digit figure can be seen in Figure 6.4 at the '7 o'clock' position.

Figure 6.4b: M&P Calculator

Figure 6.5: A section from the 1899 M&P Instruction book

```
                              LUXEUIL
                         IMPRIMERIE M. PATTEGAY
                              1899




                         PRIX DE L'INSTRUMENT
Boîte en Métal ........................................................ 60 fr.
Boîte en Argent ....................................................... 75.—

         Une petite seconde trotteuse augmente la pièce de 5 fr.
```

Lord's Pocket-Watch Calculator

Introduction

The Lord's Calculator family first became generally known to collectors via The Oughtred Society Survey of 1998[8] covering 'Watch Pocket Calculators'. This produced a number of surprises, one of which was Lord's Calculator, previously unknown as a pocket-watch type. Then to add to the pleasure, there appeared a number of variants and at least four supposed "manufacturers" or, more probably, retailers of the device. Lord's calculators appear to have been designed and made for mill managers in the spinning and weaving trades to be able to make specific relevant calculations.

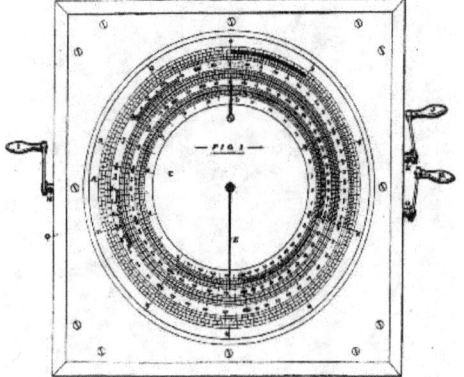

Figure 7.1: front view of Lord's desk calculator from patent 22,210

Lord's Patents

There are two patents which carry the name Lord; both are applicable to a greater or lesser extent to these calculators, the second being completely relevant to pocket-watch designs.

Patent No 22,210 of 1892 with an application date of 5th December 1892, accepted on 7th October 1893, was awarded to Lawrence Lord, Mill Manager, of 66 Devonshire Road, Burnley, Lancaster. It describes an '... improved apparatus or calculator [which] consists of a system of dial plates and concentric rings or circles ... to act after a manner of the ordinary slide- rule ... specially [sic] adapted for calculating, in textile industries, the quantities of weft, warp reed, pick, counts, length and values.'

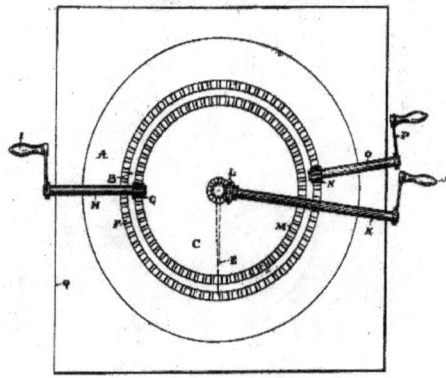

Figure 7.2: rear view of Lord's desk calculator from patent 22,210

The drawings in the patent show a large circular calculator with three handles to rotate, via spur and bevel gears, the various dials and a pointer. The detailed description goes on to describe how 'The whole apparatus may be enclosed within a neatly constructed box or case when the instrument is large ...' but does later suggest 'In smaller instruments the case is preferably in the form of a watch ...'. Having set out the alternatives, Lord goes on to say: '... I do not confine myself to the particular form of driving arrangement herein described, as it will be evident, other driving arrangements may be devised for the purpose.' The option for a number of different pocket-watch calculators is therefore briefly touched on in the patent.

The suite of scales on the various dials of the 'desk' model covered in the text and illustrated in the drawing of the front of the calculator (Figure 7.1) are as follows:

- The outer (fixed) scale has:
- a scale of the mantissa of logarithms,
- a single cycle logarithmic scale, and
- one or two small scales commencing from 56 or 84 of the inner (logarithmic) graduations and continuing in a reverse direction to 46.66 and 70 respectively.

---

[8] 'Oughtred Society Pocket-Watch slide rule survey' in *Journal of the Oughtred Society*, Vol. 7, No. 2. Fall 1998, p17

LORD'S POCKET-WATCH CALCULATOR

Figure 7.3: Desk calculator made by Elliott Bros.

The latter of these is '... specially valuable for obtaining per centages [sic.] in calculations for cotton, whilst the former is used for... woollen good' [sic].

- An inner (moveable) scale which has:
  - a single cycle logarithmic scale on both edges
- A moveable dial plate with a single cycle logarithmic scale graduated in sixteenths, this also has a cursor set at '1' which extends across all the other scales

There is also a pointer capable of separate movement. The drawings of the front and rear of the desk calculator are shown in Figures 7.1 and 7.2, and an actual example is shown in Figure 7.3. This is made by Elliott Bros. London, carries a two-digit serial number (35), another Elliott example is known with a single digit serial number.

The second Lord's patent is **No 7,081 of 1903**, accepted in 1904. The patentees are Ernest Lord of 57 Devonshire Road and Wilkinson Lord of 61 Queen Victoria Road, both in Burnley. We can only speculate that these two were sons of Lawrence, the fact that one lived 'just down the road' from Lawrence and was also a Mill Manager adds some weight to the argument but is not conclusive.

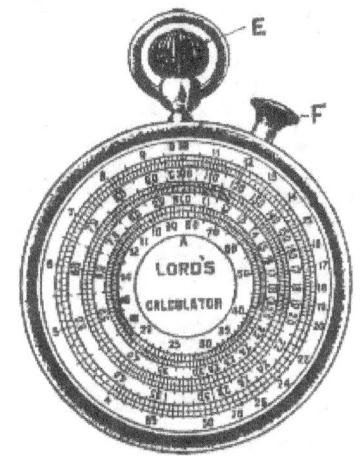

Figure 7.4: Pocket-Watch Calculator from patent 7,081

This patent emphasizes the pocket-watch form: 'The instrument is preferably in watch form ... but it may be made of any size or shape desired.'

The drawing accompanying the specification is shown in Figure 7.4. From this it can be seen that this is the design for what we have taken as the Type 1 calculator, while the other types use other different parts of the design within the patent.

Types of Lord's Pocket-Watch Calculators

Four versions of calculator are known, Type 1, Type 2 and Type 4 which have scales on one face only but are very different in layout and size, and Type 3 which has scales on back and front faces. All are in a pocket-watch style case with winders.

Type 1.
The Type 1 calculator very obviously follows the design shown in the second patent, **7081/1903**, with the same layout of scales, controls and so on. It is single sided.

Figure 7.5: Type 1 Lord's Calculator from Elliott Bros.

POCKET-WATCH SLIDE RULES

Very similar designs from Elliott Bros. of London (illustrated in Figure 7.5) and W. Waddington and R. Waddington of Coventry, and J. Casartelli & Son of Manchester in Figure 7.6. Two crowns (knobs) control the equivalent of the inner scale and the moveable dial plate described in the patent. The R. Waddington's example is quite big, being approx. 2¾" (70 mm) diameter, while the Casartelli one is a massive 3 ⅜" (86mm). The large piece of extra metalwork is nothing to do with the calculator, and is probably to allow it to be mounted near or on a piece of machinery. The others are smaller, and it is assumed that the Elliott one is smaller. Both large and small versions have the following scales:

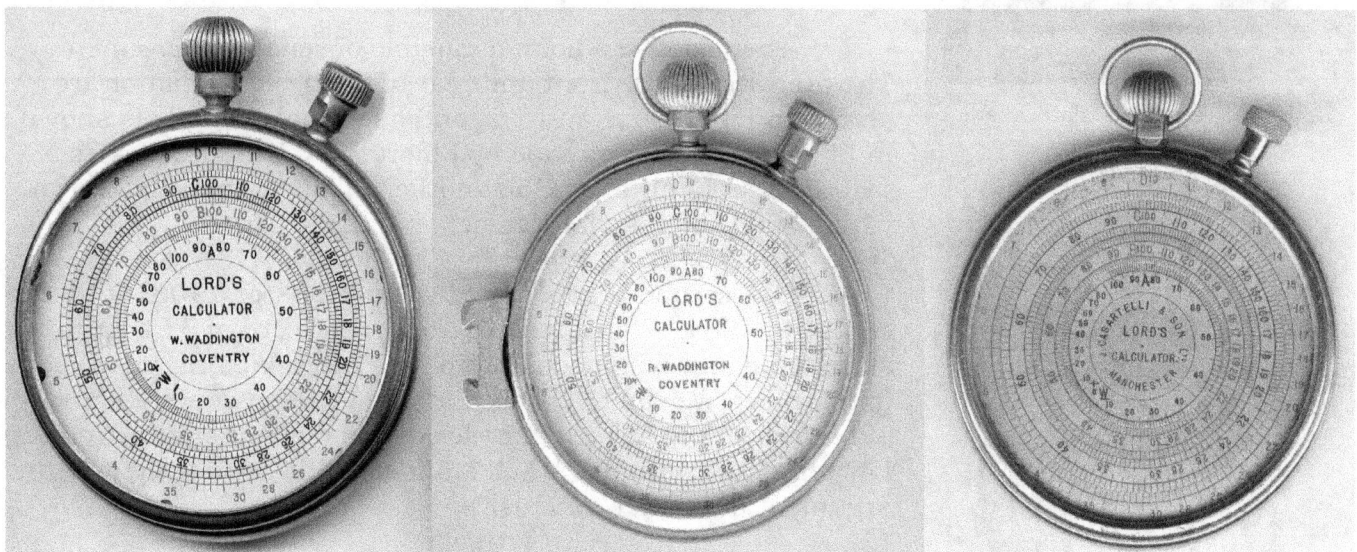

Figure 7.6: Type 1 Lord's Calculators from W. Waddington and R. Waddington of Coventry, and J. Casartelli & Son of Machester

- The outer fixed scale, labeled D, is a single cycle logarithms scale from 1 to 10, graduated in 'eighths'.
- An inner scale, labeled C, is a single cycle logarithmic scale from 10 to 100. This is rotated by one of the knobs.
- A second inner scale labeled B, with similar graduations to C, is controlled by the other knob.
- The inner fixed plate has an unusual scale from 0 to 100 in two directions, the − direction covering approx. 270°, the + direction using the remainder.

There are two rotating sets of scales, but no pointers or cursors on either model.

It is possible that all Elliott, Casartelli and Waddington calculators were made by the same unknown manufacturer. They are very similar in look and graduations only differing in minor detail such as the shape of the crowns and obviously the maker's name on the center plate. Elliott advertised themselves as mathematical instrument makers, and would have been capable of making a Lord's calculator, Casartelli made sophisticated equipment for the textile industry and may have been capable of making the calculator, nothing is known about either Waddington as possible makers. It has not been possible to date any of the examples, however it can be speculated that the Waddington examples may be older. This is simply from the look of the device and the watch furniture, but is highly subjective.

Type 2.

Figure 7.7: Type 2 Lord's Calculator, unknown maker

Figure 7.8: Type 2 Lord's Calculator, Unknown maker (2)

The evolution from Type 1 to Type 2, if indeed Type 2 is later, is not obvious. It is possible that with its moveable pointer as described in the earlier patent, Type 2 may be the earlier type. A number of Type 2 variants are known, two examples from unknown makers, and one by W. Wilson. However as nothing is known of Wilson, we are unable to verify which the earlier or later type is.

The two examples each by an unknown but possibly common maker, one in silver (Figure 7.7), the other in nickel silver (Figure 7.8) are illustrated. They are simply marked 'Lord's Patent'. Both have the scales on one face of a 2.5″ (64 mm) diameter pocket-watch case. The positioning of the two additional crowns is different on each example. The silver version has them at 35° and 77°, the nickel silver model at 30° and 70°. Both examples have the 'E' at the center, this is the same as the example from Wilson, however it is fairly probable that Wilson did not make either example, apart from the side crowns being differently placed, the hands are also different while both Wilson devices (Type 2 and 3) use the same hand with no reverse overhang.

The scales on this model are:

- Fixed outer scale, a single cycle logarithmic scale from 10 to 100 labeled A, plus the 'short' scale from 70 to 85, but which also carries an anti-clockwise 0 to 20 scale, both of which are of unknown use.
- Middle rotatable scale, is a single cycle scale from 10 to 100 labeled B on the outer edge and C on the inner edge.
- Inner rotatable scale is single cycle logarithmic, graduated in 'eighths'. There is a label D on the centre ring, which may apply to the adjacent scale or the cursor.
- There is a pointer on the central spindle, and the cursor from the top of the central disc.

The Type 2 example (Figure 7.9) made by W. Wilson of London is identical in scale layout etc to the two unknown maker examples and to one face of the Type 3. Its two crowns are at 35° and 70°. Whether the positioning of the additional keys is an indication of the maker is not certain. (See Appendix 2).

Note that while the scales, the pointer, and the cursor on the front face of this Type 2 are the same as the front face of the Type 3, the crowns may well operate different aspects of the two types of calculator.

Figure 7.9: Type 2 Lords Calculator from W.Wilson, London, front and the blank rear

It is not possible to date these two examples; they appear very similar in date with virtually identical furniture (knobs etc.). However, the Wilson device has very obvious screw heads and axles showing on the reverse, while neither the Type 1 devices nor the unknown maker Type 2 devices show the same mechanical details on the back. There appear to be a high quality suite of examples with gold knobs and a more utilitarian with gunmetal / blued furniture, and then there are the silver and nickel silver examples – a quite delightful variety of instruments to tempt the collector!

Type 3.

The evolutionary path and relative dates between this and the previous two types are also completely unknown. A two-sided version is not an obvious path that is covered by the known patents. We need more information to make any sort of informed guess on the development of the types.

One example, a two-sided model with three crowns, (at centre, 35° and 70°) also labeled W. Wilson, London, is known. This is also a smaller device, 2.5″ in diameter. The scales are as follows:

- Front face: See Figure 7.10, as previously listed for Type 2:
  - Fixed outer scale labeled A, a single cycle logarithmic scale from 10 to 100, and the short scale 84 to 70.
  - Inner moveable single cycle logarithmic scale from 10 to 100, labeled B.
  - Inner moveable scale from 1 to 10 in eighths labeled C.
  - There is a cursor labeled D which extends to '1' on the A scale.
  - The center spindle carries a pointer, maybe labeled E.

- Rear face: See Figure 7.10, right:
  - Fixed L scale.
  - Moveable disc single cycle log scale on both edges.
  - Fixed or moveable degree scale (uncertain).
  - Pointer on central spindle.

Image Courtesy of the Conrad Schure Collection

Figure 7.10: Type 3 Lord's Calculator from W. Wilson, London, Front and Rear faces

This type has two rotating discs (B & C on the front) worked from crowns, the other (center?) crown works the pointer. It should also be noted that the pointers at front and back are different – whether this is a design feature or a repair is unknown, all that can be said is that the two types of pointer feature on other single sided calculators. On the rear there is definitely one and maybe a second disc which may rotate, it is not certain if these are locked together or synchronized in any way. Again, it has not been possible to date this calculator.

LORD'S POCKET-WATCH CALCULATOR

Figure 7.11: Type 4 Lord's Calculator from W. Wilson, London, Front and Rear faces.

Type 4

Another variant of Lord's calculator has come to light which I have called Type 4. It too is made by W. Wilson of London, carries the same suite of scales as Type 2 and the front face of the Type 3, but has the subsidiary keys at 28° either side of the center key. It is a single sided variant, leaving Type 3 still as the only double sided type.

Two examples are known, one having appeared on e-Bay in 2010. The illustrated example is a silver cased example (Hallmarks on the stem) with the gold colored knobs, and uses the very elegant fine pointer with circular finial to the overhang. The second example does not have the circular finial, but is definitely silver cased with a date mark of 1897 and a maker's case mark of C.H. (for Charles Harrold & Co, of 2 and 3 St. Paul's Square, Birmingham?) on the main suspension loop stem (both sides) and on the bow. The actual marks are the Lion Rampant (sterling silver) and date letter 'b'. The case inside is marked with C.H and 7 underneath that the number 124. The item is guaranteed as all silver cased. The slide rule measures 2 3/8″(60mm) diameter. It has three sets of scales, the left hand side button operates the very inner circle with fixed blue steel hand marked C10 on dial; the center button operates the middle scales marked B10; and the right hand button operates the central pointer.

It has to be one of the very nicest pocket-watch slide rules the collector could aspire to own.

W. Wilson

W. Wilson, of 1 Belmont St., London. S.W. (though another record shows this address as London N.W.) is known as a maker of various instruments such as Spherometers, Dip Circles and so on, some of it dated as late as the second quarter of the 20th century. Some of it dated are later than expected for the Lord's calculators which seems no later than pre WW1, and thus whether this is a relevant address or not is not known.

Equally, it is not known whether W. Wilson had any relationship with the firm of Wilson and Gillie (W&G) of The Quay, North Shields, or indeed any other firm carrying a Wilson name in part. W&G were in existence in 1922, and it is not known whether W. Wilson came before or after.

Summary

A possible scenario for Lords calculators may be as follows:

- The Type 1 calculators all look to have a common maker, but which of them was it? Was it Elliott or someone else who never put their name on a calculator?
- The two 'unknown maker' examples of Type 2 do not look to have a common maker and it is probable that this was not the same maker who made the Type 1 devices. We do not know who the maker was.
- Why there are some examples of Type 2 not marked with a maker's or retailer's name when there is space is impossible to guess. One would have thought that the maker would have been extremely proud to have made and marketed such an attractive calculator.
- The Wilson two-sided version with its identical front face to Type 2 and additional scales on the rear is very different. Did Wilson also make it, or was there yet another manufacturer and was Wilson simply a retailer is not known. Is the significance more about the extra face or a different maker?
- We do not know why Wilson also made a Type 4 calculator whose only difference to the Type 2 is the positioning of the winders.
- When were they made and for how long? We can assume a start date shortly after the first patent (1892) and the Type 1 may only have followed the later patent (i.e. after 1902) and there fore have been made after the Type 2, 3 and 4.
- Who set out the various types and why?
- Do we know anything more about Lawrence Lord, Mill Manager? His ideas for a very sophisticated calculator must surely have come from an interesting background.[9]
- What, if any, was the relationship between Ernest and Wilkinson with each other and with Lawrence?
- What is known about W. Waddington and R. Waddington?

If anyone can add to this information, add other examples or resolve some of these points, I would be very grateful.

---

9   'Further information on Lord's Calculators ....' Colin Barnes in *Slide Rule Gazette*, Inaugural Issue, Autumn 2000, p69 shows that the name Lord was common in the Burnley area, and that there were a large number of people named Lord in relevant jobs in that area. The first patentee Lawrence was the second son of a preacher, well known for his mathematical ability and as a prolific inventor. Ernest and Wilkinson were his second and third sons.

Keuffel and Esser (K&E) Pocket-Watch Calculators

Introduction

K&E are the only United States company with any history of making and selling pocket-watch slide rules. They started by selling a version of the Calculigraphe, and then they took on the pocket-watch slide rule patents of Elmer Sperry and George Lange producing an attractive and unique range of pocket-watch devices. The first and so far only, effort at trying to make sense of the chronology of these pocket-watch calculators was in the JOS[10] so it makes sense to start over again with as much new information as we can muster.

K&E Catalogues

There are now a number of web-sites which carry more and new K&E information than was available when the original JOS article was written. This has to help in making new sense, amongst the best are the following, the first for the company history, http://www.antiquesurveying.com/K&E%20History.htm and then for catalogue details there is http://mccoys-kecatalogs.com/ from where you can view and download pages from virtually every K&E catalogue, an absolutely invaluable reference source.

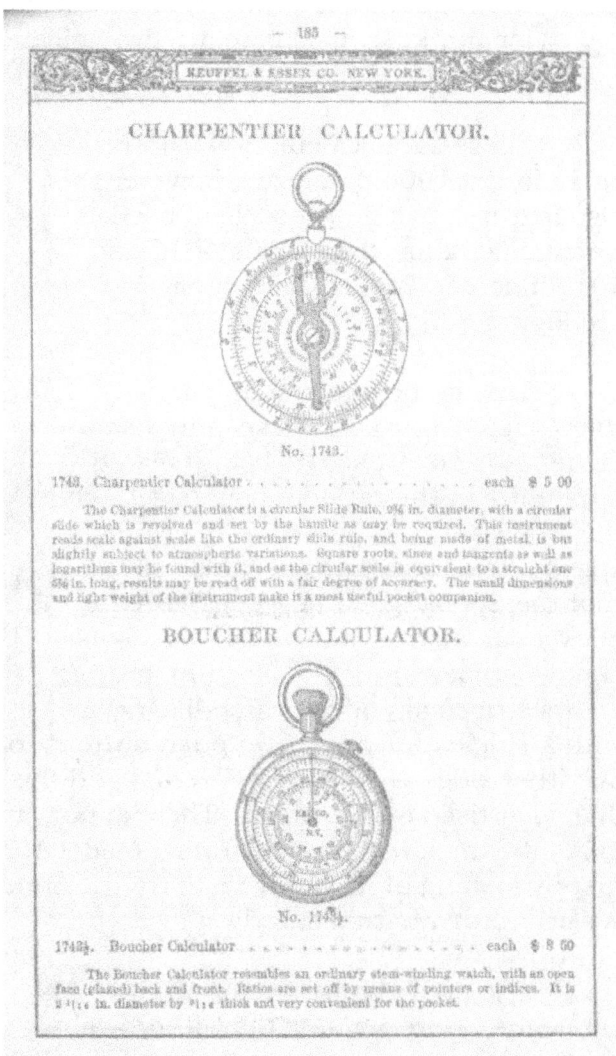

Figure 8.1: 1895 K&E catalogue

The catalogues show that K&E started selling a Boucher (Calculigraphe) calculator as Model 1743½ at the same time as the Charpentier Calculimetre (Model 1743) for the first time in 1895, for $8.50 and $5 respectively, the relevant page from the 1895 catalogue is shown in Figure 8.1. The Boucher calculator illustrated is very obviously a Calculigraphe. Whether any examples ever had the 'K&E Co NY' marking added is doubtful, but perhaps someone has an example. We have pictures of an example device sold by K&E, (Figure 8.6) it is not labeled K&E in any way.

Similar pages are in all catalogues through to 1899, and in 1901 there is the first change. First the model numbers change, the Boucher (Calculigraphe) calculator becomes Model 4022 and a new model 4024 is added. The Charpentier Calculimetre becomes Model 4020. We have to assume that the 4024 is directly equivalent to the Model 1743½ as the price is the same and we now know it had 'enameled cardboard dials', while the new Model 4022 at $14.- had silvered metal dials.

---

10   'Elmer A. Sperry and His Calculator' Bob Otnes in Journal of the Oughtred Society, Vol.6, No 2, Fall 1997 Pg 19.

The next change takes place in 1903, where the catalogue now shows two additional new models of Boucher calculator as well as confirming that the Model 4024 is a 'Calculigraph' [sic] as we have already surmised.

This is as illustrated in Figure 8.2, which is text cut from the 1903 catalogue page, see below. We have:

- Model 4022A as 4022 but with paper dials at $12.50 (why is this more expensive than the enameled cardboard dials version?)
- A new and intriguing model, the Model 4023 'with an extra hand for recording revolutions of the long hand' at an expensive $19. Never having seen such a device, unless it was a Stanley Boucher type with 'rev-counter' – but that is not what it says in the catalogue – we can only guess. There is no further explanation or illustration of this model. Even the explanation of the other models is not exactly clear and concise, one could be forgiven for thinking that there are two 'milled head keys' to operate the two sides – which is not the case.

These same calculators feature again in the 1906 catalogue, however this also features two new models of pocket-watch calculator, the Models 4016 and 4017 'Sperry's Pocket Calculator', see Figure 8.3.

4022.	Boucher Calculator, silvered metal dials, (Calculigraph)	each	$ 14 00
4022-A.	Boucher Calculator, like No 4022, but with paper dials	"	12 50
4023	Boucher Calculator, like No. 4022-A, but with an extra hand for recording revolutions of the long hand . . .	"	19 00
4024.	Boucher Calculator, enameled cardboard dials	"	8 50

The Boucher Calculators resemble an ordinary stem-winding watch and have glass covered dials back and front.

They are about 2⅛ in. diameter by ⅝ in thick; hence of convenient size for the pocket. One of the dials can be revolved by means of the milled-head key at the stem; the other is fixed. Each dial is provided with a hand or pointer. These two pointers are fixed on a common axle and move together and alike by a milled-head key on the edge of the case. A third pointer is attached to the rim over the movable dial.

The fixed dial has an outer scale of equal parts and the three inner circles are the cube roots of the numbers on the logarithmic scale from 1 to 2,154, from 2.154 to 4,657 and from 4.657 to 10, respectively.

The movable dial has an outer circle of angles from 5° 44' 39" to 90°, the sines of which are found on the next inner circle, which is the logarithmic scale. Ratios are set off in a similar manner as on the Fuller Slide Rule.

No. 4024 is similar to No. 4022, but about ⅝ in. thick. There is no second milled head key for the pointers, which are operated by the key at the stem when pressing a button on the edge.

Figure 8.2: Text cut from 1903 K&E catalogue

This is the one and only time that the Model 4016 Sperry is seen in a catalogue. It is advertised as being 'geared differently in the ratio of their scales' while the Model 4017 is 'geared to the same speed'. The catalogue sheet also says that the Sperry's is a new departure in pocket calculators' and that it was 'Patented October 25, 1904'. The illustration shows a normal pocket-watch like device with a single crown and two push buttons, one on either side. Note also the 'S' dial and the 'L' dial advertised on the sheet. There is no way of identifying a Model 4016 from a Model 4017 just by looking at it; you have to try the hands! We will return to this shortly.

SPERRY'S POCKET CALCULATOR.

S dial Nos. 4016 and 4017. L dial

4016.	Sperry's Pocket Calculator, watch pattern, diam. 2¼ in., with two engraved metal dials geared differently in the ratio of their scales, with Directions, ...	each	$ 20 00
4017.	Sperry's Pocket Calcalator, like 4016, but the two dials geared to the same speed, with Directions, ...	each	18 00

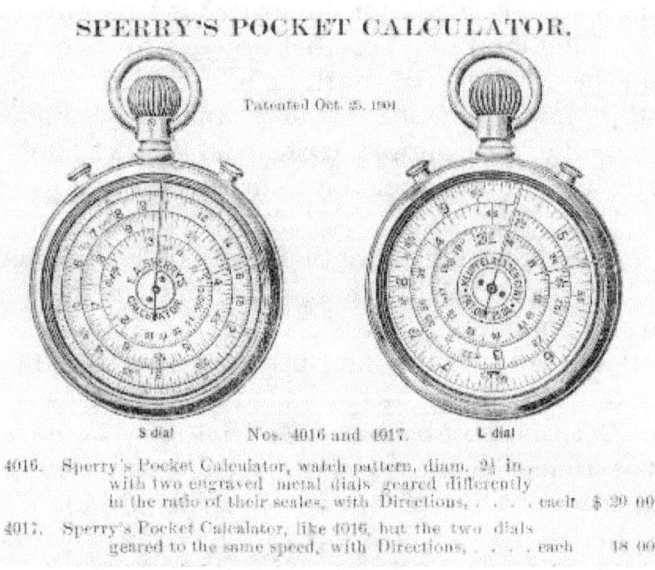

Figure 8.3: Illustration of K&E 4016 and 4017 early calculators from 1906 catalogue

The final change occurs in the 1909 catalogue. Here we note the withdrawal of the 4016 Sperry, the continuation of the 4017 Sperry and the introduction of the 4018 K&E Calculator on subsequent pages of the catalogue; see Figure 8.4.

Subsequent catalogues carry on advertising the same calculators, the 4017 Sperry through to 1939, the 4018 K&E to 1927, and the 4020 Charpentier until 1930.

Early K&E Pocket-Watch Devices

Having identified the chronology of K&E pocket-watch slide rules via the catalogues, we can now start looking at actual examples and other references, starting with the Model 1743½ (which I have seen described as Model 1743/1 and Model 1743/2 – a complete misunderstanding by those authors!).

K&E were mentioned as makers of Boucher calculators in Cajori. An illustration of the K&E Boucher calculator features as Figure 12 in the book (Figure 8.5). It is fairly obviously a Calculigraphe. No examples are known which are marked K&E. We have seen them advertise the Model 1743½ as a Boucher calculator from 1895 to 1906 – before they started producing their own Sperry Calculator and later K&E Watch calculators from 1906 and 1909 respectively.

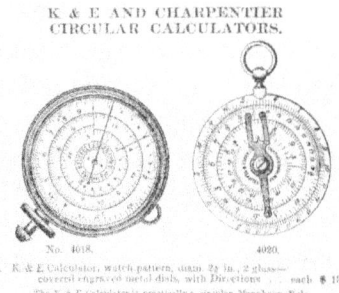

Figure 8.4: Illustration of K&E 4017 and 4018 early calculators and Charpentier 4020 from the 1909 catalog

The same picture is used in K&E's 1895 catalogue; it is surprising that Cajori, published in 1910, did not use a more up-to-date illustration.

The instruction sheet, complete with the appellation 'Boucher Calculators', 'Calculigraphs [sic]' and the K&E 127 Fulton Street, New York, address accompanying a Calculigraphe calculator confirms that K&E did supply such devices.

A closer look at the device itself in other photographs shows the 'Calculigraphe.' (front) and opisometer (back) logos for a normal Calculigraphe that have been covered in the previous chapter on them.

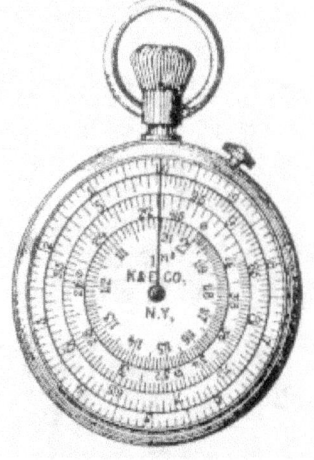

Figure 8.5: K&E Boucher from Cajori

K&E Patents

There are at least three versions of calculator which carry the E.A. Sperry name and a K&E label. There is one with a separate crown and two buttons, which is most unusual, the others use a concentric pair of nuts. These types are further detailed later.

Figure 8.6: Boucher and instructions from K&E

POCKET-WATCH SLIDE RULES

There are two different patent dates shown on K&E calculators and some examples are marked 'Pat Appd. for'. There are however three relevant patents. The patent information and the actual look and feel of the calculators, plus what is written on them is neither obvious nor logical. The third patent (Sperry's second slide rule patent of 1928) does not appear to have ever been quoted on a calculator even though it appears to be more related to the earliest Sperry devices. It is not the most logical situation.

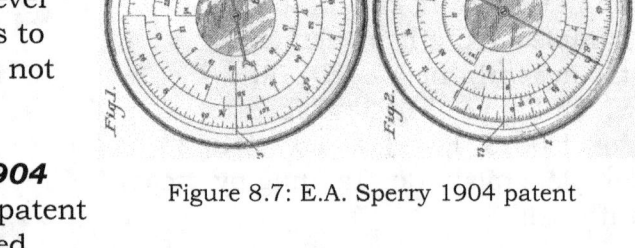

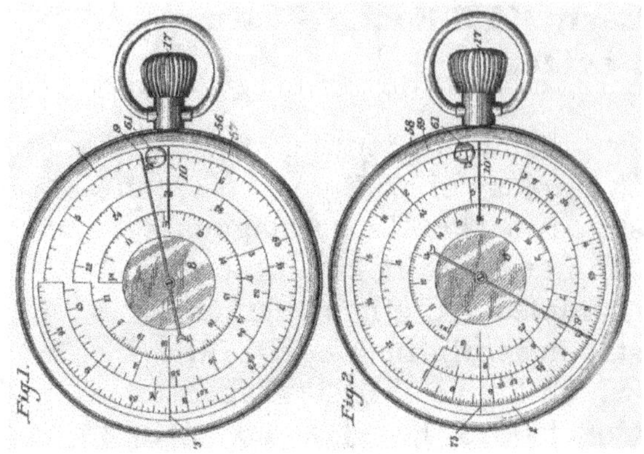

Figure 8.7: E.A. Sperry 1904 patent

Elmer A. Sperry, USA 773,235, 25 Oct 1904

The two figures 8.7 show how Sperry in his patent No. 773,235 filed 21st December 1903, and awarded 25th October 1904; intended that his pocket-watch calculator should work, with a single crown and, one of his unique ideas, was that there should be gearing to allow the functions on different sides to operate at different rates.

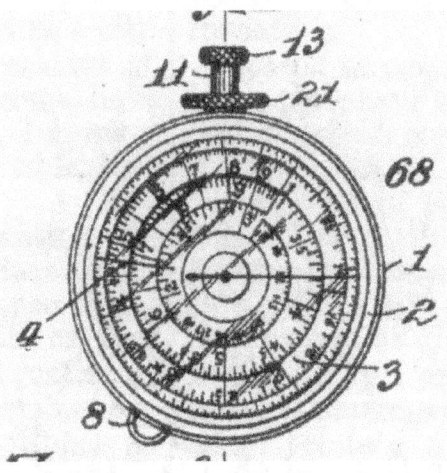

Figure 8.8: G. Lange 1907 patent

Despite this patent date being quoted on a number of K&E Sperry pocket-watch calculators none look like this and only the 4016 of 1906 has the geared works.

George Lange, USA 1,012,660, 26 Dec 1911

The Figure 8.8 is Figure 1 from Lange's extensive patent which is declared as an improvement on Sperry's 1904 patent (above) and is assigned to K&E. It is declared as a means of improving the method of manufacture and use, simplifying and reducing the number of components and so on.

This is instantly recognizable as the device with the iconic concentric nuts that carries Sperry's name throughout, even when the patent is the later one by Lange.

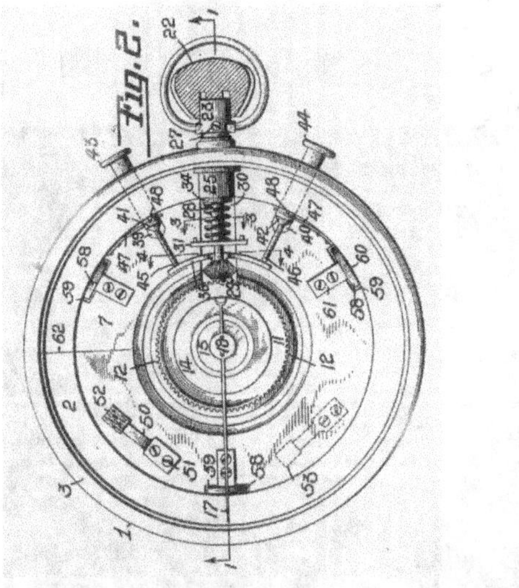

Elmer A. Sperry, USA 1,671,616, 29 May 1928

Sperry's second patent, filed on 23rd January 1922, but not awarded until 29th May 1928, some 6 years later, is also declared as an 'improving' patent on his original one awarded some 24 years previously.

Neither this patent number nor date has ever been seen on a calculator. The 'early' Sperry calculator illustrated below carries the original 1904 patent date, begging the question as to whether it is an early or late device.

Sperry / K&E Pocket-Watch Slide Rules

The following examples of Sperry and K&E pocket-watch slide rule calculators are first described in some detail, and then there is an attempt to confirm a chronology based on the first attempt by Bob Otnes in 1997 plus some new input from me.

Figure 8.9: E.A. Sperry 1928 patent

KEUFFEL AND ESSER (K&E) POCKET-WATCH CALCULATORS

Figure 8.10: Early Sperry calculator

Type 2 Calculator

The calculator measures 3″ (76mm) including the crown and is 2 1/8″ (54mm) wide by 5/8″(16mm) thick. There are two thick glass crystals, and a dial on each side that will turn with the crown on top. Each dial has a movable hand which is turned by pushing one of the side buttons and turning the top crown. There are two buttons for either right or left handed people (it says!). Each glass crystal has a red line etched on the inside of the glass. On one of the dials, it reads "E.A. SPERRY'S" "CALCULATOR". The second dial reads "KEUFEL & ESSER Co. N.Y." PAT. OCT.25.04."

Note 'S' (left) and 'L' (right) dials in Figure 8.10.

This is an unusual version of the Sperry calculator with normal crown and unusual Calculigraphe like push-buttons for control as per the last Sperry patent of 1924. It is not serial numbered, but appears to carry the Sperry scales rather than the Calculigraphe scales. The RKO/PMH Chronology puts this as Type 2, whether 2a or 2b can not be defined from the picture alone.

Type 3a Calculator

This is marked 'E.A. Sperry's Calculator', and 'Keuffel & Esser Co NY; Pat Oct 25 04'. The same as the date on the Type 2 calculator, therefore this is a Type 3a.

> **An example would need to be marked:**
> E.A. Sperry's Calculator
> &
> Keuffel & Esser Co NY Patt App[d] for

Usual watch pattern 2 1/8″ (54mm) diameter two sided with engraved metal dials, an example has an instruction booklet Copyright 1906 by K&E.

Each dial has an index hand and a stationary pointer which takes the place of a runner in a straight slide rule. The 'S' dial side is equivalent to 'A' and 'D' scales and the mantissa scale of a rectilinear rule.

The 'L' dial carries a logarithmic scale arranged in a spiral of three circuits.

Possible Serial No 378, other examples have serials 353 and 438.

Type 3b Calculator

No example of a Type 3b calculator has been found to be able to add to this chronological listing of illustrations.

Why should there be a Type 3b? We have a "Sperry" calculator with the first patent number, and a "K&E" with Pat Appd. for; is it not logical to have a "Sperry" with Pat. Appd. for?

Figure 8.11: Sperry 1904 Patent Calculator

53

Type 3c Calculator

Note that this calculator has the thumb nuts that are indicative of the Lange mechanism, but the labeling is as above; i.e. on one of the dials, it reads "E.A. SPERRY'S" "CALCULATOR". The second dial reads "KEUFEL & ESSER Co. N.Y." PAT.DEC.26.11."

This makes it a Type 3c calculator in our chronology.

'E.A. Sperry's Calculator', and 'Keuffel & Esser Co NY; Pat Dec 26. 11', labeling makes this also a Type 3c calculator as the above example, i.e. it is still a Sperry Calculator but with the later patent number.

The calculator is approx. 2 1/8″ (54mm) diameter with the two concentric adjusting nuts on the one axle, with a small loop just off-center at the bottom.

As with all the Sperry marked devices, it carries a serial number, this is discussed later.

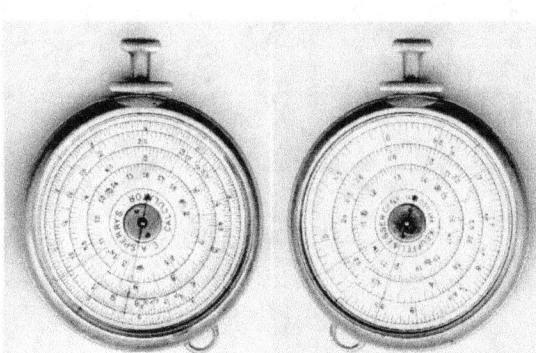
Figure 8.12: Type 3c calculator

Examples with Serial Numbers 788, S 824, and S 978 are known, the significance of the preceding 'S' is not known.

Type 4a Calculator

This is an early K&E Calculator, without the 'L' dial and no mention of Sperry's name. It uses Langes mechanism and is marked 'K&E Pocket Calculator' and 'Keuffel & Esser Co NY, Pat Appd. For'. This is a Model 4018, Type 4a.

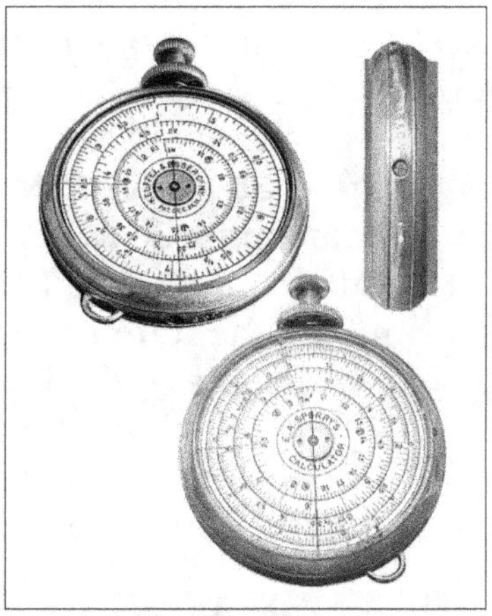

The implication is that it is probably dated somewhere between filing and award date for Sperry's first patent, i.e. before 1911. Possibly not serial numbered.

Type 4b Calculator

No example of a Type 4b calculator has been found. Whether this means that they were never so marked (with a patent number of any sorts) or not, is not known.

Figure 8.13: Sperry 1911 Patent Calculator

Why should there be a Type 4b? We have a "Sperry" calculator with the second patent number and a "K&E" with Pat Appd. for; is it not logical to have a "K&E" with the second patent number?

Type 5 Calculator

No example of a Type 5 calculator has been found.

The logic for a type 5 is that all other patent numbers are shown on a calculator type, but not the final patent number - very speculative!

Figure 8.14: Sperry 'Patent applied for' Type 4a Calculator

The discussion as to who made and who did not make pocket-watch slide rules applies as much to K&E as to any other manufacturer. It is highly likely that the later calculators were made in the K&E factory, though Joe Soper's excellent book[11] never mentions them, and it is equally true that as with their rectilinear slide rules which were first of all bought from D&P in Germany, their earliest foray into pocket-watch slide rules were via Calculigraphe devices that were bought from Henri Chatelain in France.

An example would need to be marked:
E.A. Sperry's Calculator
&
Keuffel & Esser Co NY Patt App^d for

The previously mentioned original K&E chronology published in the OSJ asks many of the same questions – where and who made them, how many of each type were made, and so on. The question of serial numbers similarly cannot be resolved. Where serial numbers have been found they have been recorded, and there may be the first signs of some sort of logic, they are shown in the table below. The original article also speculated that as many as two to four thousand may have been made. No evidence at all has been found to back that up, and instead it can be estimated that perhaps as few as 1,000 (see the known serial numbers) were made, which would make them very rare devices.

Figure 8.15: Sperry 'Patent applied for' Type 4a example 2

An example would need to be marked:
With some reference to the last patent:
1,671,616/1927

---

[11] 'K&E Salisbury Products Division Slide Rules'. Joseph L. Soper, published by The Oughtred Society, 2007. ISBN 978 0 0791477 5

Summary

| **RKO & PMH K&E Pocket-Watch Chronology** ||||||
Type	K&E Type No	Patent	Marking		Serial Numbers	Comment
			Front	**Back**		
1	None	773,235/1904	-	-	n/a	Single key as per first Sperry patent, none made
2a	Early 4016	773,235/1904	E.A. Sperry Calc	K&E N.Y. Pat Oct 25 04	No serials	1906 Cat, Figs 145, 152 2-buttons
2b	Early 4017	773,235/1904	E.A. Sperry Calc	K&E N.Y. Pat Oct 25 04	No serials	1906 Cat, Figs 145, 152 2-buttons
3a	Later 4017	773,235/1904	E.A. Sperry Calc	K&E N.Y. Pat Oct 25 04	353, 378, 404, 438, and 500	Lange mechanism
3b	Later 4017	Pat App^d For	E.A. Sperry Calc	K&E N.Y. Pat Ap^d For	No example	Lange mechanism
3c	Later 4017	1,012,660/1911	E.A. Sperry Calc	K&E N.Y Pat Dec 26 11	788, S 824, and S 978	Lange mechanism
4a	Model 4018	Pat App^d For	K&E Pocket Calc	K&E N.Y. Pat Ap^d For	548 and 680	Lange mechanism
4b	Model 4018	1,012,660/1911	K&E Pocket Calc	K&E N.Y Pat Dec 26 11	No examples	Lange mechanism
5	?	1,671,616/1927	?	?	No examples	?

'Scientific Publishing' Pocket-Watch Calculators

Introduction

John Knott[12] and Jenny Wetton[13] have previously covered the history of Fowler, both articles give the Scientific Publishing Company (SPC) as the root from which Fowler & Co. grew. The range of 'Fowler's' calculators has also been previously covered[14], and pocket-watch type calculators carrying the SPC name are mentioned. In this chapter we attempt to define the chronology, and show how the range started with one pocket-watch calculator, 'The Mechanical Engineer', and then expanded via a small range of SPC calculators to the extensive range of calculators that were later available under the 'Fowler' brand names. It is very unlikely that SPC initially manufactured calculators, but we do know from later information that when they became Fowler they did assemble them.

History

William Henry Fowler set up the Scientific Publishing Company in 1898, his son Harold Fowler became involved in 1905. SPC were best known for the publication of a range of technical pocketbooks for architects and the engineering disciplines. William Henry was also the editor of a weekly news magazine, 'The Mechanical Engineer' which was published from 1898, initially at 6d. per week, and later (by 1909) had reduced to 3d. per week. The availability of a pocket-watch calculator from SPC was advertised during 1898[15]. The various Fowler's Pocket Books advertise many different Fowler watch type calculators over the years. A chronological list of addresses for the Scientific Publishing Company are as follows:

      1898: Corporation St. Manchester, England
      1901 - c1915: 53 New Bailey Street, Manchester
      1908: Workshop in the Family home, Sale Lodge, Sale, Cheshire
      Pre 1914: Oakleigh, the Avenue, Sale, Cheshire
      c1915: Fowlers & Co. 53 New Bailey Street, Manchester

Pocket-Watch Type Calculators

Calculators which are known to have been made or sold under the name of the Scientific Publishing Company are fairly rare and to date only include the following types:
- The Mechanical Engineer (single scale)
- The Mechanical Engineer (only one version carrying the SPC name) in various sizes
- The Mechanical Engineer, desk version
  (No known examples, but advertised by Halden in 1902)
- Fowler's Patent Pocket Calculator
- Type T textile calculator
- Type O Calculator – a later version of the Fowler's patent calculator?

We can now look at these in greater detail to establish their chronology and to get a better understanding of which models were available under the SPC label and when.

---

12   'Fowler and Company, 1898 – 1938'; J.V. Knott in *Journal of The Oughtred Society*, Vol. 4 No 2, Fall 1995, p16-17.
13   'Scientific Instrument Making in Manchester, 1870 – 1940', iii- Flatters and Garner & Fowler and Company; Jenny Wetton in *Bulletin of the Scientific Instrument Society*, No 53, (1997), pp 15-18.
14   'Fowler's Pocket-Watch Type Calculators'; Peter Hopp in *Journal of The Oughtred Society*, Vol. 7 No 2, Fall 1998, pp 43 - 49.
15   Wetton (above) states 'In 1898, the *'Mechanical Engineer'* carried an article on a circular calculator, under the same name, which had been developed by the proprietors'. She goes on to say 'Records do not show who designed this instrument or where it was made; it was sold via the Scientific Publishing Co.'.

POCKET-WATCH SLIDE RULES

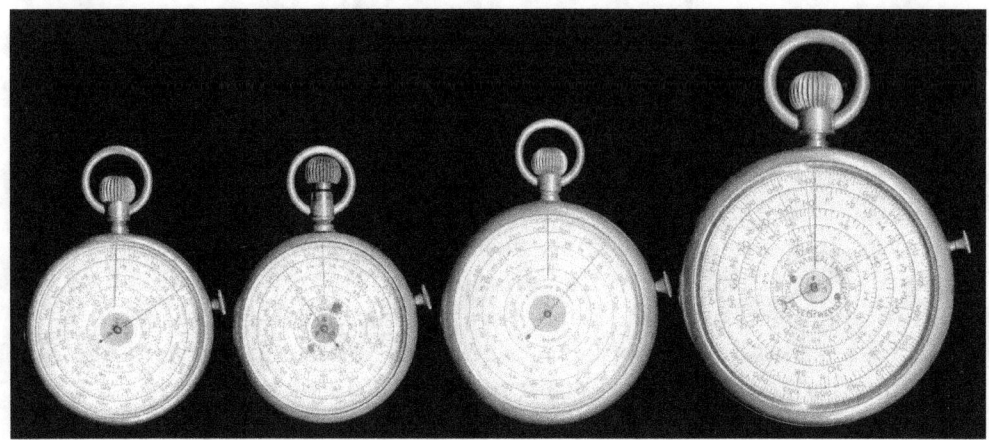

Figure: 9.1a, 9.1b, 9.1c and 9.1d: SPC 'Mechanical Engineer' calculators various

The 'Mechanical Engineer' (ME) Calculator

There has been some speculation as to who made the 'ME' calculator. A previous article[16], identified the apparent anomaly of a 'Swiss' marking on some examples, though the majority of known examples show no obvious maker's name. However we have now found enough examples which do carry a 'maker's name' i.e. Scientific Publishing or 'The Mechanical Engineer' so that we can now be certain that SPC were the retailer if not the actual maker. Four examples are shown in Figure 9.1; this appears to cover all known major variants with multi scales. Here we have an example with no maker's name and no model name (9.1a), a second example marked 'The Mechanical Engineer' but no makers name (9.1b), a third marked 'Scientific Publishing Company, Manchester' (9.1c), and finally one marked 'The Mechanical Engineer Price 6d. weekly' (9.1d). While many SPC adverts state that the calculator was available in two sizes, we now know that they actually came in three sizes, the scale diameters of 1¾", 2" and 2½" being obvious from Figure 9.1. The chronology of the models is more difficult to ascertain.

Subsequently we have also found what appears to be a 'single scale' Mechanical Engineer pocket calculator, a device that only carries the second scale of the 'normal' ME, i.e. the 'calculating scale' of the ME. Why SPC should decide to make such a simple calculator, and when, is not known, but we can try some theories and see how they work out:

Image Courtesy of the Conrad Schure Collection

Figure 9.2: Single scale ME

The device has 2" (51 mm) diam scales in a 2½" (62 mm) diameter single sided case and carries all the other characteristics of an ME, including the furniture etc , and it also carries the clearest Scientific Publishing Co., Manchester; labeling. As with the ME, the crown turns the scale and the side knob the pointer.

Note also that a 1902 Halden catalogue advertises a desk version of a Mechanical Engineer, there is neither description nor illustration, but it is priced the same as an F-C Calculigraphe with a nickel case. This is a curious device as it has not been seen advertised anywhere else, and no examples are known.

---

16   'The Mechanical Engineer'; Bob De Cesaris in *Journal of The Oughtred Society*, Vol. 7 No 1, Spring 1998, pp 23 - 24.

With this[17] and other evidence ([4] and [5]) we can now be sure that the ME was sold by the SPC, and is in all probability the earliest design made and sold by them starting from 1898. Exactly what 'made' entailed is still open to debate. We know from contemporary photographs (c1908) in the Bolton Museum that Fowler assembled pocket-watch calculators (see Fowler chapter). From this we can assume that either he had the components made to his designs, or that he bought off-the-shelf (pocket-watch?) components from any of a variety of sources; and hence some could have been 'Swiss'. Note that the calculator in Figure 9.1d has 'Swiss' stamped into the axle, (Figure 9.14) and Figure 9.3 is marked 'Swiss Make' on the dial. We do not know what this link was. Figure 9.1 appears to cover all known variants of multi-scale ME, and Figure 9.2 is yet another in their range of calculators, the single scale calculator.

Figure 9.3: ME marked 'Swiss Make' on dial

Dyson. An example of Dyson Textile calculator very much looks to have been made by SP, (see later chapter). Whether it is a variant of the ME, or whether it is another type of SP calculator remains unknown without seeing the mechanisms. It is more fully described later.

SPC made three sizes of ME. If we take the SPC adverts at face value, i.e. that there were two sizes of calculator available at any one time, but with the caveat that this might have been <u>any two</u> sizes at one time, then we can possibly estimate a chronology. The 1901 edition of 'Fowler's Mechanical Engineers Pocket Book' carries an advert (Figure 9.4) which shows a calculator marked 'The Mechanical Engineer' and gives prices for the 1¾" and 2½" scale diameter sizes available. Pickworth [5] shows the same advert and an 'early' (undated) edition of 'Watch Calculator' [4] shows the same two sizes with the same markings. A 'later' edition of [4] (also undated) shows a small (1¾") calcula-

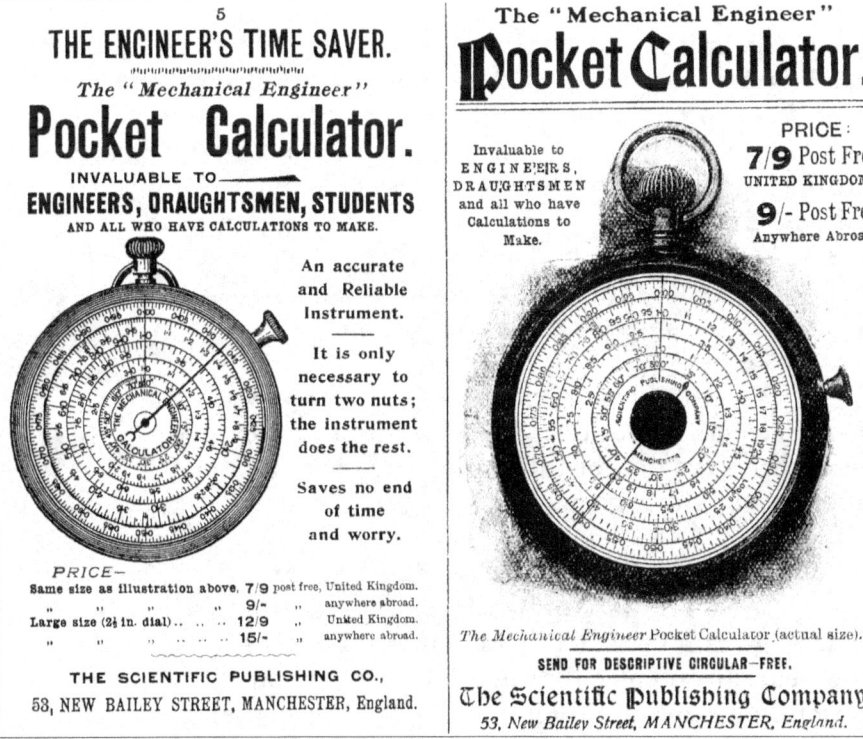

Figure 9.4: 1901 SP advert   Figure 9.5: 1909 SP advert

tor marked as described earlier, and a larger (2") calculator marked 'Scientific Publishing Co, Manchester'. The 1909 edition of 'Fowler's Mechanical Engineers Pocket Book' carries an advert (Figure 9.5) which shows only one size of calculator, the 2" version, marked SPC, Manchester, and priced the same as the smaller version in the 1901 advert. The 1908 issue of 'Calvert's Mechanics' Almanac' (typeset in 1907) also carries the same advert, hence we can estimate 1907 as a possible earliest date for the advent of the SCP marked 2" models.

---

17   'Scientific Instrument Making in Manchester, 1870 – 1940', iii- Flatters and Garner & Fowler and Company; Jenny Wetton in *Bulletin of the Scientific Instrument Society*, No 53, (1997), pp 15-18.

POCKET-WATCH SLIDE RULES

The 'no name' version of the 1¾″ ME remains an enigma - were they intended to be sold by independent retailers in parallel with the marked versions, or were they the earliest (or latest) version available? We do not know, hopefully future evidence will answer the question. From the evidence above it is possible to estimate a chronology for the ME:

- No name (Fig. 1a) 1¾″ diam.   1898 - 1900 (assuming that they were the earliest model)
- 'Mech Eng' (Fig. 1b) 1¾″ diam.   1900 - 1907 (Pickworth etc. adverts all show calculator marked ME)
- 'Mech Eng 6d.' (Fig. 1d) 2½″ diam.   1900 - 1907 (or possibly earlier)
- SPC (Fig. 1c) 2″ diam.   1907 - 1910

Note that the 'No Name' versions may have been produced throughout their history for other retailers to sell, they are not uncommon. By not carrying any marking they have caused confusion as to what the device is, and others (see Davis in 'Other slide rules' later) have engraved the back of the calculator, or named them in some other way.

Other SPC Pocket-Watch Calculators

Having established that SPC started with the Mechanical Engineer as their first design, and that at least one model was produced with SPC as the 'makers name', what calculators followed the ME and when? The intermediate chronology is not obvious; however we can also be fairly definite about the calculator which superseded the ME. This has to be Fowler's Patent Pocket Calculator, patented in 1910. This also became the Type 'O' later still under the SPC name.

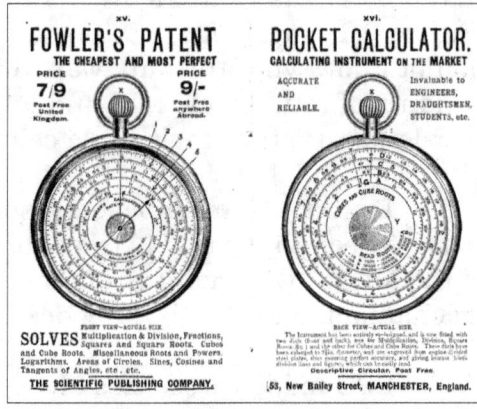

Figure 9.6: 1913 SP advert for the 1910 patent calculator

We also have an example of an early type of Textile calculator and its later evolution under the SPC name; we do not think that any other models also existed during this time.

Fowler's Patent Pocket Calculator

The 1910 date of patent 5,528 granted to W.H. Fowler gives a very strong indication that this was the next chronological design following the ME, which in all probability it superseded. The patent covers the very characteristic and unique calculator with center button on the obverse and pointer driven from the single crown. It was advertised in the 1913 Fowler's Electrical Engineers Pocket Handbook, see Figure 9.6.

Figure 9.7 shows an example of Fowler's Patent Calculator, it is not clear whether this particular example with its three clips are a home-made addition to stop the glasses falling out of the cast case, or whether these were part of the original fit.

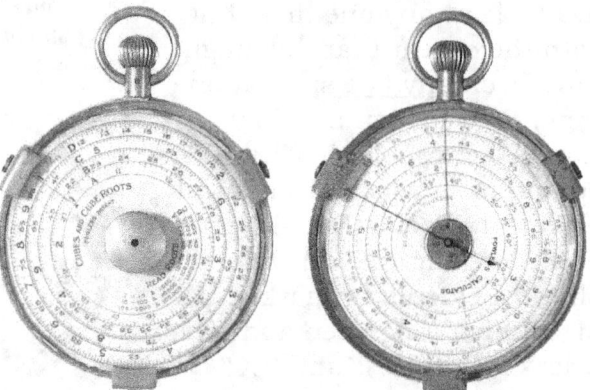

Figure 9.7: Fowler's Patent Calculator by SPC

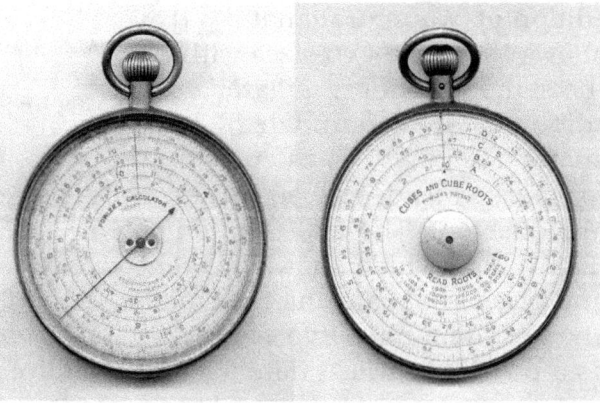

Figure 9.8: Fowler's Patent Calculator

'SCIENTIFIC PUBLISHING' POCKET-WATCH CALCULATORS

Figure 9.9: Scientific Publishing Type O (the Patent Pocket Calculator)

I believe that they are a home-made cure for a problem. A second example shown in Figure 9.8 does not have the clips. All three clips on the example are very similar leading to the suggestion that they might have been available as a DIY cure for the problem.

A later version with two crowns instead of the center button is called a Type 'O', this being written where the center button used to be. (Figure 9.9.) This is the first evolution from the Patent Calculator. An example of the next evolution, another of what became the more usual two-crown device (known as the Type H) made by Fowler & Co. which is covered by patent 20,416 of 1912 by W.H. & H. Fowler, has a date of '11.11.1915' written inside it. It is accompanied by an SPC instruction manual which is for the earlier style of calculator with center button, but has a stuck-in overprint to the effect that the scales: '... are rotated by a nut at the side instead of a button at the center, but this does not affect the instructions for making the calculations'. This calculator, the Type H, was still being advertised in the 1925 Fowler's Mechanic's and Machinist's Pocket Book. This is further evidence that by 1915 SPC had definitely become Fowler & Co. and was producing pocket-watch calculators under that name rather than SPC, and we can now be sure that the SPC model of the Patent Calculator was made and sold from 1910 through to 1914 or 1915.

Later patents, 3,638/1914 and 15,990/1914, cover anti-backlash mechanisms and a calculator which does not use crowns at all but is rather more like Halden's Calculex utilizing thumb nuts on both sides, it was probably never manufactured. These patents were at the very end of the SPC period.

Scientific Publishing Textile Calculator

This is a variant of the Patent Calculator complete with the center button, Scientific Publishing name, and tables on the rear that would soon turn into the slightly later Type T with its side key as shown below.

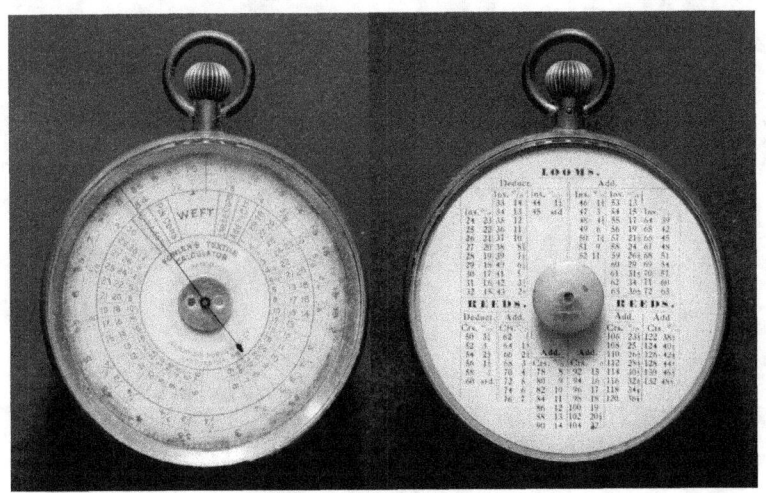

Figure 9.10: Scientific Publishing Textile Calculator

Type T Textile Calculator

The Type T Textile calculator is shown below (Figure 9.11). Apart from carrying the Scientific Publishing Co maker's name, it is very obviously from the same period characterized by the very thin pointer, the prominent axle, and the cast metal case with the two spokes carrying the mechanism. Note that the anti-backlash mechanism shown in Figures 9.12 and 9.13 is covered by patent 3,638/1914 from which we can more accurately deduce that the change from SPC to Fowler took place around the time of the patent grant (May 1914).

POCKET-WATCH SLIDE RULES

This Type T textile calculator is thus from very late in the SPC period (c1913?). When they started making Type T Textile calculators is not known, however the general style would evolve for years to come as part of the 'Fowler' range, see next chapter. I am not aware of a Type T calculator in the 'Fowler' range.

Figure 9.11: Scientific Publishing Type T Textile Calculator

Figure 9.12: Type T Textile Calculator with yellow lens and showing mechanism

Fowler's Type M Textile Calculator

This Fowler's calculator has been included in the Scientific Publishing section to give an indication of when Scientific Publishing ceased to exist. An example of this calculator dated late 1914 is shown in Figure 9.13. The style of this device and the mechanism is extremely similar to the earlier Type T (Figure 9.11) and other SPC calculators; however this Type M carries the Fowler & Co. name. The pencil annotation on the back of the scale says 'Repd. 6/12/1914. HF'. Was this calculator repaired by Harold Fowler himself? Probably, but we will never know. However this is further evidence that no later than December 1914, and probably slightly earlier as this was a repair to a 'Fowler' calculator, SPC had become Fowler & Co., Manchester.

Figure 9.13: Fowler & Co Type M Textile calculator

Summary

We can now conclude that the ME was the first pocket-watch calculator made (or at least assembled) by The Scientific Publishing Company, and that it was made from 1898 and continued to be made in various guises until 1910 when the patent for Fowler's Patent Calculator was taken out, and SPC started to manufacture that calculator instead. The Patent Pocket Calculator with the center button was made and sold under the SPC name from 1910 until about 1914, and then evolved to have two crowns when it was sold under the Fowler name. Whether the two-crown version was made with the SPC name is not known. We can reliably speculate as to the chronology of the SPC Type T textile calculator and for how long it was made, there is no hard evidence available to date it.

Other calculators carrying the Scientific Publications Company name were available for a short time, from about 1907 to 1914. Only a very limited range of models carried this name, one version of the Mechanical Engineer, a Textile Calculator and the Type T Textile and Fowler's Patent Pocket calculator (later Fowler Type H) are the only ones known to date. However, by 1915 all pocket-watch calculators carried the Fowler & Co. name.

Figure 9.14: ME marked 'Swiss' on the axle

Fowler's Pocket-Watch Calculators

Introduction

Any description of the Fowler's product range follows seamlessly on from the description of the Scientific Publishing range, it being self-evident that the same products (in some cases) now sold as Fowler's calculators. An early attempt at a full classification of Fowler's calculators[18] has been subsequently updated[19] and now, starting from 1915, we can examine the prolific range of pocket-watch calculators that are known to have been sold.

The earliest designs use the cast sintered Aluminum alloy case, and of course there are also Fowler's versions of the Scientific Publishing cast case 'Calculator' with the center button.

Fowler's Patents

Neither William Henry nor Harold Fowler were prolific patentees; however their five patents all reflect solutions to problems that would have had to be overcome during the manufacture of these devices.

| \multicolumn{3}{c}{*Fowler's Pocket-Watch Slide Rule Patents*} |
Date	Patent No.	Patentee Information
1910	UK 5,528	William Henry Fowler of 53 New Bailey Street, Manchester, Engineer.
1913	UK 20,416	William Henry Fowler of Sale Lodge, Sale, Cheshire, Engineer, and Harold Fowler, of 'Alston' Old Hall Road, Sale, Cheshire, Engineer.
1914	UK 3,638	William Henry Fowler of 'Oakleigh' The Avenue, Ashton-on-Mersey, Cheshire, Engineer, and Harold Fowler, of 'Alston' Old Hall Road, Sale, Cheshire, Engineer
1914	UK 15,990	William Henry Fowler of 'Oakleigh' The Avenue, Ashton-on-Mersey, Cheshire, Engineer, and Harold Fowler, of 'Alston' Old Hall Road, Sale, Cheshire, Engineer.
1924	UK 215,648	William Henry Fowler of Station Works, Sale, Cheshire (British) and Harold Fowler, of Station Works, Sale, Cheshire (British).

William Henry Fowler's first patent, No. 5,528, applied for on 5th March 1910, and accepted very quickly thereafter on 23rd June 1910, is supposedly to simplify the construction of calculating instruments and to avoid 'derangement or fouling of the gearing or pointers'.

This is very obviously the patent for Fowler's Patent Pocket Calculator and the unique calculators with the single crown and a milled knob at the back of the calculator that was used on at least two designs of calculator illustrated in the Scientific Publishing section.

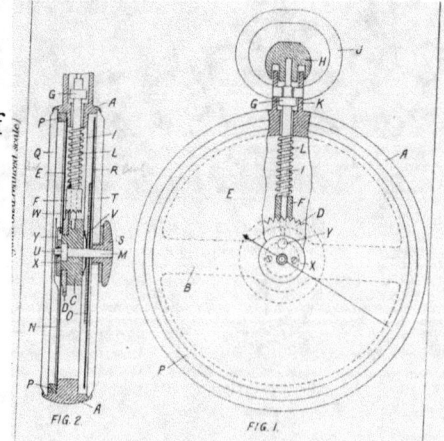

Figure 10.1: Fowler Patent 5,528

---

[18] 'Fowler's Pocket-Watch Type Calculators'; Peter Hopp in *Journal of The Oughtred Society*, Vol. 7 No 2, Fall 1998, pp 43 - 49
[19] 'The Fowler Calculators – A Catalogue Raisonné'; Rick Blankenhorn & Bob de Cesaris in *Journal of The Oughtred Society*, Vol. 11 No 2, Fall 2002, pp 3 - 12

FOWLER'S POCKET-WATCH CALCULATORS

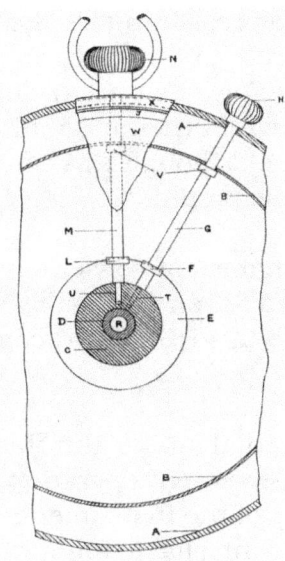

Figure 10.2: Fowler Patent 20,416

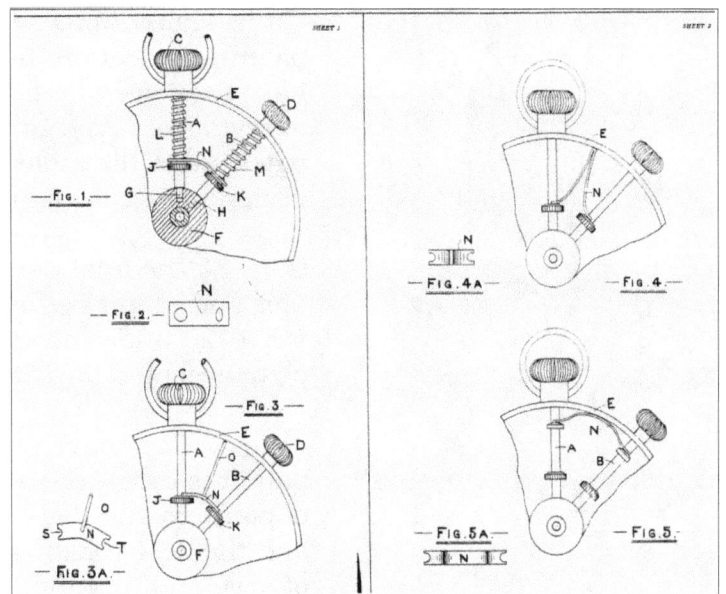

Figure 10.3: Fowler Patent 3,638

The first joint patent No. 20,416 from William Henry Fowler and Harold Fowler, both living in Sale, Manchester. The patent was applied for on 7th September 1912 and was awarded on 27th February 1913.

The patent covers a method of reducing the expense of the design and improvements to enable the radial shafts (which replaced the milled knob) to be better fitted and more reliably 'rendering the boss immovable, and at the same time secure extreme accuracy in the readings of the instrument'. It is not easy to understand why they took out this patent; the Mechanical Engineer calculators would have used such a construction 15 years previously.

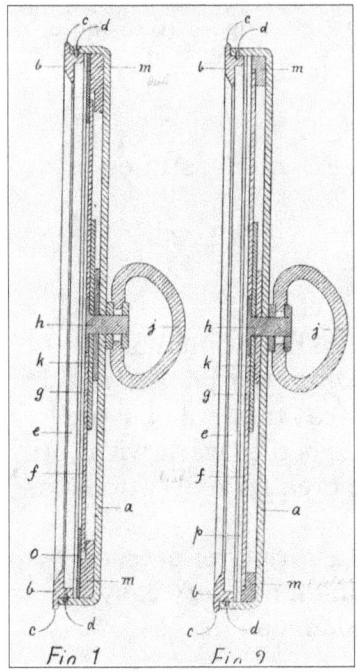

Figure 10.4: Fowler Patent 15,990

Patent No 3,638 applied for on 12th Feb 1914, and awarded 21st May 1914 is also in the joint names of Fowler father and son still living in Sale, and is the first of two patents awarded in 1914 for improvements to the design of the calculators.

The drawing at left shows 4 of the 5 designs of anti-backlash designs that were suggested and obviously implemented as can be seen in the illustrations of the internals of the Fowler calculators in this and the last sections.

Albeit that they did succeed in avoiding the 'inexact movements' that are mentioned in the object, there is nothing truly novel in the design and therefore rather difficult to understand why the patent was issued.

Patent No 15,990 applied for on 4th July and awarded 3rd December 1914 in their joint names is the second patent of 1914 and applies to 'improvements in the method of operating circular calculators or watch forms of slide rule.'

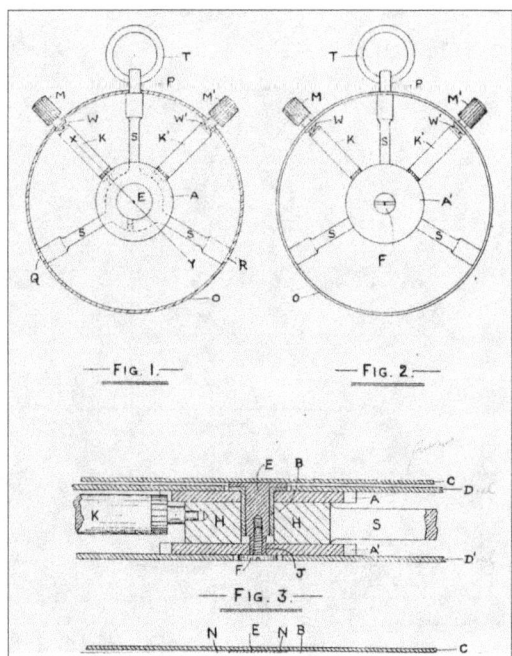

Figure 10.5: Fowler Patent 215,648

It is again difficult to understand the reasoning for the patent application, no types of slide rule to this design have been seen, and it looks as if the Fowler's were trying to revert to a type similar to that shown in their original patent with the milled knob at the back, though this design uses a form of ring to rotate the pointer.

The final patent in the joint names of Fowler senior and junior is No 215,648, applied for on September 6th 1923 under provisional patent No 22418/23 and complete accepted on 15th May 1924.

They have reverted back to radial shafts and this patent is intended to improve the independent operation of pointers and dials on the two sides of the instrument, and the design allows a definite and controllable amount of frictional resistance to the circular movement of the wheels rotating on a common axis.

Once again it is possible to recognize later designs of Fowler's calculator in this patent, those where the loop was attached to a separate point on the rim and two entirely independent knobs working on radial shafts.

It is always interesting to be able to follow the application of such as a patent in the designs that followed afterwards. This is definitely so here.

Figure 10.6: Fowler Calculator Logo

Fowler design evolution is difficult to establish. The earliest designs used a cast sintered aluminum alloy case which is actually very brittle and must have been extremely difficult to take to pieces in the event of requiring repair. However we know that this did happen as we have dated examples which have been repaired.

A Fowler's logo which was used for a short time, is an intertwined FC, one assumes standing for Fowler's Calculators.

Fowler's Design Changes

The earliest Fowler calculators (and indeed all of the Scientific Publishing Calculators apart from the Mechanical Engineer in its various forms which comes in a proper pocket-watch case) were assembled in a case that was made in some type of sintered (heat treated) cast aluminum alloy. This is very distinctive, and must have been economic and good to work with, but repairing such devices must have created real problems.

Figure 10.7: Construction of early calculators

Later calculators came in a variety of pressed steel case designs (Figure 10.8) which are very easy to take apart and repair the mechanisms as necessary.

Finally Fowlers reverted back to another form of cast alloy case; this had a more 'chromed' appearance (though the early calculators can be highly polished).

Fowlers sold at least one special tool for unscrewing the axles of the majority of their designs. This spanner is illustrated in Figure 10.9, it has a pair of lugs at the broad end which would fit into the two holes in most axles, and likewise the thin end has a pair of similar lugs but perpendicular to the body of the 'spanner'.

For the non-purist, a pair of needle nosed pliers can be pressed into service if required.

Figure 10.8: Cast and pressed steel cases

Serial Numbering

Serial numbers are found on many Fowler calculators, on the case, the back, and very often on the axle. We have been unable to discover any logic to the numbering.

Calculator Types

The following list of Fowler's calculators with a picture wherever possible, and short description of some of the features is mainly alphabetical.

A Fowler's Electrical Engineer's Pocket Book from 1946 quotes: 'These Calculators are made in three sizes, the smallest approximately 2½ ins. (63.5 mm) in diameter for carrying in the waistcoat pocket, and fitted with either one or two dials; the medium size, of which the "Universal" and "12/10" are examples (see separate advertisements), with single dials approx. 3 ins. (76 mm) in diameter; and the "Magnum," the largest instrument made, having a single dial approx 4½ ins. (114 mm) in diameter.'

A similar description appeared in all the Fowler's Pocket Books (Mechanics' and Machinists', Electrical Engineer's, Mechanical Engineer's are the usual three titles that are quoted; later there was an Architects' Builders' and Contractors' and special books such as the Stationary Engine book) right through to the latest editions, with minor changes in size and detail.

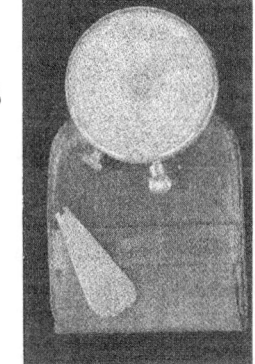

Figure 10.9: Fowler spanner

Fowler's Calculator

'Fowler's Calculator' is a generic name covering several versions, (Figure 10.12). This one shows all the characteristics of an early Fowler made calculator. It has a cast case, the 'bulls-eye' center and the shape of the early furniture. The scales are: C,A and then four scales whose function is not obvious, while on the verso, we have C,CI and then 4 trig scales (sin & Tan). The scales are, in fact, those of a Type RX, even though this is nowhere stated. Figure 10.43, which shows an even earlier version with fine pointer.

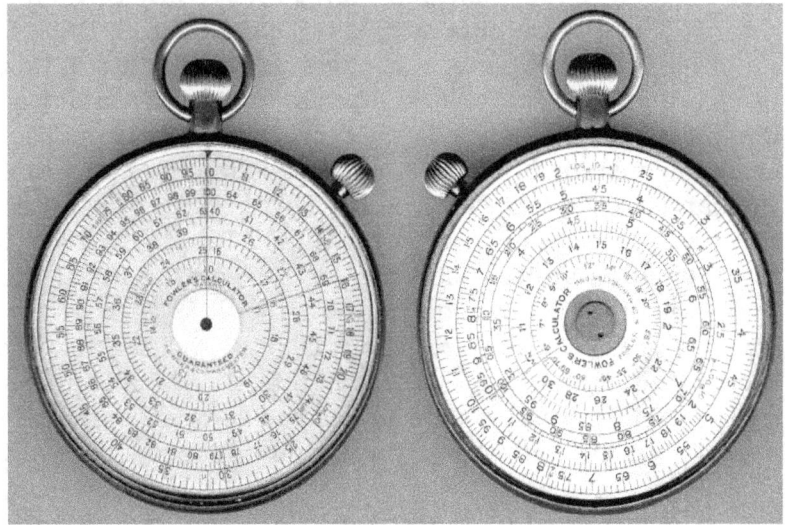

Figure 10.10: Fowler Calculator

67

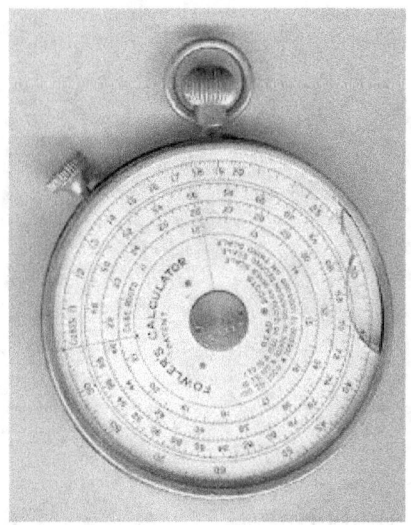

Figure 10.11: Fowler Calculator (later version) Type R

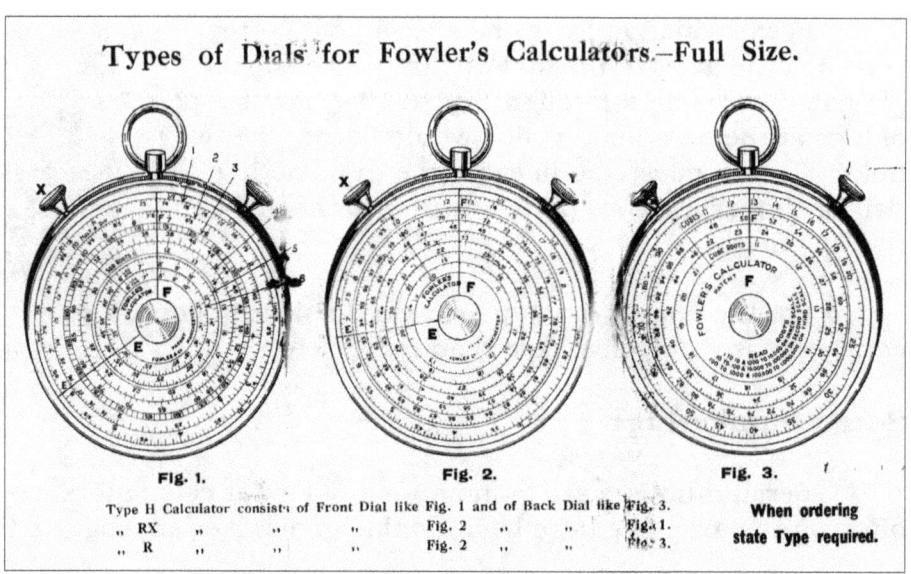

Figure 10.12: Type H, RX and R Fowler Calculators

This example has the later axle and furniture, but otherwise is not very different to the earlier version.

Some of the confusion regarding certain Fowler Calculators may be clarified by reference to the diagram above taken from an undated 'Fowler's Calculators' advertising leaflet. It also contains the description of these types as follows:

The following three types of Fowler's Calculators are formed by a combination of two of the three dials shown full size on page 3. [of the Advertising leaflet].

Type H Calculator (Front Dial as Fig. 1, Back Dial as Fig. 3).- The Front Dial comprises six scales : (1) Multiplication and division : (2) Reciprocals : (3) Logarithms : (4) Square Roots (it extends over two circles and can be used like the long scale on Type RX : (5) Logarithmic Sines of angles : (6) Logarithmic Tangents of angles. The Back Dial is a scale of Cubes and Cube Roots. The type is generally preferred by Students.

Type RX Calculator (Front Dial as Fig. 2, Back Dial as Fig. 1).- The Front Dial comprises an outer scale complete in a single circle, which can be used for Multiplication and Division in the same way as in Type H. The six remaining circles constitute another similar scale 30 in. long. his six circle scale is used in the same way as the single outer scale, though the outer scale is convenient for finding the precise circle on which to read the result. The Back Dial is the same as the front of Type H. This is a very useful combination for Engineers and Draughtsmen, as it gives Squares, Roots, Sines, Tangents, Logs and Reciprocals from the Back Dial, while multiplication and division can be done on the Front Dial with the long or short scale, according to degree of accuracy required.

Type R Calculator (Front Dial as Fig. 2, Back Dial as Fig. 3) - The difference between this type of Calculator and Type RX is that the Back Dial gives cubes and Cube Roots as in Type H, and is preferred by those who desire a long scale for accurate multiplication and division (as in Type RX) combined with a dial giving direct readings of Cubes and Cube Roots.

While the Type H and Type RX have examples shown against their descriptions, we have not been able to find examples of the Type R calculator.

FOWLER'S POCKET-WATCH CALCULATORS

Note that FJ, Camm's 'Newness Slide Rule Manual' [6] carried a description and instructions for use of the Fowler Calculator (and was illustrated with diagrams of a Calculator – Fig 1 in Figure 10.12) from the first edition of 1944 right through to the final 7th edition of 1963, as well as later impressions [of advertising leaflet].

Type A

This illustration shows a fairly early calculator with 'bullseye' marking and a fine pointer and early furniture. It is a 2½″ (63.5 mm) diameter double-sided calculator with

Image Courtesy of Conrad Schure Collection
Figure 10.13: Fowler Type A Calculator

Type H front dial (6 circles): 'Short Scale', Reciprocal Scale, Logarithm Scale, Square Root Scale (2 circles), Sine Scale (5° 45' - 90°), Type SR1 Conversion Scale back dial (5 circles): Inches, Millimeters, Whit[worth] Pipe Threads (3 half-circles), Whit[worth] Bolts (3 half-circles).

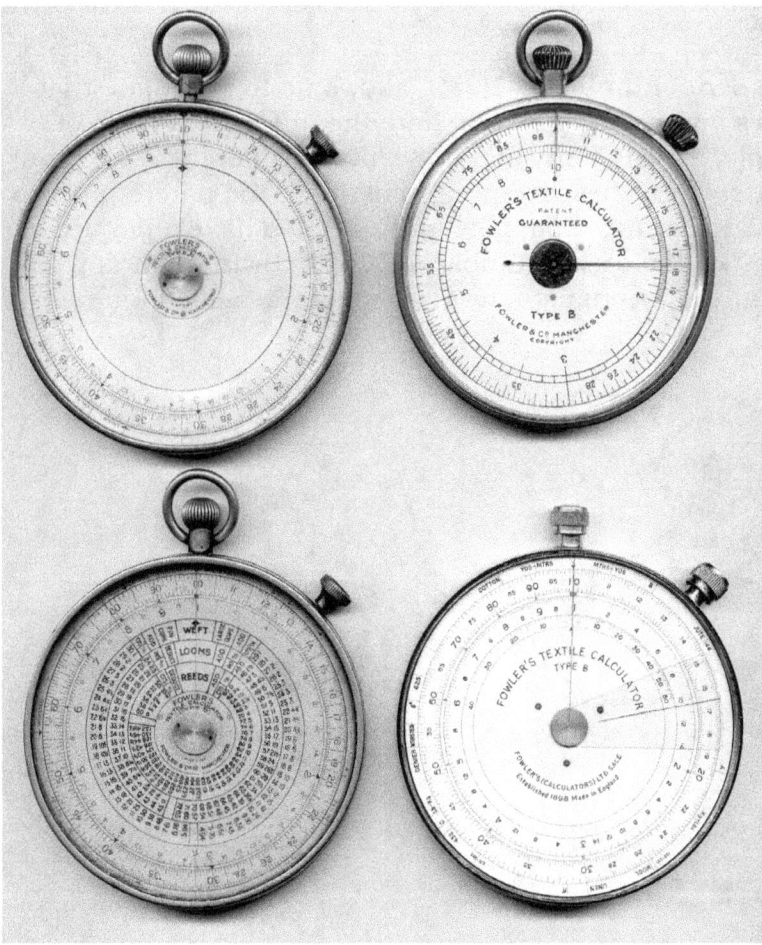

Type B (Textile)

This was a single sided calculator throughout its life. The earliest version (Figure 10.14) shows the Scientific Publishing parentage with its thin pointer and an early version of pressed steel case. This is smaller than the 3½″ (90 mm) diameter pressed case with two scales and gauge points around the outside of the outer scale that the remainder used. The central crown rotates the scale against the red index at 12-o'clock; the second knob rotates the cursor. The second version (top left) has a label around the center axle which says 'Fowler's – Textile Calculator – Type B' working inwards towards the axle. Other versions (difficult to date) through to the latest type which has reverted to a cast case again (bottom right) are similarly labeled but carry very different versions of the scales and the data table on the bottom left version are unusual. It is interesting to note the 'Established 1898' notice which sadly proves nothing other than this may be the date for the earliest SP calculators.

Figure 10.14: Fowler Type B Textile Calculator various.

POCKET-WATCH SLIDE RULES

Type E1 (Textile)
This early example in its sintered metal cast case with its hand-written serial number (420) and date of 26th March 1915, and a later dated repair (15.3.1917), both possibly signed by Harold Fowler allows us to date the possible start of the 'bulls-eye' version of pointer to 1915 or just before.

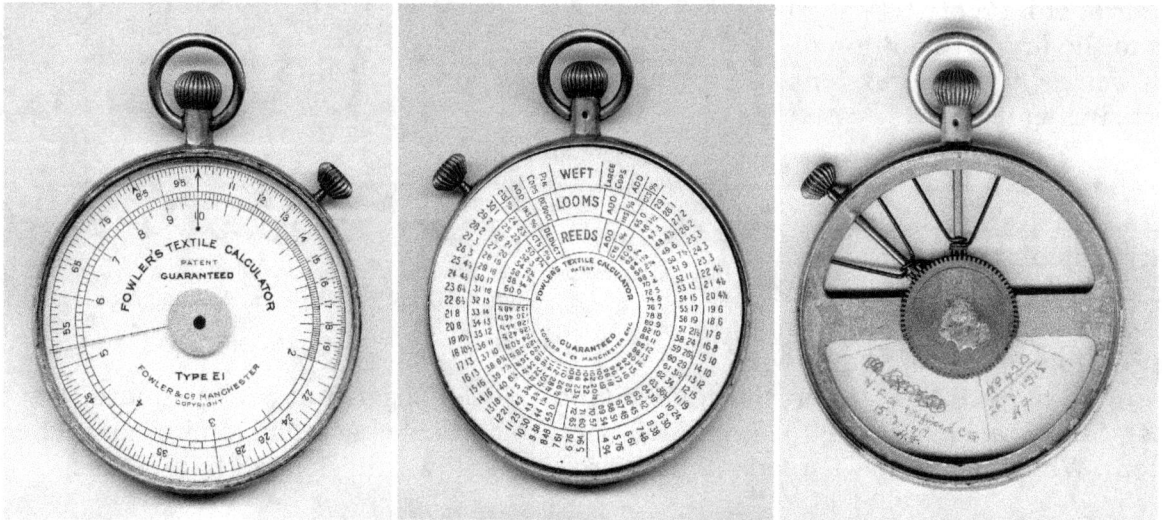

Figure 10.15: Fowler Type E1 Textile Calculator

This later version dated 1919 with a serial number of 2,959, allows us to speculate that the 'bulls-eye' was in use for at least 5 years and possibly more. Note the different version of anti-backlash springing used in this example. The Patent No 3,638 with its different versions of anti-backlash mechanism was dated 1914, so both these examples post-date the patent, and do not seem to provide any clue to more accurate dating. Coincidentally, we also have a picture of another example made during October 1919 with a serial number of 3009 showing that at least 50 devices were made in the month and that the mechanism was probably the same for at least that month.

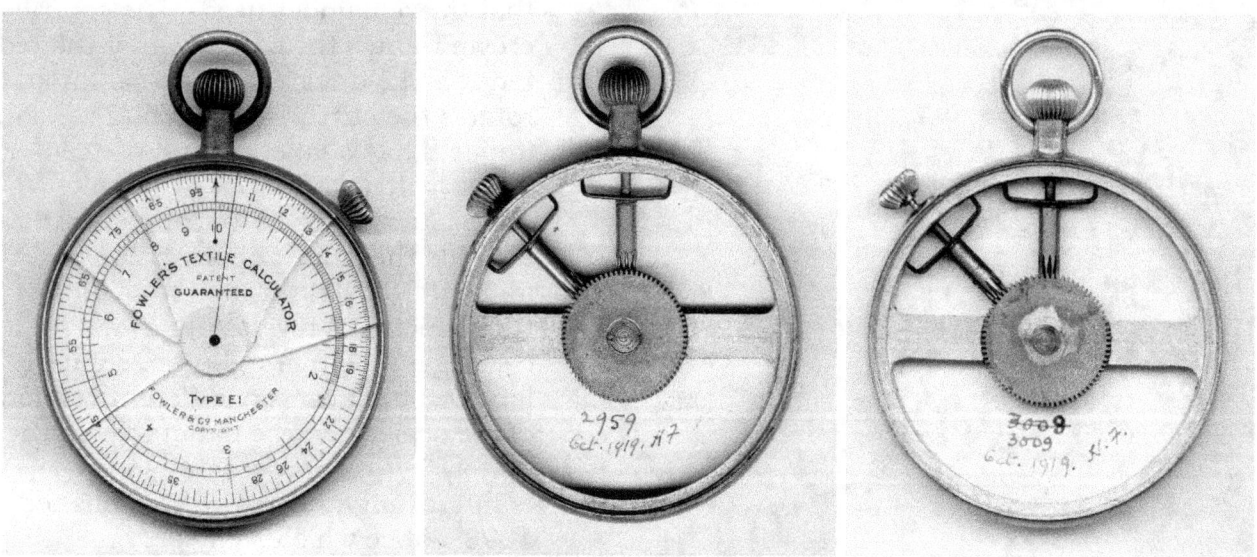

Figure 10.16: Fowler Type E1 Textile Calculator, different mechanism

FOWLER'S POCKET-WATCH CALCULATORS

Type H (early)
This early version is almost 'Scientific Publishing' in design. It has the fine pointer, and is also in a cast case. The 'early' i.e. rounded rather than square watch furniture is also characteristic of an early design.

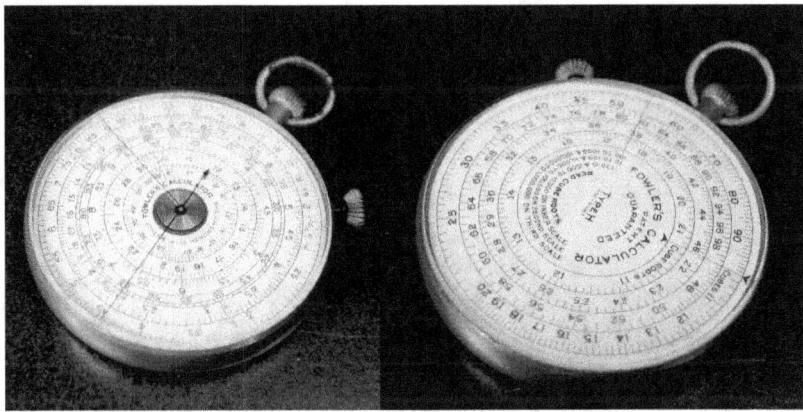

Figure 10.17: Type H Textile Calculator (early)

Type H (later)
This calculator is in a cast case 2⅝" (68 mm) diameter. It could be argued that it is the same calculator as the Scientific Publishing, 'Fowler's Patent Calculator', see Figure 9.7, where the Center Button would have covered the 'Type H' label. The 'bulls-eye' sticker has already been mentioned as an early Fowler feature and is synonymous with other calculators in a cast case.

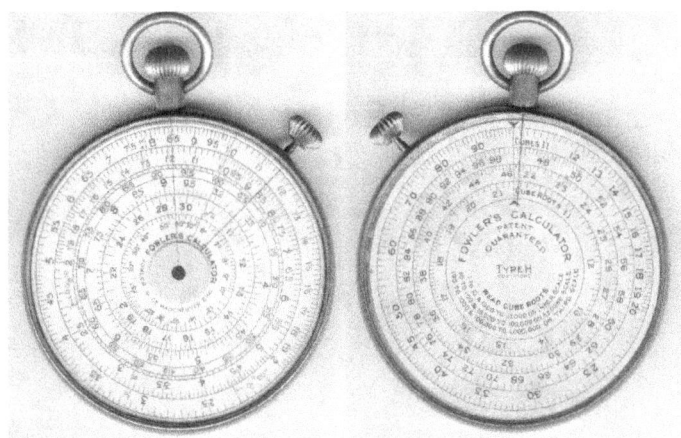

Figure 10.18: Type H Textile Calculator (later version)

Note this calculator is also sometimes referred to as a 'Vest Pocket Calculator' Type H, see later.

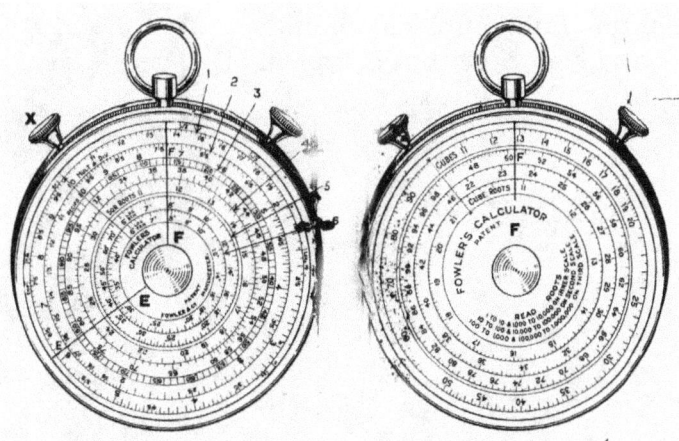

Figure 10.19: Type H from the Fowler leaflet

71

POCKET-WATCH SLIDE RULES

Type M (Textile)
This is also illustrated in the Scientific Publishing section and is an excellent example of a 'transitional calculator' which has all the SP characteristics but carries the Fowler name. It is probably a very early example of Fowler calculator with a repair date of 1914 and no obvious serial number.

Figure 10.20: Fowler Type M Textile Calculator

Type O
The Type O is actually a Scientific Publishing calculator, and pretty rare. It has the fine pointer and cast case that is typical of the type. I am not aware of a type O with a Fowler label.

Figure 10.21: Fowler Type O Calculator

Type T (Textile)
The Type T Textile is also a Scientific Publishing calculator, and fairly rare. It has the fine pointer and cast case that is typical of the type. I am not aware of a Fowler labeled Type T Textile.

Figure 10.22: Fowler Type T Textile Calculator

FOWLER'S POCKET-WATCH CALCULATORS

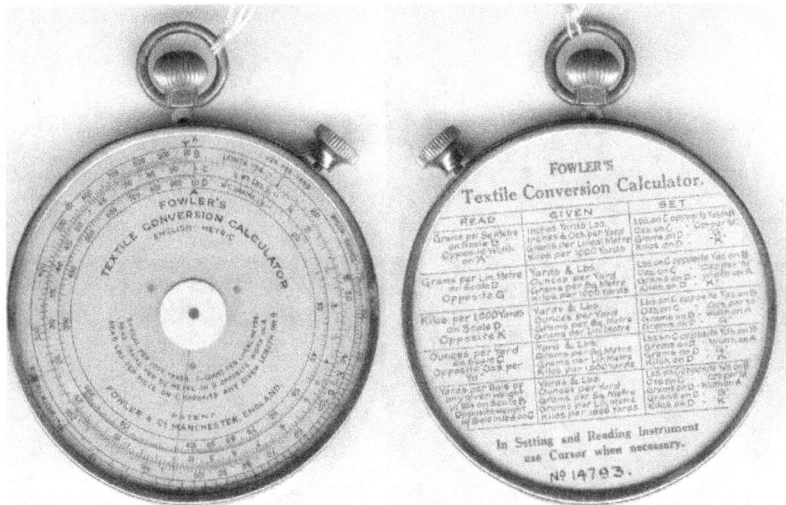

Figure 10.23: Fowler Textile Conversion Calculator

Textile Conversion Calculator

This is an early type of Fowler's calculator with the paper 'bulls-eye' label shielding the axle on the front of the calculator. While this is an earlier form of calculator, it is a transitional design as it is in a pressed steel case rather than the cast aluminum alloy case that would have been typical.

Figure 10.24: Fowler Short Scale Textile Calculator (early)

Short Scale Textile

Figure 10.24 is the early version of Short Scale textile calculator, and below is the later version recognizable by the shape of the knobs, but it is not the latest cast case variety which normally featured such knobs, but in this case is a pressed steel case. In between is a mid period calculator.

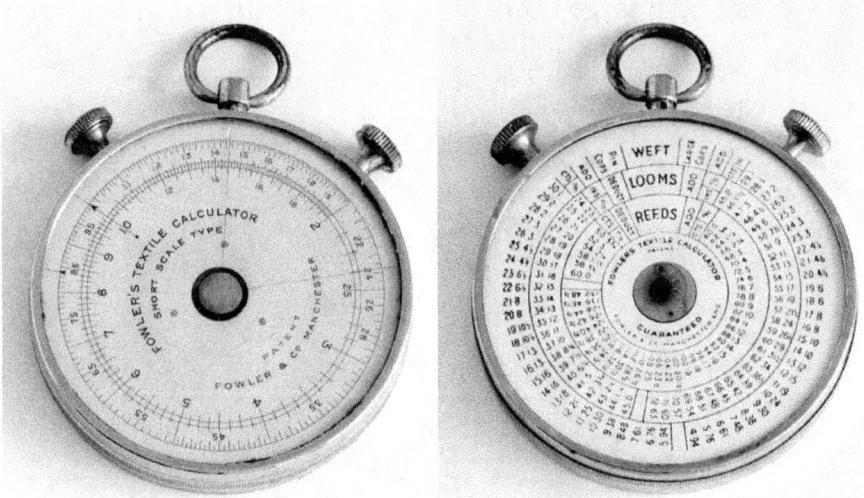

Figure 10.25: Fowler Short Scale Textile Calculator (mid)

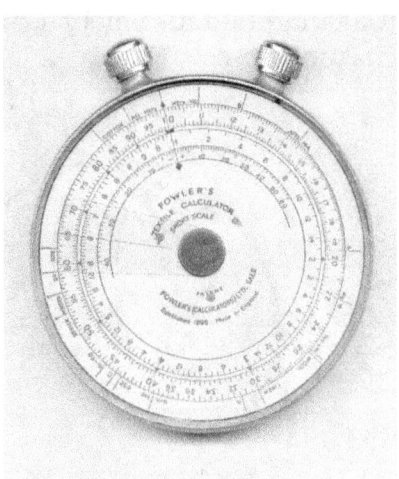

Figure 10.26: Fowler Short Scale Textile Calculator (late)

73

POCKET-WATCH SLIDE RULES

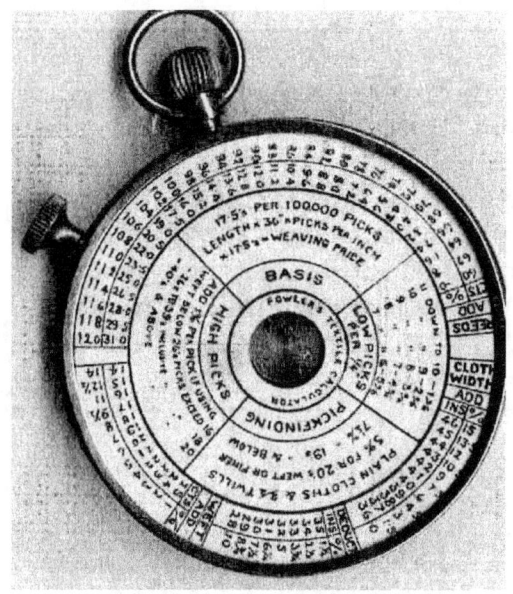

Figure 10.27: Fowler Long Scale Textile Calculator (pick finding)

Figure 10.28: Fowler Long Scale Textile Calculator

Textile (Long Scale Type) Pick Finding Variety

I am not an expert in weaving or the processes that might benefit from the use of such a calculator, however pick finding appears to be something whereby breakage of the yarn in weaving causes problems, and being able to calculate what to do can improve the quality of cloth surface and ease the operation. (Figure 10.27)

Textile (Long Scale Type)

Comparing the calculators in Figures 10.24 and 10.28, it can be seen that the rear of the two types carried identical sets of tables. These were extremely similar to other textile calculator tables; see Type T and Type M. They were often supplied in a metal box.

'Magnum' Textile

Two versions of the 'Magnum' Textile calculator are illustrated with considerably different scales and markings. The example on the left is the earlier version (Fowler & Co. Manchester) with a simple double scale and very few gauge points, while the later center example (Fowler's (Calculators) Ltd. Sale) has additional scales and a large number of gauge points round the outer circumference.

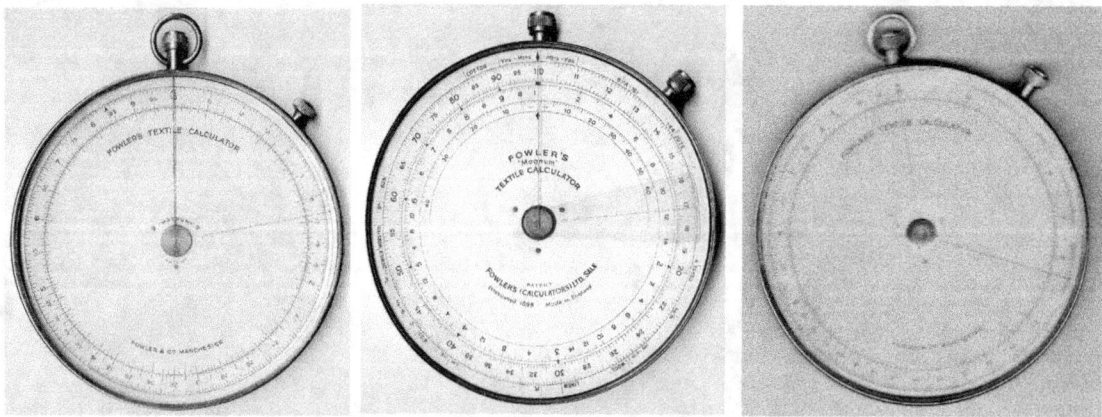

Figure 10.29: Fowler Magnum Textile Calculator

FOWLER'S POCKET-WATCH CALCULATORS

The poor picture at the far right of Figure 10.29 shows a variant of the left hand version which does not have the 'Magnum Textile' marking round the center spindle and could be taken as a separate type of calculator if we had not pictures of the other variant.

Yet another variant (though this does have the 'Magnum' appellation) is shown as a separate type in Figure 10.30, and is actually an earlier version (cylindrical knobs) and has the table from the Long Scale Textile calculator included.

Fowler's Textile Calculator
See Figure 10.30

Vest Pocket Calculator, Type MD
This and the following two types of Fowler's calculator are described in a Fowler's Pocket Book dated 1946[20] where a paragraph titled 'Fowler's Single Dial Vest Pocket Calculators' states:

'These can be supplied fitted with either the front, or the back dial of the Long Scale Instrument, or the front dial of the 'Circular Slide Rule.' They are known respectively as Types 'MD'; H (SD); and C.S.R. (SD). Type 'MD' is useful for those who desire to perform multiplication and division only.'

Image Courtesy of the Conrad Schure Collection

Figure 10.30: Fowler Textile Calculator (type 2)

Identifying these devices becomes a worthwhile challenge! I do not believe I have ever seen a Type MD, and the same applies to a picture of one.

Vest Pocket Calculator, Type H
See illustrations earlier under Type H. This name 'Vest Pocket Calculator' appears to be an alternate way of referring to the calculator when used in various advertisements.

Vest Pocket Calculator, Type CSR
See later illustrations under 'Circular Slide Rule' which this would appear is an abbreviation of, as it uses the front dial only.

Universal Calculator
See Figure 10.31

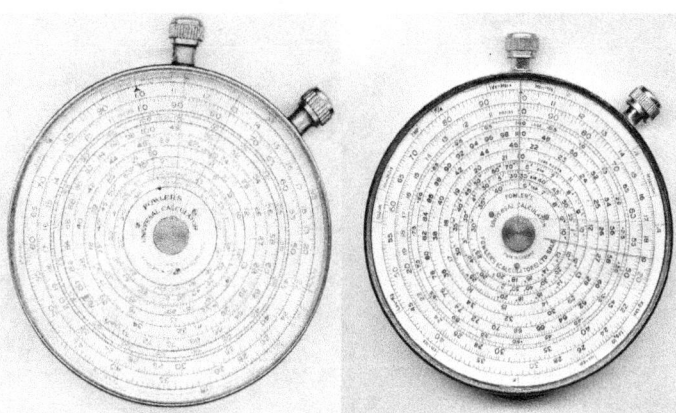

Figure 10.31: Fowler Universal Calculator

---
20 'Fowler's Electrical Engineer's Pocket Book. 1946', page xliii

POCKET-WATCH SLIDE RULES

'Twelve-Ten' Calculator (12-10)

Three variants of the 12-10 calculator are illustrated, the earliest (Figure 10.32) is likely to be the version with the Bakelite back, next is a version with a steel back (Figure 10.33), and finally the Rexine covered back (Figure 10.34) of the final version. Note that this is a single sided calculator produced throughout Fowler's life.

Figure 10.32: Fowler 'Twelve-Ten' Calculator
(Bakelite back)

Figure 10.33: Fowler 'Twelve-Ten' Calculator
(Anodised back)

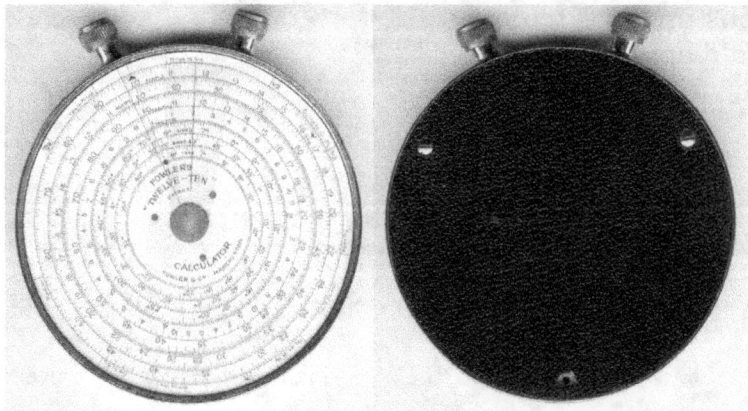

Figure 10.34: Fowler 'Twelve-Ten' Calculator (Rexine back)

We have never been able to fathom out the secrets of Fowler's serial numbering – i.e. is the serial number per type or universal across all types – however in the case of the 12-10 there is a serial number on the back, whatever the type, three digits on the Bakelite, four digits on the steel back, and not obvious on the final one.

Magnum' Long Scale
See Figure 10.35

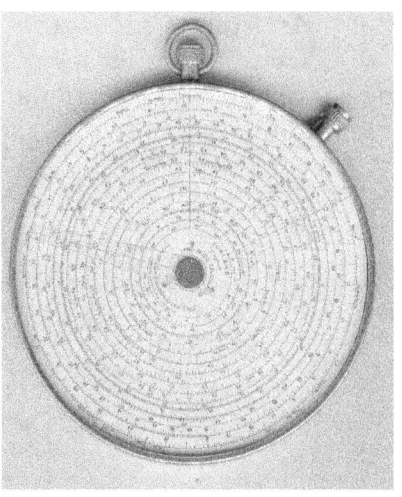

Figure 10.35: Fowler 'Magnum' Long Scale Calculator

Jubilee 'Magnum' Extra Long Scale
A large, single-sided calculator, the first two pictures illustrate one example with its Rexine covered back, the third picture of a slightly later version (Figure 10.36).

Figure 10.36: Fowler Jubilee 'Magnum' Extra Long Scale Calculator

Nautical Calculator
The Fowler Nautical calculator (Figure 10.37) is one of the special application pocket-watch slide rules they produced for various times, these included the Artillery, Nautical, and Navigator's.

Fowler describes the instrument in a publication from approximately 1957 as: 'providing a quick and easy way of accurately solving the calculated altitude, azimuth etc, as described in the "Nautical Magazine" of July 1952. It is double sided 4¼″ diameter, with the scale equivalent to a slide rule 6′ 6″.

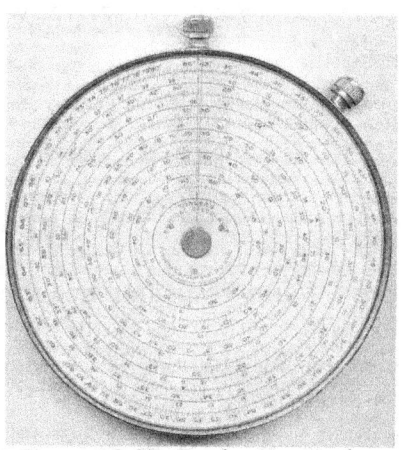

Figure 10.37: Fowler Nautical Calculator

POCKET-WATCH SLIDE RULES

Artillery Calculator

There are at least two versions of the artillery calculator (Figure 10.38). The scales are the same across all versions, but the layout and furniture differs depending on the age of the calculator.

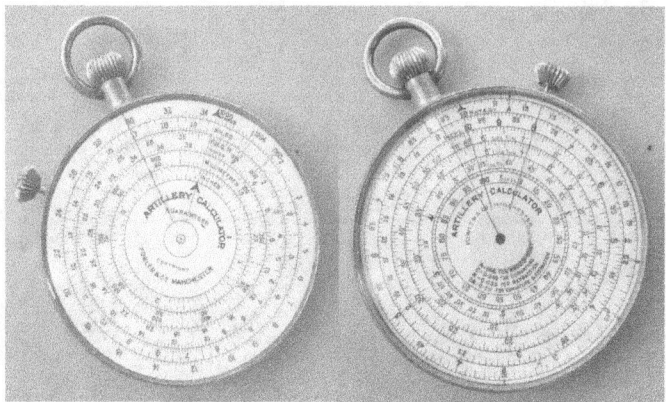

Figure 10.38: Fowler Artillery Calculator (early)

Figure 10.39: Fowler Artillery Calculator (later)

In the 'early' version, we can see the traditional 'early' bulls-eye (Figure 10.38) on a cast case and the early rounded furniture, while below that is a later version with the more usual prominent axle, completer with a serial number, and a pressed steel case.

Long Scale Type R

The Type R continued to be described right through to 1922 when it featured in a Joint Instruction Manual with the Type H (Figure 10.40). The same description was also to be found in 'Newness Slide Rule Manual' [6] by F.J. Camm through its life from 1944 to the end of publication in the 1960's.

Figure 10.40: Fowler Type R from the advertising leaflet

Long Scale Type RX

This is one of the earliest designs with fine pointer and cast case also early furniture, a later variant with the Type RX engraved into the axle is shown in Figure 10.43.

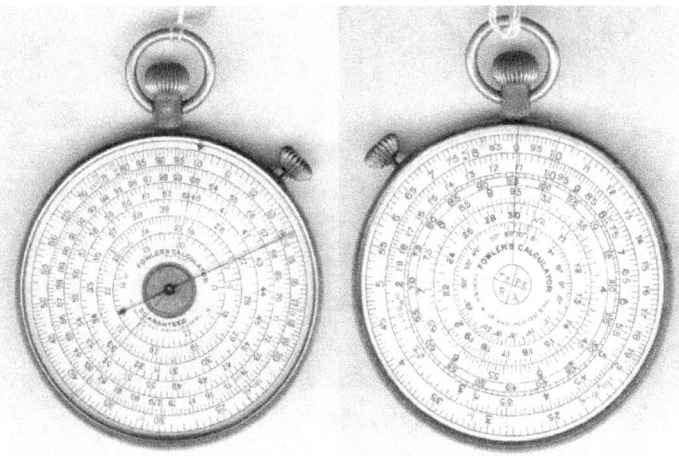

Figure 10.41: Fowler Long Scale Type RX

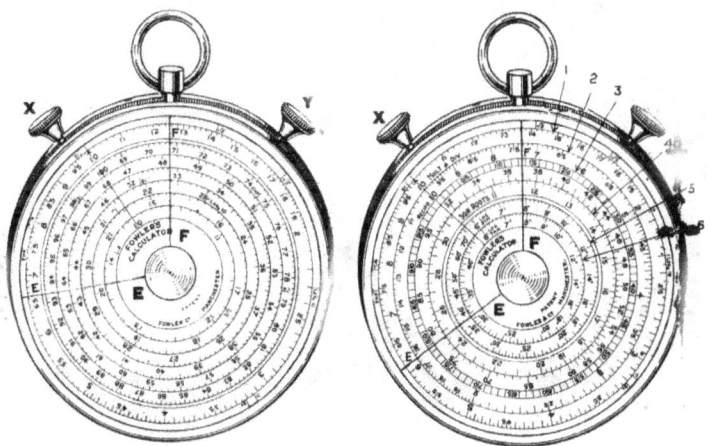

Figure 10.42: Fowler Type RX from the advertising leaflet

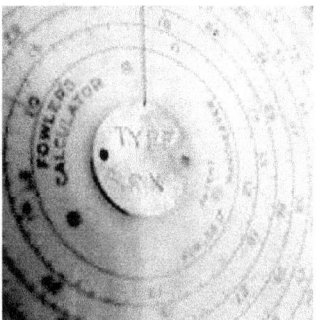

Figure 10.43: Variant with Type Marking on the axle

Long Scale

One of the most popular and common of Fowler's calculators, the Long Scale was in production for such a long time that all variants can be found starting with the standard early type with loop, central key and one side key as shown, (Figure 10.46) working through to the later versions with two keys and no central loop. There are also minor variations to be found as shown below, with and without logo and with and without plastic finger cursor.

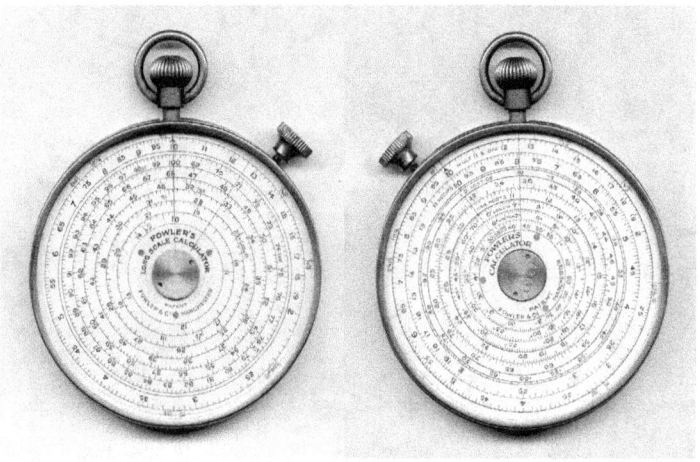

Figure 10.44: Fowler Long Scale Calculator (early)

POCKET-WATCH SLIDE RULES

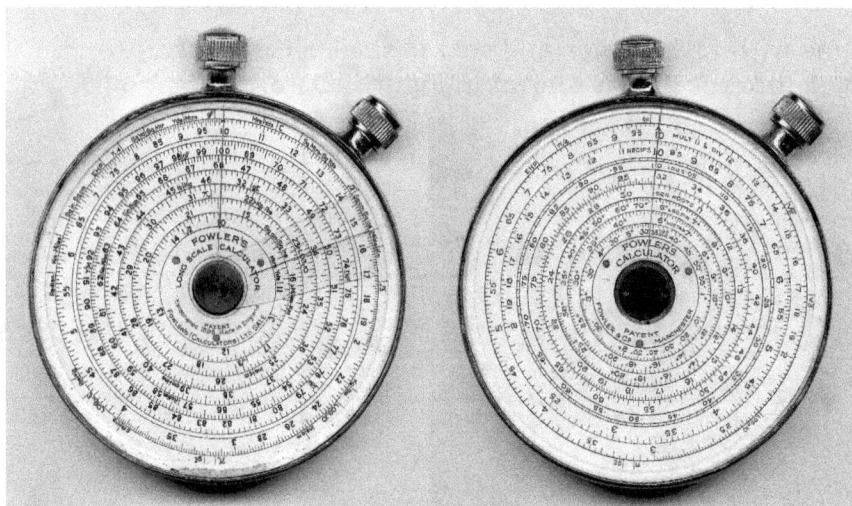

Figure 10.45: Fowler Long Scale Calculator (late)

Two versions – early (Figure 10.44) and late (Figure 10.45) – of the very popular Long Scale calculator, are distinguished by different types of case and furniture.

Figure 10.46: Fowler Long Scale Calculator (variant)

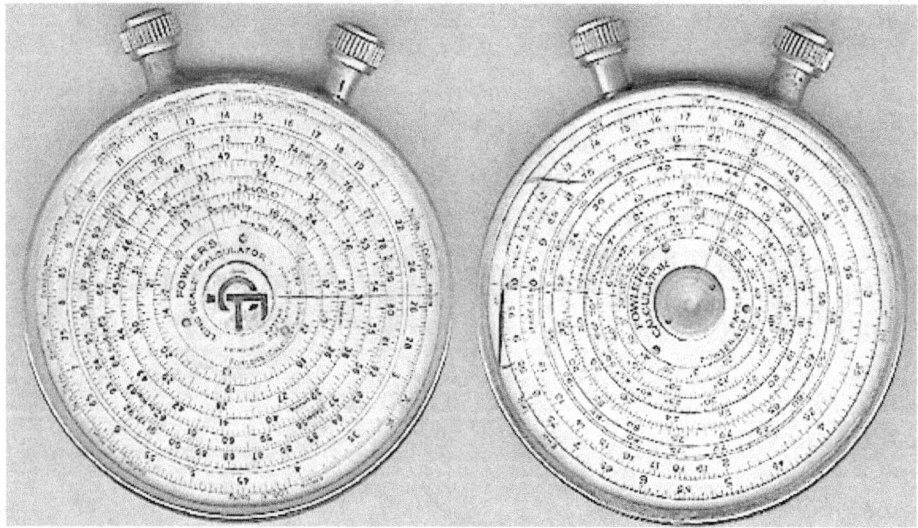

Figure 10.47: Fowler Long Scale Calculator (variant 2)

The two illustrations show, (Figure 10.46), an unusual variant with a plastic cursor separate to the more usual sheet pointer and Figure 10.47, a more normal version in pressed steel case with normal plastic sheet cursors, but this one has the 'FC' logo.

Circular Slide Rule

Confusingly, this is also another name for the Fowler Junior calculator illustrated later under 'Junior Calculator', and it may also be that the Type CSR (abbreviation for Circular Slide Rule) is yet another variant of the name. However, there also was a pocket-watch rule carrying the same name as shown below. Whether this should be catalogued as a variant of the Fowler's Calculator or Circular Slide Rule is a moot point, I have opted for the latter as the former is also used as a generic title, see Type RX etc.

Figure 10.48: Fowler Circular Slide Rule / Fowler's Calculator

'The Mechanical Engineer' Pocket Calculator

This device has been covered in considerable detail in the Scientific Publishing chapter where it is more accurately placed. A Mechanical Engineer calculator labeled 'Fowler' would be a real rarity and a considerable find!

Junior Calculator

In no way can this unusual device be called a Pocket-Watch calculator, but as it was the only non-watch type calculator made by Fowler it is included for completeness and to show how similar the scales are to some pocket-watch designs, and thus it owed some of its parentage to the rest of Fowler's product line. The two sided device is called a Fowler's Circular Slide Rule on one side and Fowler's Junior Calculator on the other, a situation that can (and does) cause considerable confusion.

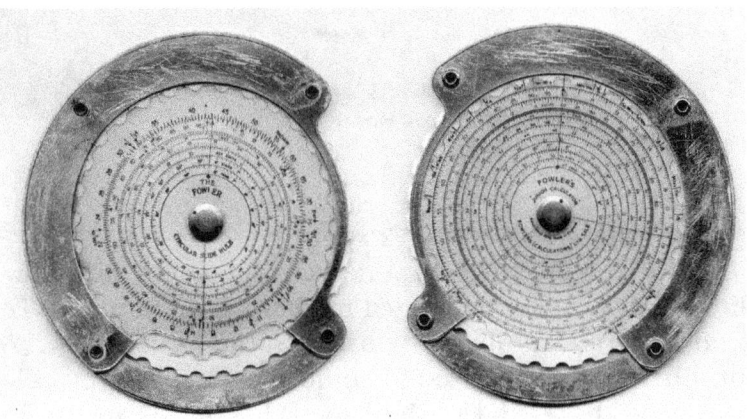

Figure 10.49: Fowler Circular Slide Rule / Junior Calculator

Kearns Machine Type Computer

Fowler made a small number of specialist pocket-watch calculators; The Kearns device is unusual and rare. An example has been described in JOS[21].

A single sided pocket-watch slide rule, specifically designed to calculate cutting times on Kearns Boring Machines[22], sometimes supplied in a tin box.

Figure 10.50: Fowler Kearns Machine Type Computer

---

21   'H.W. Kearns & Co Ltd. – Machine Time Computer by Fowler'; Rick Blankenhorn in *Journal of The Oughtred Society,* Vol. 13 No 2, Fall 2004, pp 19
22   W Kearns & Co Limited was a long established (pre World War 1) machine tool maker in greater Manchester and were known by this name till 1967 when they were taken over, and became Kearns Richards.

Mackay Paper & Board Calculator

The Mackay[23] Paper and Board Calculator is one of the more common specialist devices made by Fowler, and can be found with a number of minor variations as illustrated in Figure 10.51 and Figure 10.52. Perhaps only a specialist in paper science would be able to appreciate the subtleties of the differences.

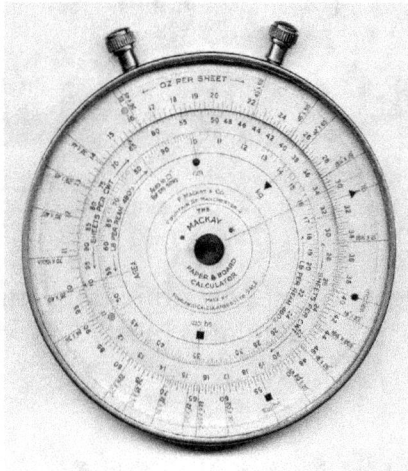

Figure 10.51: Fowler Mackay Paper & Board Calculator

Figure 10.52: Fowler Mackay Paper & Board (variant)

Fowler Bakelite Cases

From the information available so far, we know Fowler produced calculators with Bakelite backs in all single-sided models of the day, e.g. Textile Type B, 12-10, and Universal. The known serial numbers are listed in the table below. At first sight, it would appear that the serial numbers were allocated in some specific order by calculator type number rather than randomly. However, the #1464 in the Type B list, # 881 in the 12-10 list and the #845 in the Universal list shows that it is probably not so straightforward. We have not been able to come up with a logical order within the limits of the available serials, and we have also been unable to date when this happened other than saying it was fairly early in the manufacturing life, an assumption taken from the shape of the furniture. Where we know that a Bakelite case (Figure 10.56) was supplied with the Bakelite backed device, this is shown in the list with an asterisk by the serial number.

What is definitely true is that the Bakelite backs appear to be identical across all models including screws and the wording, color differences are probably from the different batches, and serial numbers are not always in one specific place, though most are at the top.

Fowler Model	Serial Numbers of Bakelite Backed Examples
Type B Textile	33*, 117*(?), 254, 821, 1464
12-10	633, 881
Universal	1061 between 845 ,10611, 1214, 1423, 1540, 1923, 1971

---

23 No records can be found relating to F. Mackay and Co of Fountain Street, Manchester 2, but it seems safe to assume that they too were in existence between about 1950 and 1960.

FOWLER'S POCKET-WATCH CALCULATORS

Figure 10.53: Fowler Bakelite Backs

Also shown here is an even more unusual variation – a carrying case in Bakelite, with the Bakelite back of the Textile Type B calculator that fits into the case shown beside it. Two examples are known.

Figure 10.54: Fowler Bakelite Case

POCKET-WATCH SLIDE RULES

Fowler as Manufacturer

Fowler appears to have been the only true English company who we can be absolutely certain 'manufactured' and sold his pocket-watch slide rules, but even here we have to add the rider that he may actually only have 'assembled' parts that had been bought in!

The 'Swiss' markings on some early Fowler (actually Scientific Publishing) pocket-watch slide rules remains unexplained, unless Fowler sourced standard pocket-watch parts from Swiss manufacturers which were then assembled. However, I cannot confirm this as I do not know enough about the manufacture of pocket-watches and the parts that are needed, to know whether this is a sensible approach.

An interesting article by Colin Barnes[24] includes descriptions of the watch making cottage industry in the midlands and elsewhere in England and an illustration of a watch making factory in Coventry where the Waddington versions of Lord's Calculator came from. Whether it was the Waddington's or indeed anyone else who made that type remains unknown.

Originals of the following photographs are available from the Sale Library, Cheshire; they show the Fowler factory as described in Jenny Wetton's excellent series on instrument manufacturing in Manchester at the end of the 19th century in the SIS Bulletin[25]. Fowler's 'factory' is hardly the ultimate in manufacturing capability. The photo shows a room with peeling ceiling paper and an open fire, and some rudimentary tools are available for 'fettling' the instruments they were assembling. Assuming it is Harold Fowler in the foreground, he has about 30 calculators laid out in front of him, and a further large pile of parts to his left. How long it would have taken to assemble these would be interesting to know. From the hand-written dates inside two opened examples we know that at least 50 Type E1 calculators were made in one month, how typical this was and what else might have been made in parallel is not known.

Figure 10.55: Harold Fowler and unknown assistant assembling calculators in the workshop at Oakleigh about 1917.

---

24   'Lord's Calculator & W. Waddington - an appendix' by Colin Barnes in the Proceedings of the International Meeting 1999
25   'Scientific Instrument making in Manchester 1870 – 1940, III: Flatters and Garnet Limited and Fowler & Company' by Jenny Wetton, Bulletin of the Scientific Instrument Society, No. 53 (1997).

The next photo shows the constituent parts with a completed calculator and illustrates just how sophisticated this slide rule was, and yet it was extremely cost effectively made, selling for 21/- in 1934.

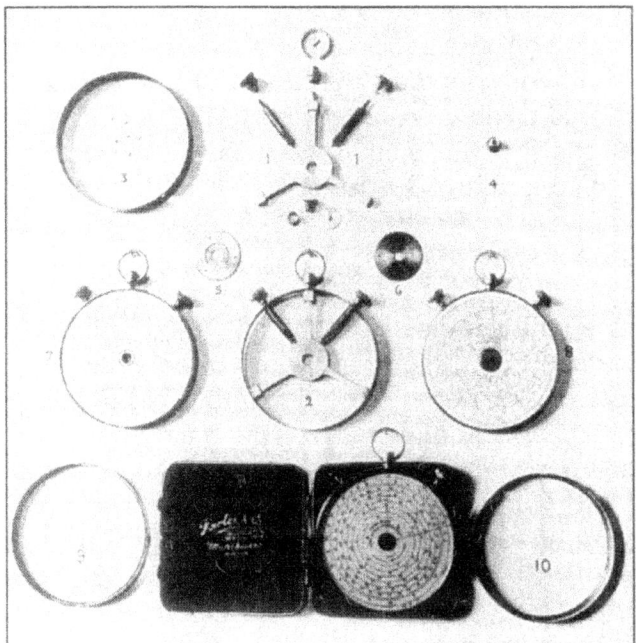

Figure 10.56: Parts for the construction of a Long Scale calculator, with a completed example, probably taken at the Station Works in around 1929.

Figure 10.57: Cutting head of the machine used for marking out the steel die for a calculator scale, c1929

Halden's Calculex

Introduction

Halden's Calculex is one of those delightful watch-pocket devices (not pocket-watch, as it does not (usually) have a crown) that make the slide rule collectors lot such a pleasurable one. It is much more like a traditional circular slide rule and is operated by the 'thumb nuts' through the glass faces. These drive the inner scale of a traditional circular rule, supported by a rich collection of supplementary scales. The Calculex is probably even more robust than the other watch designs as it has no cogs or other mechanism to go wrong. On the other hand it is not as accurate as the other designs such as Fowler long-scale. Lord's Calculator has similar circular slide rule scales; however these are driven from a winding stem.

The Calculex is available in a number of variants including a 'desk' model which has to be one of the ultimate slide rule collectables. The standard Calculex is ubiquitous; many retailers sold a version in the UK and Europe as well as in the USA. A very small number of models appear to have been 'specials' which were only available via the one retailer. It is particularly interesting that it is only known as Halden's Calculex when the earliest patent is due to Edward Wilson in 1903, an early example of branding! The history is further confused in that there are at least two other patents for 'Calculex' type devices and how they relate is completely unknown and even very difficult to speculate.

The device recognizable as a Calculex was sold by many retailers, some under their own name, most retained the Calculex name. Others advertised, and some claimed, to have converted the basic Calculex mechanism with its unique 'thumb nut' into a pocket-watch case with a suitable mechanism that was their own design. These will be investigated in this chapter. The fact that there may have been an obvious development path adds to the interest, this too will be investigated.

Calculex Type Patents

Joseph Halden always referred to their Calculex devices as a 'Patent Circular Slide Rule (Halden Calculex)' both in advertising material, on the majority of the calculators themselves and also the instruction manuals. However, nowhere is the actual Patent number or a patent date quoted. Various authors have speculated that the patent was 'about 1910'. This turns out to be a complete guess which stemmed from publications that quoted numbers sold as well as the earliest dates when adverts for the Calculex appeared, both in the UK and abroad. The earliest Calculex advert found is 1908.

However, for this section a more detailed study has been made, and firstly a number of possibly competing patents have been found, and secondly, adverts with an earlier date have also been catalogued. Looking at the patents, we have the following:

Calculex Type Slide Rule Patents		
Date	Patent No.	Patent Information
1903	UK 14,533	Edward Wilson – this is actually the Calculex patent, passed to Halden at some time.
1904	UK Prov. Pat. 19,061	H.T. Hinks, UK Provisional patent, see below for the full US patent. Not seen full UK patent.
1907	USA 845,463	H.T. Hinks, a slide rule with electrical and normal scales in pocket-watch format which also looks extremely similar to a Calculex. It is doubtful that it was ever made
c1910	UK n/a	Halden's supposed patent date for the Calculex – quoted by Halden. It has never been separately identified and may actually be a reference to Wilson's 1903 patent, see above.
1912	USA 1,017,719	H.R. Watts. Another device that is instantly recognisable as a Halden Calculex, see also Edward Wilson 1903, and H.T. Hinks 1904 & 1907
1913	USA 1,056,775	D.W. Brunton, Circular slide rule with a watch loop and glass face – not a true pocket-watch rule.

Edward Wilson's Patent

Edward Wilson, Engineer of Commercial Road, Exeter, in the County of Devon, applied for a patent in June 1902, filed the complete specification in March 1903 and was granted patent number 14,533 in June 1903. The patent describes a device that is instantly recognizable as the Calculex, a simple, compact and highly effective design for a two-sided circular slide rule with rotatable glass covers which carried 'hairlines' – the cursor.

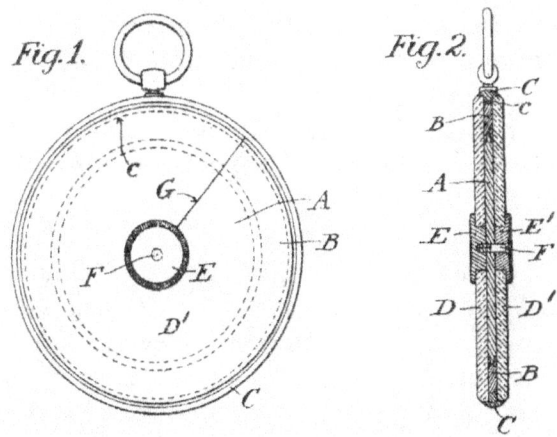

Figure 11.1: Taken from Wilson patent

To anyone who has ever taken a Calculex to bits, the cross section (Figure 2 in Figure 11.1 above) is instantly recognizable, and when you also read in the description: 'The scale disc may be turned to any position by holding the nuts between the finger and thumb, the ring being held in place by a small pin in the outer or metal ring'.

A Wilson Device

The Wilson device was actually made. At least one example is in a collection and it is instantly recognizable as a Calculex though labeled 'Wilson's Slide Rule Calculator, Patent'. There are no clues as to who actually made it, which will remain a mystery. However, whoever made it also made the earliest version of Calculex, a comparison of a Type 1 Calculex and the Wilson device shows identical devices, apart from the labeling, also makes this the obvious starting point for the type.

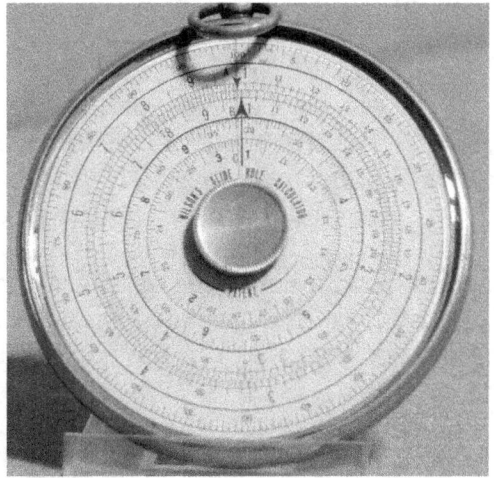

Image Courtesy of the Conrad Schure Collection

Figure 11.2: A Wilson Calculex

Harold Thornthwaite Hinks' Patent

H.T. Hinks of Chester, an electrical engineer is the next producer of a patent which was very like Wilson's patent for the Calculex. Fig. 5 and Fig. 6 within Figure 11.3 below are taken from the full US patent No. 845,463 of 1907, originally applied for in May 1905, but not awarded until February 1907. In the US application he quotes a provisional British application No 19,061 dated September 1904. It has not been possible to find a related full UK patent award, which in all probability means it was never awarded. It is entirely possible that there was no full UK award because the design is so extremely similar and within two or three years of the Wilson patent that it must have infringed it. However, as we have not found an equivalent to the Wilson patent filed in the USA, the Hinks patent would have been the first for such a device filed there and in all probability would have had no problem in being awarded, albeit after the delay which we have noted.

Herbert Richard Watts' Patent

Herbert Richard Watts, an Englishman from the county of Chester (a strange coincidence – see Hinks above) filed an American patent in January 1911, and was awarded patent No. 1,017,719 in February 1912. This is so incredibly similar to the UK Calculex, including a single screw in one side of the device and the double screws in the other, as well as the shape of the 'Thumb nuts' the rotatable glasses, virtually identical scales and so on, that it is hard to understand how Watts patent could be awarded when the Wilson UK patent already existed, but more so is its similarity to Hinks' US Patent of only a few years earlier.

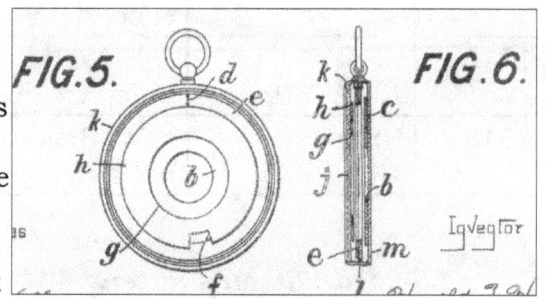

Figure 11.3: H.T. Hinks patent calculator

Figure 11.4 below shows all diagrams from the Watts patent. There can be few better sets of working drawings for a Calculex! However, I have never seen a device bearing the name of Watts, so whether there was a relationship with any 'Calculex' type devices is not known at all. It may be that this patent covered the later versions of Calculex (Type 3) but nothing is recorded.

David W. Brunton's Patent

The final 'Calculex look-alike' is US Patent No 1,056,775 in the name of David Brunton of Denver Colorado, filed in November 1912 and awarded in March 1913. The similarities are not as strong when considered in the detail which a Patent Attorney would have to consider, nevertheless at first sight there are enough similarities to at least cause some surprise. The patent drawings can be seen in the earlier chapter, page 12.

Here then are four patents which could be 'the' Calculex patent. However I would submit that Wilson's patent is the starting point for the design, and as it was actually made in enough numbers for at least one to survive this is the 'prototype' which would ultimately

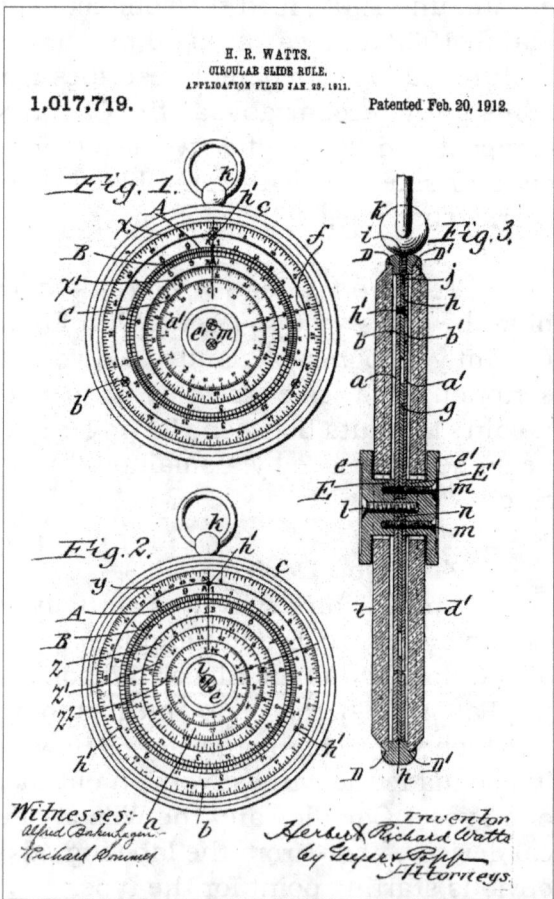

Figure 11.4: All Figures from H.R. Watts US Patent of 1912

become the Type 1 Calculex. The shame is that we are unable to put any dates to either action, other than it was sometime in the 3 years between the Wilson patent award date of 1903 and the earliest mention of a Calculex in 1906, [3] or maybe the first advert in 1908.

Calculex Developments

Despite the original patent being applied for in 1902, it was several years before the Calculex came into any form of prominence. Whether Wilson tried to sell the device on his own and did not succeed we do not know at this remove. The existence of a 'Wilson' device makes this a strong possibility. What Hinks, Watt and possibly Brunton actually contributed is also unknown, however with the advent of Joseph Halden, an established slide rule maker, and the very catchy Calculex name, the device seems to have taken on a new lease of life and continued to be sold for many years through to the 1950's.

Calculex Types

Halden produced several variants over the years the Calculex was manufactured; these are delightfully idiosyncratic, and almost impossible to date.

However, as a first attempt to provide some dating information, we can look at the adverts for Calculexes (Calculii?) that were used by various retailers in the UK as well as Halden themselves, starting with the adverts in Pickworth[26]. We can also look at Halden Calculex adverts used by other retailers in Europe and in the USA.

Recording the variants that have been seen, we can put together a first estimated chronology.

Adverts for Halden's Calculex Devices							
Pickworth				**Other Reference**			
Edition	**Date**	**Pickworth Slide Rule Advert**	**Cost**	**Company**	**Date**	**Rule**	**Cost**
06	1900	Stanley Boucher Mech Eng	n/a 7/9d; 12/9d				
07	1901	Stanley Boucher	n/a				
08	1903	Stanley Boucher	n/a				
09	1904	None					
10	1906	Stanley Boucher Patent	n/a	W. Harling: Halden Calculex	1906	Cajori item 211 [3]	
11	1908	Calculex T1 Dietzgen Calculex	12/6d n/a				
12	1910	None					

---

26 Pickworth – see footnote 4 on page 20. It is very useful to be able to use consecutive editions of Pickworth as a record of how information changed over a range of dates.

13	1915	Calculex T1 Desk Calculex	12/6d £1.17.6d	Halden	1915	Calculex T1 Desk Calculex	2/6d £1.17.6d
14	1916	Calculex T1 Desk Calculex	12/6d £1.17.6d				
15	1917	Calculex T1 Desk Calculex	16/- £3.3.0d				
16	1919	Calculex T1	25/-				
17	1920	Calculex T1	27/6d	Halden	1925	Calculex T3	£1.1.0d
18	1927	None		C.F. Casella	1930	Calculex T3	£1.1.0d
19	1930	None		J.H. Weil	1930	Calculex T1	
20	1935	None		W. Harling	1930	Calculex T1	£1.1.0d
21	1938	Calculex T3	21/-	F. Weber	1931	Calculex T1	$7.50
22	1941	None		Dietzgen	1938	Calculex	$9.00
23	1942	None					
24	1945	None					

The dates in the above table may not be accurate; the problem being that the same 'copy' was often used for advertisements over a number of years. For example the Halden Type 1 advert featured virtually unchanged from the first time in the Pickworth 11th edition of 1908 through to the 17th edition in 1920, and was replaced by an advert for the type 3 in the 21st edition in 1938 with a gap in between when there was no advert. However the same Type 3 artwork was used separately by Halden and Casella in 1925 and 1930 respectively, while Weil and Weber in the USA and Harling in the UK continued to use the 'old' Type 1 artwork in 1930 and 1931. However, the earliest mention is on page 75 in W.H. Harling's 'Drawing Instruments', 13th ed. 1906 as mentioned in Cajori [3], as also recorded above.

We can thus speculate that the Type 1 device might have been first marketed in about 1906 (4 years after Wilson's patent) and could have been phased out sometime between 1920 and 1925, as we have a Halden 1925 catalogue with the Type 3 device illustrated.

Calculex Type 1

We can hypothesize that this is the earliest Type 1 version because it most closely resembles the Wilson device and Wilson's patent. It is 60 mm (2 3/8″) diameter, 4.75 mm (3/16″) across the glass, and 7.5 mm (5/16″) across the 'thumb nuts' – which themselves are extremely thin and joined with a single central screw, (Figure 11.5) as shown in Wilson's patent. The band on which the ring is fixed via a 5.9 mm ball, is 4 mm thick, i.e. the ball is wider than the band. The glass is not beveled, and the scales appear to be applied via some sort of anodizing or photographic process. The labeling, only on one side, is 'Patent Circular Slide Rule' above the nut, and '— Halden's "Calculex" —' below. The Type 1 Calculex weighs a mere 35 grams, the lightest version by far.

A Type 1a has been recorded. This has thin beveled glass, almost as if the slightly crude Type 1 above had been tidied up. It is noticeably heavier and the dimensions are tending towards those of the Type 2, but it still has the single screw through fixing. (Figure 11.5 end image of the Type 1) neither 1 nor 1a is the _″ thickness mentioned in the early adverts.

Figure 11.5: Halden Type 1 Calculex

Calculex Type 2

We can further hypothesize that the Type 2 Calculex version is the similar but more robust design illustrated above. It is 62 mm (~2½″) diameter, 7.7 mm (5/16″) across the glass, and 12 mm (½″) across the 'thumb nuts' which are much larger with heavier knurling on the 'thumb' surface, and now have a single screw on one side and two screws on the other side, (Figure 11.6). It weighs 71 grams. The band, on which the ring is fixed via a 5.4 mm ball, is just less than 5.8 mm thick. The glass is slightly beveled and is proud of the band on both sides. The scales are engraved and filled onto plastic discs. This version has 'Patent Circular Slide Rule' on the bottom circumference of a circle at the center, and 'The Halden Calculex' on the upper circumference of the same circle, i.e. it is opposite to the first and third versions, and has different words.

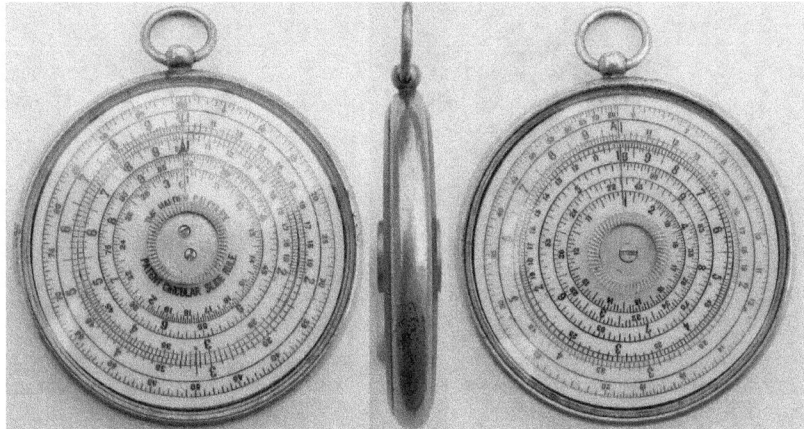

Figure 11.6: Halden Type 2 Calculex

It is noticeable that this version of Calculex does not appear to feature in any of the 'Full Size' advertisements that were used by Halden – or so it appears as it is extremely difficult to be specific about this. However, where we have no difficulty in identifying a Type 3 Calculex with its heavily beveled glass, and what appears to be a Type 1 Calculex with its very thin and simple outline, this is not the case with the Type 2.

Yet another version of Type 2 Calculex, perhaps better described as a pre-Type 2, or a Type 1b, has been recorded. This is heavier yet, has beveled glass, but not as the Type 3, and again is getting slightly heavier and more 'robust' i.e. the dimensions are increasing. (Is this like increasing human age when everything gets fatter?). It is noted in the table of variants.

Calculex Type 3

The Calculex Type 3 is another robust device. It is 60 mm (2.375″) diameter, 8.7 mm (~.375″)across the glass, and 14.7 mm (.5625″)across the 'thumb nuts' and weighs 78.3 grams. These nuts are the larger form, but with knurling on the 'thumb' surfaces which are now beveled, and have the single screw on one side and two screws on the other side, (Figure 11.7). The band has shrunk considerably and is itself knurled. The ring is fixed via a 6.1 mm ball, and the band is just under 2.5 mm thick, the ball holds a 'V' shaped washer which is bent over the top bevel of the glass on both sides, both very distinctive features. The glass is thick and heavily beveled and is the most recognizable feature of this version of Calculex. The scales are metal, and in common with what I have called the first version, have 'Patent Circular Slide Rule' on the upper circumference of a circle at the center, and '— Halden's "Calculex" —' on the bottom circumference of the same circle.

POCKET-WATCH SLIDE RULES

Calculex Variants

It is relatively easy to describe variants to the three basic types identified earlier. The chronology is not so easy to establish. A version is known which has a knurled bolt through which the ring is passed ('Calculex' on the upper circumference) which looks to be a variant on the Type 2 (Type 2a) – Figure 11.8.

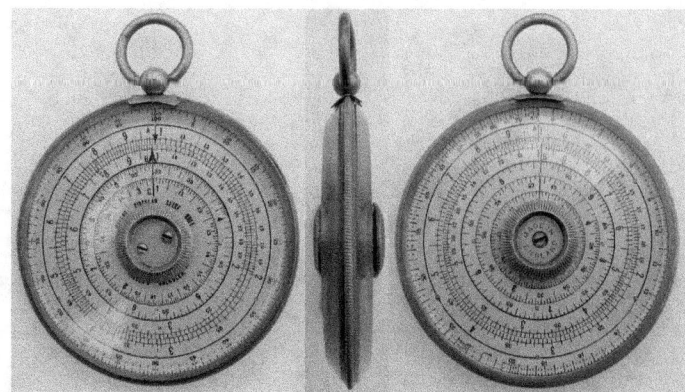

Figure 11.7: Halden Type 3 Calculex

Figure 11.8: Variant Type 2 Calculex

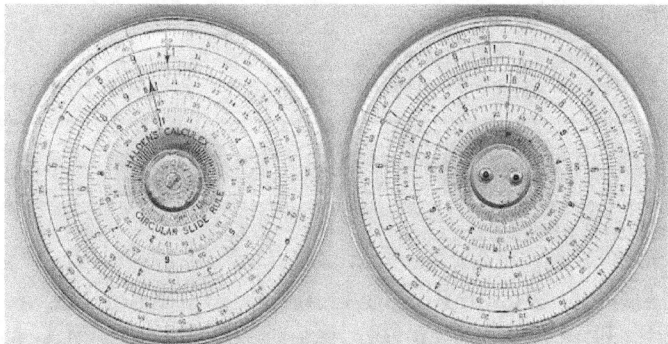

Figure 11.9: Variant Type 3 (3a)

Figure 11.10: Another variation of the Type 3 (3b)

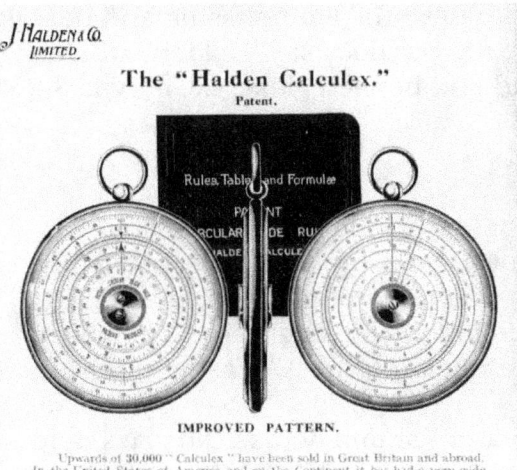
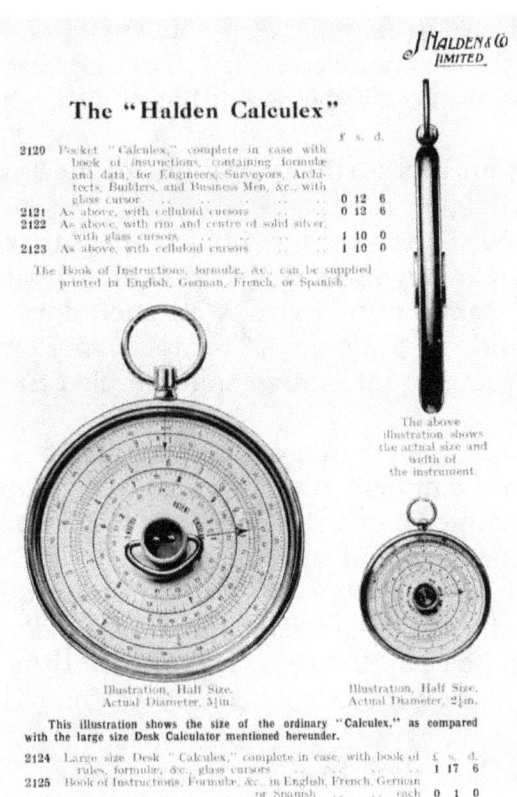

Figure 11.11: 1915 Halden catalogue adverts

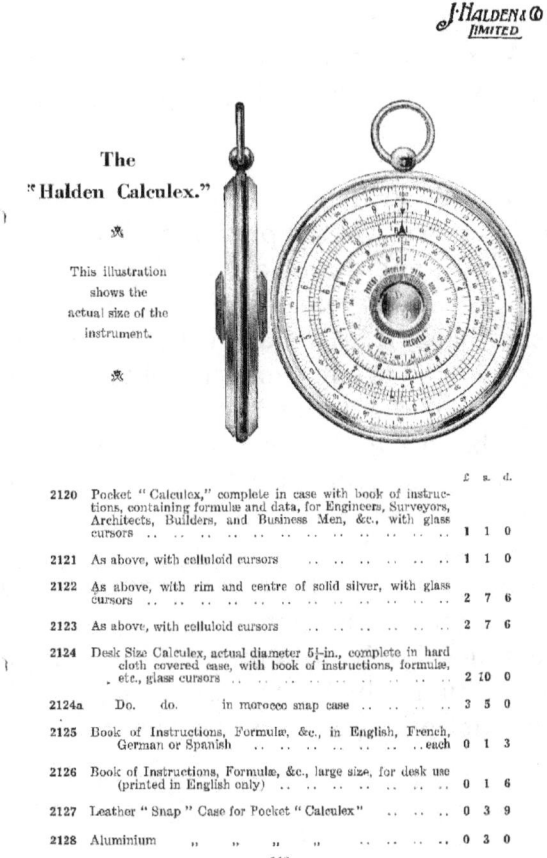

Figure 11.12: 1925 Halden catalogue adverts

Another variant, an example of which just happens to have the loop missing and the two smaller screws (lost), does not say 'Patent' Circular Slide Rule, but does say 'Halden's "Calculex"'. This is a variant of the Type 3 as it has the thin band and beveled glass, i.e. a Type 3b.

Summarizing these and yet further variations of the Type 3:

- Type 3a – (above) does not mention the patent and only says 'Halden's "Calculex"
- Type 3b – which has only been seen in pictures (above), has only a single screw fixing between the thumb nuts, has a 'V' washer, does not mention the patent and again only says 'Halden's "Calculex". This is a complete anomaly. The single screw makes it 'early', larger and square rather than beveled thumb nuts and the 'V' washer implies type 3.
- Type 3c – which is 16.5 mm across the thumb nuts and 7.5 mm across the glass, and has very prominent dished washers between glass and nut on each side to accommodate the different dimensions. This still has a 2.5 mm knurled ring 60 mm diameter and is identical in marking and scale material. It weighs 73.8 grams.
- Type 3d – which is 12 mm across the thumb nuts, 7.5 mm across the glass, but has no knurling on the 60mm diameter ring and no 'V' washer under the ball carrying the loop. Both 3b, and 3c carry the same labeling, but the 3c could have paper scales rather than the metal scales on the other types. It weighs 61.6 grams.

Evolution of the Calculex and Numbers Made

It is interesting to compare two Calculex adverts from Halden catalogues published in 1915 and 1925. (Figures 11.11 and 11.12) We can see that the earlier (1915) advert is for a Type 1 (or should this be Type 2?) device and includes both pocket and desk varieties, with both glass and celluloid cursors and silver and non-silver rim and centers. It also repeats the statistic of 'upwards of 30,000 sold' and shows that our previous estimates of when they started saying this are not so far wrong. We can also confirm the wording on the devices.

The second (1925) later advert shows a Type 3 device with its iconic beveled glass, and advertises but does not illustrate a desk device. It gives the statistic of 'upwards of 60,000 sold, perhaps somewhat later that we had previously estimated. Otherwise both adverts are remarkably consistent in content and outlook.

What is interesting is that the Calculex advertised in the 'early' advert is not obvious as either Type 1 or Type 2, due to the similarity of the dimensions and design, but it does have the single / double screws holding it together as Type 2. The thumb nuts appear extremely thin (as Type 1), while the band appears slightly thicker as Type 2, also the glass appears beveled as Type 2, so it may be that the Type 1 Calculex may have been very short-lived and had already evolved into the Type 2.

There is no indication anywhere of any of the variations we have recorded. Both adverts talk of an 'improved' Calculex, nowhere have we seen a non-improved type, whatever that may have been. But this might be the improvement from Type 1 to the Type 2 design. There is some logic to this train of thought; the Wichmann catalogue of 1910 definitely shows a very obvious Type 1 device in its illustration, with its single screw.

Calculex Specifications					
Type/ Variant	Diameter mm	Thickness mm.		Ring Thickness mm	Weight gms	Comment
		Across Glass	Across Nuts			
Type 1	60	4.75	7.5	4	35	Single screw
Type 1a	61	7	9.4	4.5	50	Single screw, beveled glass
Type 1b	62	7	11	5.7	63	Single screw, beveled glass
Type 2	62	7.7	12	5.8	71	Heavier ring
Type 2a	-	-	-	-	-	Nut for loop
Type 3	60	8.7	14.7	2.5	78.3	Beveled glasses
Type 3a	-	-	-	-	-	No mention of patent
Type 3b	-	-	-	-	-	No mention of patent Single screw
Type 3c	60	7.5	16.5	2.5	73.8	Prominent dished washers
Type 3d	59.5	7.5	12	2.5	61.6	No 'V' washer or knurling on ring

Halden themselves were perhaps guilty of at least gentle exaggeration when they advertised the numbers sold at various times. Joseph Halden published four books on 'Graphic Statics' all of which contained adverts for the Calculex as well as other instruments they sold. As with many publications at that time there is no publication date, and we have to apply a bit of guesswork:

Edition of 'Graphic Statics' and Other Source Calculex Sales						
Part/Vol	Edn.	Date of Preface	Contents	Calculex Type	Estimated Year	Claimed Sales
Part 1	4th	No date	>WW1	T1	1915	>30,000
Part ll	2nd	?1900	Last ref 1899	T3	1918 / 1925	>60,000
Part lll	1st	March 1909	1909	T1	1909	>10,000
			Practical Mechanics		1951	Est. 250,000

POCKET-WATCH SLIDE RULES

From this data and simple extrapolation, as shown in the graph below, it is not impossible to estimate that something in the region of one-quarter of a million Calculexes were made and sold. This should hardly make them rare, and either there is many tens of thousands of examples in the back of people's drawers or else there was considerable exaggeration in the numbers claimed to have been sold.

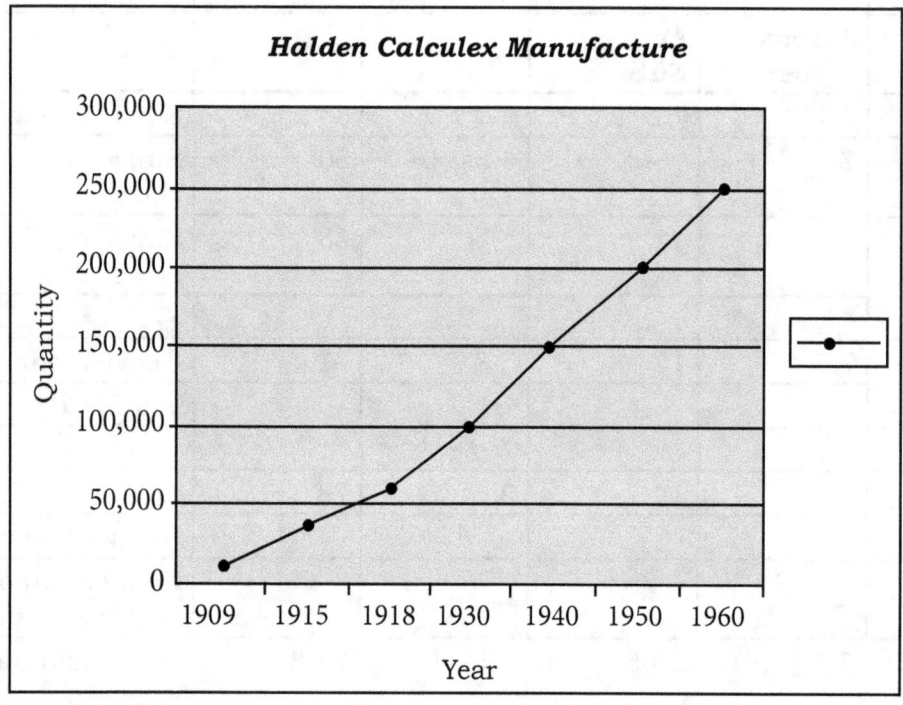

Figure 11.13: Halden Calculex manufacture

Other Calculexes

Gebr. Wichmann Calculexes

Some while back in an exchange of correspondence with another collector my interest was piqued by the description of a 'Fowler being sold by Wichmann', a fairly unlikely event as Fowler only appear to have made very specific designs to be sold under another name – e.g. Dyson, Mackay. As the correspondence continued, more detailed study of various papers and copies of adverts showed that the scales on the device were those of a Halden Calculex, and that the 'watch' format, complete with key, was the unique feature.

I believed at the time that this was a complete fabrication; however the final very surprising result is described in more detail in the Wichmann chapter.

Eugene Dietzgen USA

Dietzgen's details are given elsewhere in this book and as a well known seller of slide rules in the USA it is not surprising that they were an agent for Halden and the Calculex, though why they appear to be the only one selling a version with the rear cursor in yellow (amber) glass is not known.

Figure 11.14: Yellow Calculex ex Dietzgen

These may have been for use in bright sunlight, or (as they say, see high-lit sentence in Figure 11.19, but I can't understand why) to distinguish front from back.

Hughes-Owens Company Limited, USA

The Hughes Owens Company Limited catalogue, 1937 edition, describes a Calculex Type 1 under a model number 1775.

A. West & Partners

36 Broadway, Westminster SW1 England

West & Partners in their 1953 edition catalogue describes a Calculex Type 3 under a model number M2620.

H. Morin

11, Rue Dulong, Paris, France

Morin advertise a Cercle Halden (unillustrated) under part No. 9116 in the 1911 catalogue which makes them another early advertiser of the device, and also their 1925/26 catalogue. This has no part number but says that they can be supplied with the interesting caveat that due to problems with supplying replacement glasses, these are no longer covered by the guarantee.

The 'Desk' Model Calculex

This is surely one of the most glorious Pocket-watch slide rules, though at about 5¼" diameter one would need large pockets, or certainly deep pockets to pay for it!

Figure 11.15: Both sides of a Desk Model Calculex

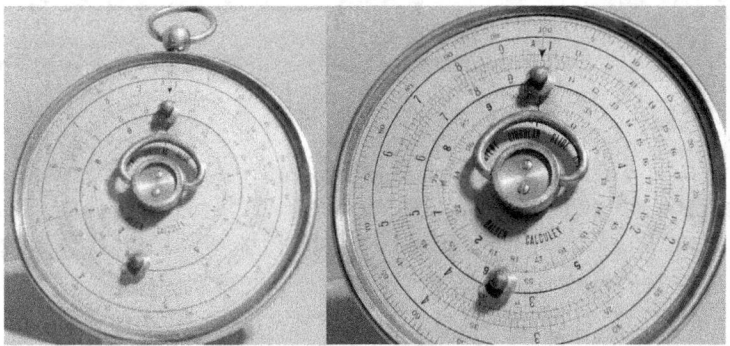

Images Courtesy of the Conrad Schure Collections
Figure 11.16: Details of a Desk Calclex,

POCKET-WATCH SLIDE RULES

The second pair of images show a variant with metal 'bubbles' on the glass to assist with turning the cursors for calculating purposes. It is an unusual addition; most desk versions are as the previous image.

Figure 11.17: Desk Calculex in its case

The Halden catalogues and other adverts imply that the Desk Calculex was not sold much after the First World War, and that may not be surprising as it was considerably more expensive than the pocket version. However a good condition one in its velvet lined case, then as now, must have been a source of great pride to the owner when it was displayed to best effect. The pocket Calculex was advertised as equivalent to a 10″ linear slide rule ($\pi d = \pi 2.25″ = 7″$) which was perhaps a touch fanciful, however the Desk version at 5¼″ diameter gave a scale length of about 16″ which would have been more than adequate for day to day calculation.

Scales:
L, C/D, $\sqrt{}$, $\sqrt{}//°$, $^3\sqrt{}$, $^3\sqrt{}$, $^3\sqrt{}$ (n.b. 2-turn square root and 3-turn cube root)

Instruction Manuals:
The tiny 94 page instruction manual 2¼″ (57 mm) square, which was designed to go into any of the carrying / protection cases the Calculex could be supplied with is a marvel of the printing trade.

Figure 11.18: Halden Calculex handbooks

However an identical manual exists for the Wilson device, and the Calculex manual was certainly translated into French for the 'Cercle Halden' and may also have been translated into other languages. There was also a 'Revised' version, but I have not carried out a detailed comparison.

F.J. Camm's 'Newness Slide Rule Manual' [6] carried a description and instructions for use of the Halden Calculex (and was illustrated with diagrams of a Type 3 Calculex) from the first edition of 1944 right through to the final 7th edition of 1963 as well as later impressions.

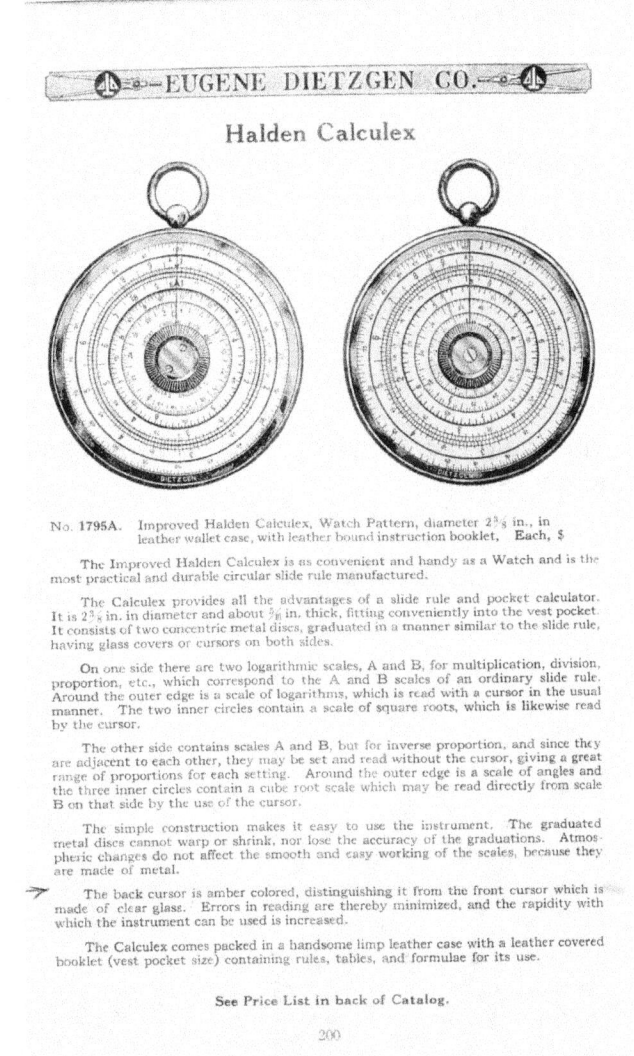

Figure 11.19: Advert from 1931 Dietzgen catalogue
(with a note that the rear cursor is amber coloured)

In addition to the early plastic pill boxes, Calculexes were supplied in a variety of simple and also more sophisticated leather wallets with a pocket for the instructions and also a tin box. What dates these occupied we have not been able to ascertain.

Figure 11.20: Early single-screw
Calculex in plastic pill-box case

Gebr. Wichmann's Pocket-Watch Calculators

Introduction

Gebruder Wichmann (Wichmann Brothers) was established in 1873, in Berlin and is still in existence today. Along the way they appear to have taken over some of the other German members of the slide rule industry such as Reiss. As with Schacht und Westerich, they are a pre-eminent example of a German company who sold a wide range of pocket-watch slide rules, but equally may not have actually made them.

Wichmann Catalogues

We can see what they sold and roughly when by looking at adverts from their c1910, c1920 and c1939 catalogues as follows:

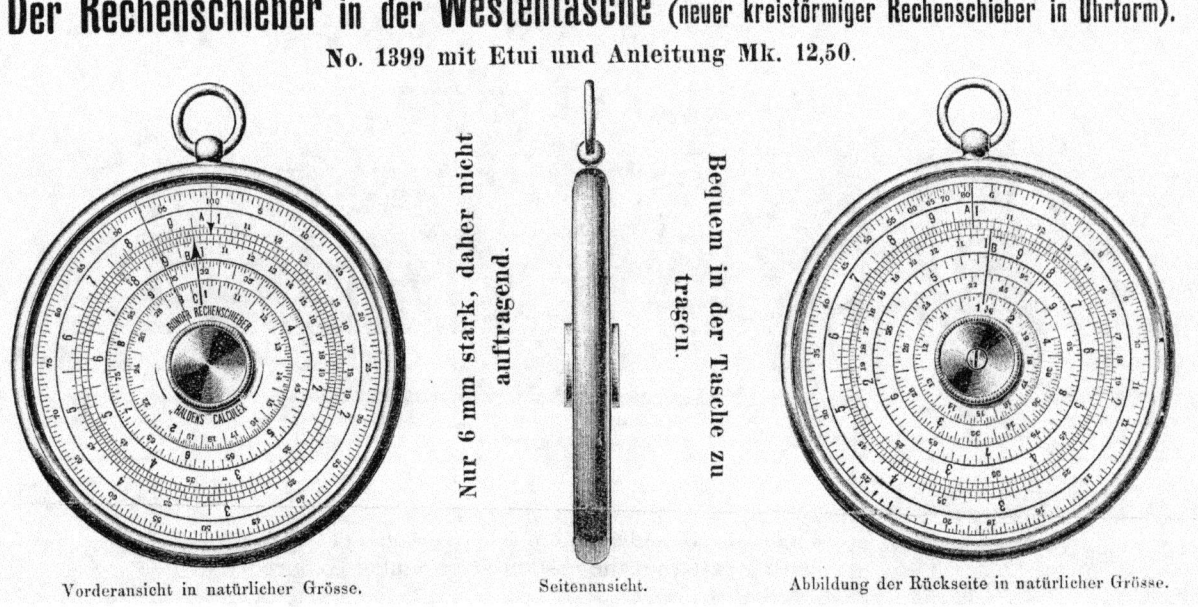

Figure 12.1: 1910 Gebr. Wichmann catalogue

The 1910 catalogue illustrates a Type 1 Calculex; it has the very thin thumb nuts and very narrow cross section, but most of all it only has the single screw fixing for the thumb nuts. This is one of the very few adverts that show a single screw, it may yet be the only true Type 1 advert we see. The advert shows the words 'Runder Rechenschieber' (Round Slide Rule) above the Thumb Nut, and below the Nut we have „Halden's Calculex" - note the European quote marks, below at the start of the words and above at the end of the words, but similar to what would be expected on a Type 1 Calculex. This appellation has never been seen on an actual example.

Any agreement with Wichmann for them to become agents or sell the Calculex must have taken place very early in the Calculex manufacturing life. Note also that the part number of this Type 1 Halden's Calculex is 1399. The product using this part number changes somewhat during its life.

Fact or Fantasy - Gebr. Wichmann Calculexes

The correspondence exchanged with a fellow collector on a 'Fowler being sold by Wichmann', has been covered earlier, and as the exchange continued various adverts were part of the discussion, amongst the first is the Wichmann 1920 catalogue, Figure 12.2, which showed that what was being discussed was actually a Halden Calculex (from the scales) and then most interestingly, that this Calculex was in a pocket-watch case, albeit a slightly thicker case at 8mm, and was complete with winding crown – a complete fabrication I believed, and once more using the 1399 part number! This, to me at the time, showed just how much 'science fiction' there was in some of these catalogues, and illustrated perfectly why it is so difficult to sort out fact from fantasy, and manufacturer from retailer.

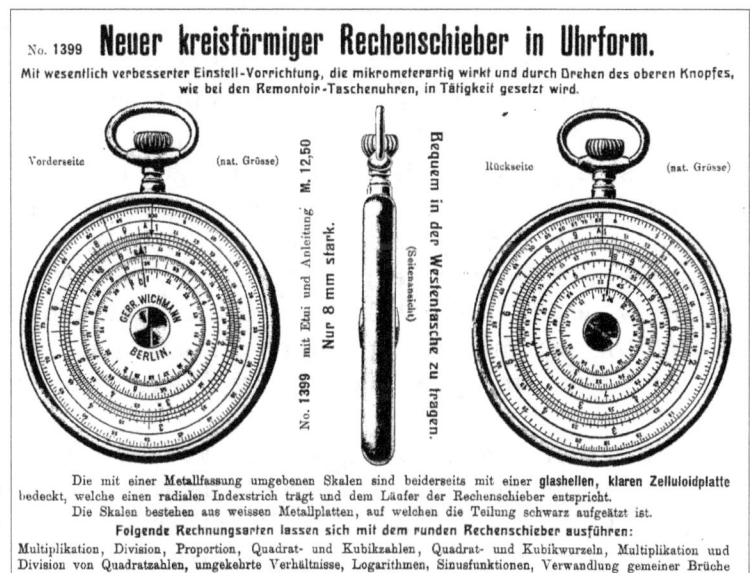

Figure 12.2: 1920 Gebr. Wichmann catalogue

Then came a page with illustrations of the three 'Kreis-Rechenschieber' from Wichmann's 20th edition of their 'Haupt-Katalog' dated 1939, (Figure 12.3) where once again a calculator under part number 1399 is recognizable as a Calculex, albeit in a different and unusual case with a very thick rim and no loop. The calculators with part numbers 1399 and 1400 are the two devices that are supposedly made by Molter as described in the JOS[27], 1400 has also previously been described as Schacht u. Westerich in an earlier JOS. Part number 1396 is yet another unusual device, I am not aware of any in a collection – and no, I do not think it is a pocket-watch slide rule. The full story on these is yet to be discovered!

However, we can do some speculation of our own. The address, 'look', printing, etc of this 1920's catalogue sheet looks to be much more like the version which is believed to be from about 1910 – about the time that the Calculex was supposedly designed or invented.

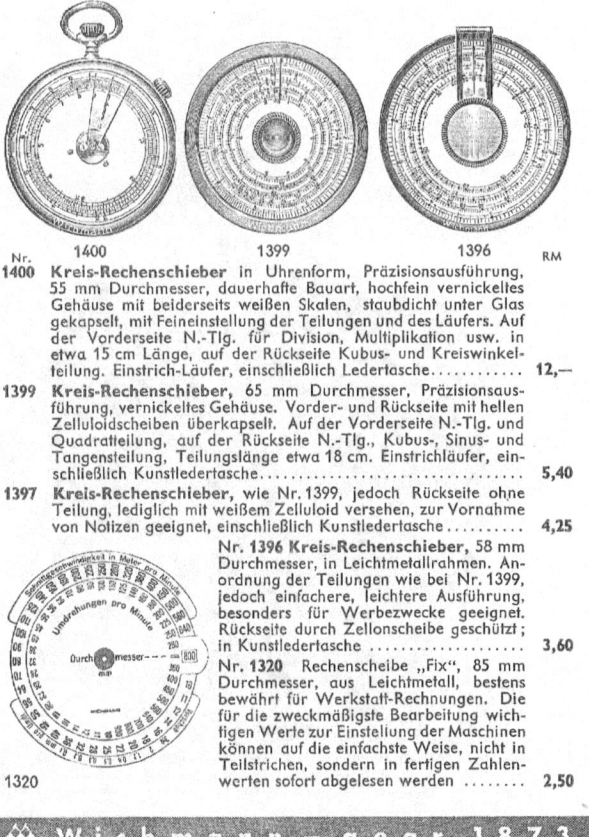

Figure 12.3: 1939 Gebr. Wichmann catalogue

---

27   'The Molter Slide Rule' Rodger Shepherd and Dieter von Jezierski in Journal of the Oughtred Society, Vol.8, No 1, Spring 1999 Pg 3.

POCKET-WATCH SLIDE RULES

The 1938/9 version looks very different. Perhaps the 1910 version where the Calculex is accurately drawn is taken from Halden's advertising copy which is recognizable as being similar in look and content to a number of other retailer's offerings world wide.

It is possible that the 1920's catalogue may be a lot earlier in date, and the illustrations may have been drawn before they actually got an example from Halden. However at about this time Wichmann had agreed to be their German agents and sell an 'Uhrform' (watch form) calculator. So they got their early 1900's equivalent of PaintShopPro (a man with pen and ink) to mock up a picture of said 'Uhrform' device in an 'Uhr' (watch) case! All this speculation is pure fun. Nothing explains why or how all versions happen to have real or at least usable scales! Interesting anyway to try and guess why all were different.

And then something happens that renders our fun guesswork null and void, – but still is part of the delight in collecting these devices. During 2002 a device was sold on e-Bay, see Figure 12.4. This is an example of Wichmann's Calculex as advertised in the 1920 catalogue, complete with Calculex scales and a winder in a 2_" (68mm) diameter case, $7/16$" (11mm) thick across the screw.

The e-Bay description is minimal, describing it as 'a rare pocket-watch calculator for Wichmann, Berlin. Probably made in the 1930's and measures 2½" (65mm) in diameter'. It continues saying: 'the scales are discolored [sic] with some edge parts illedgible. [sic] However the unit is fully working and can easily be used'. In action we find that the crown does the same job as the thumb nuts, rotating the central scales.

Figure 12.4: Wichmann 'Calculex'

Figure 12.5: Labelling on Wichmann 'Calculex'

The hairlines on the glass are rotated using the fingers on the glass as with a Calculex. The very prominent screw heads play no part in its calculating use. The labeling is shown in Figure 12.5. A second and a third example is now also known. Here we have a larger pocket-watch Calculex.

The 'glass' on the Wichmann 'Calculex' is yellow celluloid, and is the cause of the strange orange-green colouration. The scales were originally while painted copper with black markings (evident under the screws) which became discoloured blue from the celluloid out-gassing. This shows as orange-green. The calculator is fully working after a gentle cleaning.

The final and so far unanswerable question is – who actually made it for Wichmann?

An undated advertising leaflet from Wichmann shows the pocket-watch slide rule as Nr 1400, but also a lesser model without the 'micro adjustments' as Nr. 1399 E. This is yet another version of pocket-watch calculator with that number. Compare this with the items offered in Figure 12.3.

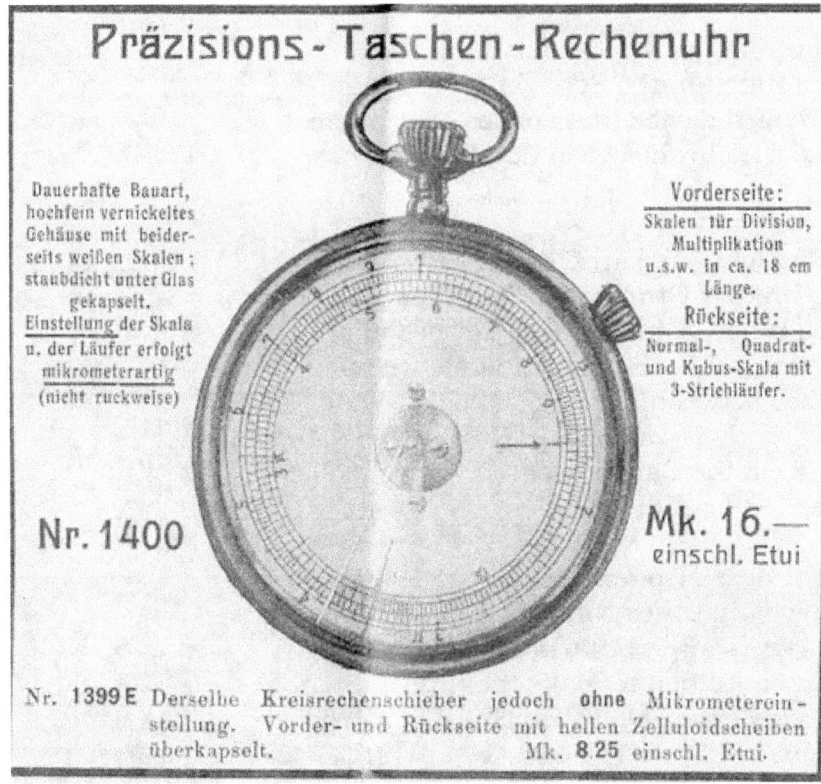

Figure 12.6: Undated Wichmann advertising flyer

POCKET-WATCH SLIDE RULES

Molter Pocket-Watch Calculators

Introduction

Ingenieur Wilhelm Molter's Technisches Büro in Nuremberg would appear to have been at the center of the German pocket-watch slide rule business as most German pocket-watch examples we have seen appear to have Molter somewhere near their roots. However it is difficult to prove this and some of the evidence does not stack up. We shall look at this in more detail later.

History

Formed in 1921 in Nuremberg[28], and so far the evidence shows that it was in 1923 that they made their first pocket-watch device, which would appear to have been the Halden type device we have listed and illustrated under Wichmann as that is the label the known example carries. The page below of the first page of the instructions for the 'Calculex' device under their part number 8406 gives remarkably few clues as to when it was made, and likewise the DRGM and DRP notations have proved elusive if not non-existent!

So we have to ask, who made the Calculex based device, the pocket-watch device, and the Wichmann Calculex with the crown?

The device described in the instruction leaflet (above) has been illustrated in the Schacht U. Westerich section as the only named device that carries that name, and it is easier to see the chronological developments in one place.

The previously mentioned article in the JOS mentions that Wilhelm's brother Otto emigrated to the USA in 1925, and may explain how some of these devices may have arrived there, but apart from these instructions we have been unable to find any link between the S u. W pocket-watch device (other than apparently it was in a 1925 S u. W catalogue, now missing) and indeed the Calculex based device as having been made by Molter.

That the two devices also featured in the 1939 Wichmann catalogue implies that they continued to be made (and sold?) for at least 14 years after, but whether Molter ever made them or indeed continued to make them until then, or whether they were made either by, or for, S u.W and Wichmann is also not clear.

Figure 13.1: First page of Molter's instructions.

Image Courtesy of the Conrad Schure Collection
Figure 13.2: Molter calculator made for maskin a.b.

---

28 'The Molter Slide Rule' Rodger Shepherd and Dieter von Jezierski in Journal of the Oughtred Society, Vol.8, No 1, Spring 1999 Pg 3.

Summary

Nowhere have we found any evidence to say that Molter had the manufacturing capability to make any of the devices he has been credited with. Equally we have no evidence to say that he even could have assembled the devices. Our only evidence is the instruction leaflet for the Calculex variant. We urgently need more information before we can be absolutely definitive.

Pocket-Watch Slide Rule

As this is supposedly made by Molter, this seems to be the obvious place for a comparison table of the various versions available from German retailers:

'Molter' Pocket-Watch Slide Rule				
Maker/Retailer	**Date**	**Part Number**	**DRP?**	**Price (Reiches Mark RM)**
Heckendorf	?	1959	?	16.-
Reiss	1925	5148	Yes	?
S u. W	1925	8406	?	8.25
Wichmann	?	1400	?	16.-
Wichmann	?	1399E #	?	8.25
Wichmann	1939	1400	?	12.-
Wichmann	1939	1399 #	?	5.40

Image Courtesy of the Conrad Schure Collection
Figure 13.3: Pocket-Watch, unmarked

Note #: Against the 1399E, the advert states 'ohne mikrometerein stellung' (without micrometer adjustment). This implies (to me) that there were two versions, one of which was a cheaper alternative to the micrometer adjustable version, though what the details of the differences were is not known. Whatever, they resulted in a version that was variously nearly 50% and about 25% cheaper than the full spec version which had a consistent price of 16RM in 1925 when perhaps it was first available. The 1939 Wichmann Model 1399 is a different device altogether, and could be the device shown in Figure 13.2.

These devices are like a thick pocket-watch, 2¼" (56 mm) diam, with 1⅞" (36 mm) scales, ⅝" (16 mm) thick. If it carries a name it is generally only on one side, the other is completely blank. The crown rotates the scale, the side winder rotates the pointer. This seems a pretty standard layout for a number of German pocket-watch slide rules, made by an unknown maker, possibly Molter, but with no definitive evidence for or against.

Figure 13.4: A. Leitz version of the Molter calculator

The A. Leitz version of the Molter calculator illustrated in Figure 13.4 sold on e-Bay in late 2010, It may be explainable by the fact that when Wilhelm's brother Otto emigrated to the USA in 1925, he may have formed a relationship with Leitz, however this is pure speculation and not supported by any known facts! The calculator is marked 'Made in Germany', nevertheless it is interesting to note the differences between this version and the one made for Maskin in Figure 13.2, which is not so marked. This one appears to be of higher quality with the chromed bezel and transparent rotater buttons.

POCKET-WATCH SLIDE RULES

Schacht und Westerich's Pocket-Watch Calculators

Introduction

Established in 1826, Schacht und Westerich (S u. W) of Hamburg exists to this day. S u. W did not produce or sell a specific family of calculators as with the previously described families of calculators. Rather, they are a 'family' in that this one company advertised over a number of years the extremely eclectic range of pocket-watch slide rules that are shown here.

There has been considerable discussion as to whether S u. W. actually made any of these devices, or whether they were simply retailers. The Halden Calculex chapter mentioned their Calculex-like offering, which may have actually been made by Molter of Nuremberg as discussed in the previous chapter.

Types of Calculator

Here follow three examples of a Calculex type device that is similar to the Wichmann type 1399 from 1939. One is marked 'Schacht & Westerich', and the next two examples, one with a customers name and another with no name are left in this section to enable direct comparison. We now know after considerable correspondence that they were made by Molter in Germany. They are discussed here only because one is labeled S. u. W, and it is useful to be able to compare 'early' 'middle' and 'late' versions in one place. Not a lot is known of Molter (see previous chapter and listing in the database) but it is believed that the first device is an early version, and its relationship to a Calculex is very obvious.

'Very Early' Type

It has the knurled thumb nut held together with a single screw as per Wilson's patent. This turns the center set of scales against a stationary set which is held in the hand. A glass 'cursor' with red index on each side can then be rotated separately. The small 'buttons' (there is one on one side and two on the reverse in the illustrated version) act as buttons to assist with rotating the cursors as well as a magnifying lens to help with setting.

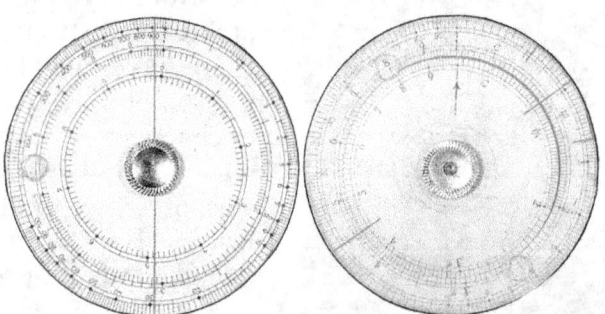

Figure 14.1: Schacht U. Westerich (Molter) 'very early' Calculator

Features of the following 'very early' version illustrated below are:
- No rim,
- Similar sized thumb nuts with a non-slotted screw holding them together,
- Scales of K,C,L on one side with index going the full diameter; and A,C/C on the other (front) with index only crossing the rotating elements, are very distinctive.

See Figures 14.2 & 14.3 for comparison, with this version which has no name or surround

'Later' Type

The 'later' type looks to be a more complete and robust device, and differences between this and the in-between type are minor.

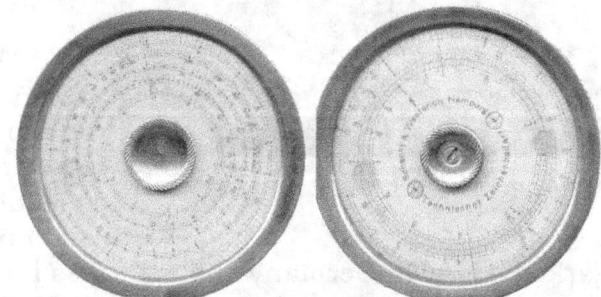

Figure 14.2: Schacht U. Westerich (Molter) 'later' Calculator

SCHACHT UND WESTERICH POCKET-WATCH CALCULATORS

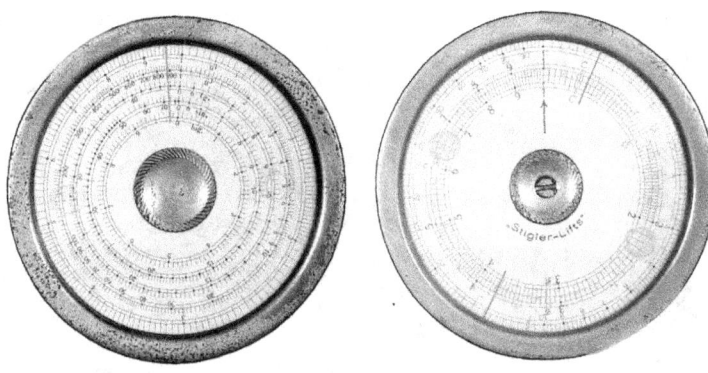

Figure 14.3: Schacht U. Westerich (Molter) 'later' Calculator II

S. u. W marked vest pocket slide rule type 8406 (Figure 14.7 from 1925); as Wichmann type 1399 from 1939, or Molter Type 8406. Perhaps Molter did make them?

As above, but marked „Stigler Lifts" who were probably a customer of either Molter or S u. W. Note that the labeling includes European quote marks, but an English word - 'Lifts', surely this would have been 'Aufzug' had this been German?[29]

The two examples of pocket-watch slide rule shown in Figure 14.2 and 14.3 are likely to both be 'late' versions, with the following characteristics:

- Very distinctive metal rim,
- Dissimilar sized thumb nuts (the back, non-screw one is bigger) with a slotted screw holding them together,
- Scales of C, n^3, tan, sin and M on back side with index only covering the scales; and A, C/C on the other (front, screw) side as 'early' version with index only crossing the rotating elements, are again very distinctive.

Another variant (Figure 14.4) – from the picture it is not possible to tell whether it is 'Mid' or 'Late' does not appear to have a red hairline, whether this is due to the glass being a replacement is not known.

S. u. W. / Molter Pocket-Watch Slide Rule

This quite delightful device (Figure 14.5) featured on the front of an early Journal of the Oughtred Society[30] and quite correctly carried the description of it being a 'Schact [sic] & Westerich, Hamburg – Technisher Zeichenbedarf' device as that was what was marked around the pivot on the reverse of the rule. It was not until a later Journal[31] that we were told that it (and indeed the first illustration of the other device listed in this section) were not made by S. u. W. but by Molter of Nürnberg in Germany. Both these devices were covered in that short article. I remain to be convinced that S. u. W. made the device as I have yet to see anything that 'proves' this statement. However, I agree that it is entirely possible that it was made by Molter as they were formed in 1921 and could have made all the devices.

Figure 14.4: Schacht U. Westerich (Molter) 'later' Calculator variant

---

29   http://www.theelevatormuseum.org/ind2.php gives Stigler Lifts as an Italian firm, formed by Augusto Stigler in Milan in 1860 as a mechanical engineering office, who installed their first elevator in 1898, and went on to world wide recognition so that by 1947, the firm had installed almost 45,000 lifts, slightly over half of which were in Italy. The remainder was installed throughout Europe and as far away as Rio de Janeiro, Buenos Aires, Seoul, Tokyo, Bombay and Cairo. The manufacturer's name became synonymous with "lift" and a lady not wishing to climb the staircase would say, "I'll take the Stigler!"
30   'Schact & Westerich Calculator' [sic] Al Bennett in Journal of the Oughtred Society, Volume 4, No 1, March 1995. Cover and p26.
31   'Slide Rules by Molter' Dieter von Jezierski in Journal of the Oughtred Society, Volume 7, No 2, Fall 1998. 24.

POCKET-WATCH SLIDE RULES

Figure 14.5: Schacht U. Westerich (Molter) 'pocket-watch' Calculator

Figure 14.6: S u. W. System Thomas 'Rechenuhr' 1923

We have been unable to find any S u. W catalogues, and only two advertisements for S u. W. This first advert is out of a VDI newsletter of 1923 where S u. W are advertising a 'Rechenuhr' System Thomas, which on closer inspection is a circular slide rule and not a pocket-watch side rule. The advert says it is shown ½ natural size, which would make it approx 4″ diameter.

And then out of the same VDI newsletter but in 1925 we have:

Figure 14.7: S u. W 8406 1925

This is probably the 'Molter' / Calculex device with a part number 8406, but the illustration is not particularly clear, and the calculator is not obviously that one.

Russian Pocket-Watch Calculators

Introduction

Russian Pocket-Watch calculators all appear to have the same unknown manufacturing parentage, and have then been retailed by a number of different organizations in the former Soviet Union, which might have included the manufacturer. I am not aware of a definitive work on the various logos; the most comprehensive to date by Colin Barnes[32] has been used to give the information on maker/retailer in the examples below.

Russian Pocket-Watch calculators, which generally seem to carry the type number KL-1, work in much the same way as any other. Each of the two winders drives a different feature of the calculator. In my 'Sunrise' example the winder with the black 'pip', which is directly above the fixed hairline, rotates the front (with logo) scale and the winder with red 'pip' rotates the two pointers, the front one being red, the back one being black, though from the pictures it can be seen that most examples seem to have red pointers on both sides. A translation of the instruction leaflet is included in Appendix 1.

The front face generally carries an outer 'A' scale and an inner 'C' scale and carries a 'π' gauge point. The obverse has an outer 'C' scale with a 'π' gauge point, an adjacent sine scale, and a nearly 2-turn spiral tangent scale marked 'T'. Some versions of the Sunrise variant are described as having light-brown faces. Whether this is true or is fading, is up to you to decide!

Types of Calculators

All calculators which have included an instruction leaflet carry a date in the late 1950's and the 1960's. However the Russian 'Matsku' version is so called from the logo shown on the calculator in Figure 15.1. This has been suggested as a Moscow factory mark.

Figure 15.1: Russian 'Matsku' Calculator

Matsku appear to have been the most prolific maker with several variants noted, as illustrated below. They also made a version of perpetual calendar for 1969 to 1990 using the same case and only a single winder. One of these examples appears to be an earlier design. Sadly the chronology is not known.

This looks to be a variant of the 'Matsku' device and appears the have a slightly different logo (but this is marginal) and a rotating set of center scales and additional different scales.

The front has 'C'/ 'D', 'A' and a mantissa scale, the back has an 'A' scale and very prominent red trigonometric scale markings, with red sine values and a sine, tangent and sine/tan central scale.

Figure 15.2: Russian 'Matsku' Calculator variant

---

[32] 'Some notes on Rules from the Former Soviet Union' Colin Barnes, Journal of the Oughtred Society, Vol. 7, No 2, Fall 1998. Pg 13.

POCKET-WATCH SLIDE RULES

Another version has a logo of two arrows chasing each other round a circle. According to Barnes, this rule is designated as KL-1 from the 'Organization for Technical Demand' in Moscow, with the trade name 'Sunrise'. Some versions of the Sunrise variant are described as having light-brown faces. Whether this is true, or is fading of the scales, is up to you the reader to decide!

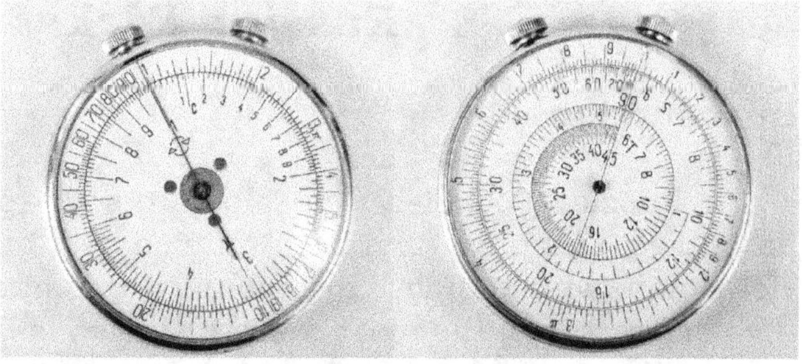

A very similar rule is known to have come from a plant in Oberwolga (Overvolga), another dated 1964 from factory 'Vladimar-7'.

Figure 15.3: Russian 'Sunrise' Calculator

Krougovaia Logarifmioueskaia Model Lineikaia KL-1. This is a variant of the circular arrows 'Sunrise' logo seen above with an additional 'ueha3p10k' (price 3 rouble 10 kopek) marking underneath.

Another has been seen with the note 'Moscow "Kontrolpribor"' (Moscow Control device).

Yet another dated 1968 is from 'The Technical Organisation Rassret', at 8 Octriavakava Street, Moscow A-57.

All of these slide rules are generally supplied in a plastic 'pill-box' case which comes in many different colors, this version being yellow. These seem to have taken the brunt of all knocks in the various examples I have seen, and in many cases are either very battered or missing entirely.

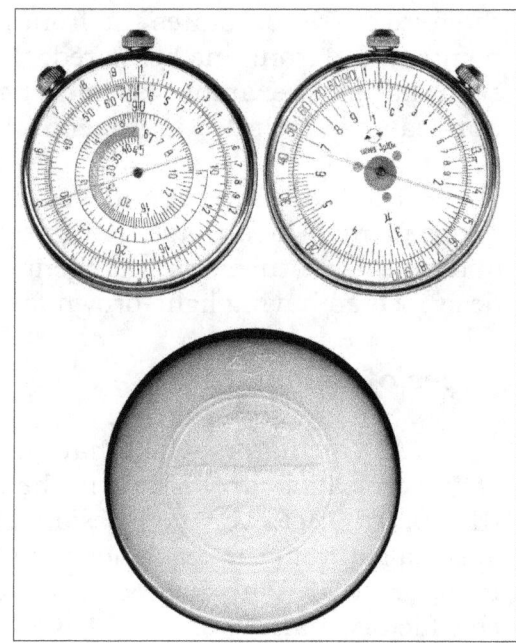

Some examples were also supplied in quite a sturdy cardboard box.

Figure 15.4: Russian KL-1 Calculator

The third variant is undoubtedly an earlier version of these calculators, exemplified by the different knobs and a pointer with circle on the end, but with no obvious logo or name (Figure 15.5). IT can be seen that it has a different plastic rim on each side, in contrast to what appears to be a chromed metal rim for all other types.

The scales are also very different, the front has an outer mantissa scale and a 'C' scale, the obverse only a sine scale, marked 'S' and a tangent spiral, marked 'T'.

Figure 15.5: Early Russian Calculator

RUSSIAN POCKET-WATCH CALCULATORS

Finally we have a version with a difficult to describe logo (a heart?) which is obviously from the same manufacturer but carries this different logo (Figure 15.6). It may also be a KL-1 and also come from Moscow.

Other variants seen, particularly on e-Bay where they are commonly and inexpensively available, include one with leather case and where the face of the rule has the dates 1917–1967 on the face as well as what appears to be the tower of the University of Moscow as does the embossed leather case, it is probably an October Revolution commemoration model, see Figure 15.7.

Figure 15.6: Russian 'Heart' Calculator

Other examples carry a mixture of marks; the 'heart' and the 'Sunrise' mark on instructions for a 'Matsku' device, but maybe examples and instruction leaflets got mixed up.

There are six Russian 'makers' or 'retailers' shown here, I am sure there must have been others. It would be most interesting to know what other variants may exist, and to see what can be deciphered from the collection of images of the instruction leaflets I have managed to collect.

Figure 15.7: Unknown Russian Calculex look-alike

The excellent translation of the Russian instruction sheet for a KL-1 Pocket-Watch slide rule included at Appendix 1, shows the large range of mathematical calculations which these devices can be used for.

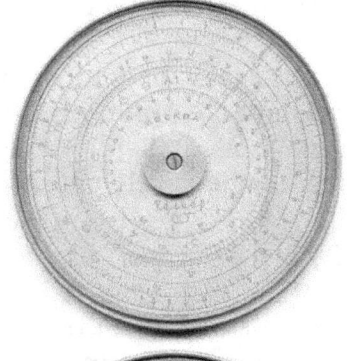

Russian Calculex

This device is totally different to the variants of the KL-1 which precede it, but it is labeled 'Moscow' and has another retailers name and another logo as well.

This also does not have a watch loop, nor winders, it is obviously operated by the 'thumb nuts', so really it might be better catalogued under the vest-pocket section, however as it also looks like another copy of a Calculex with its thumb nuts, and is similar to the Rechen-Max device shown in the chapter on 'other' makers later, and it is Russian so here it is catalogued.

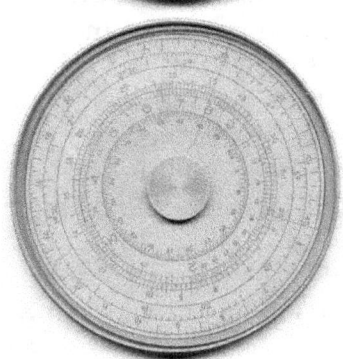
Figure 15.8: Unknown Russian Calculex look-alike

111

Other Pocket-Watch Calculators

Introduction

There are a number of makers or retailers of pocket-watch calculators that do not obviously fit within any of the 'families' that have been previously described. In alphabetical order, we now have a selection of other makers or retailers and their offerings.

Breitling

Breitling are better known as suppliers of extremely high class and expensive wrist watches, a number of which included a slide rule bezel.

Not so well known is their stop-watch slide rule. There are two versions of the Breitling Chronoslide stop watch with a slide rule bezel, as best as can be ascertained, they date from either the late 1960's or 1970's, and may carry a model number 1677 (right) with central 'totaliser' dial, and 1577 (left), with a separate small dial. (Figure 16.1)

Figure 16.1: Breitling Stopwatch

John Davis & Son

An otherwise unmarked 2″ (51mm) dia. Mechanical Engineer Calculator made by Scientific Publishing must have been sold by John Davis and Son, who engraved the back; c1900. (Figure 16.2)

It has been previously speculated that the reason SCP produced unmarked devices was to allow other retailers to mark their offered devices, Davis more expensively engraved the back.

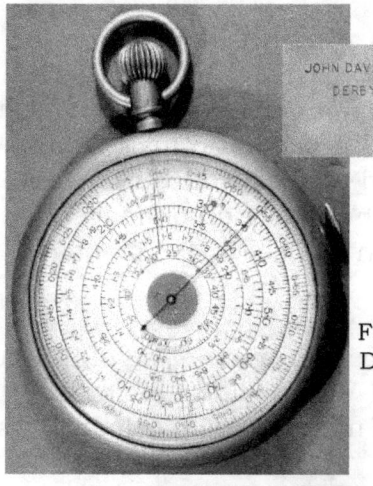

Figure 16.2: John Davis Mechanical Engineer Calculator

Dyson

This has all the hallmarks of being a device made by Scientific Publishing, the furniture looks identical and the 2½″ (63 mm) diameter watch case is distinctive, and the single sided device has the scale rotated via the crown, and the pointer via the side winder, however there is no 'proof positive' so for the present we are including this as 'another' pocket-watch type slide rule. The largest scale diameter is 2″ (53 mm) diameter.

There is another piece of evidence which may indicate a company other than SP - it has a winder angle closer to 85° which is not the same as SP used on the ME. See Appendix 2 later.

Image Courtesy of the Conrad Schure Collection
Figure 16.3: Dyson Calculator

The function of each of the 3 scales is not obvious either.

OTHER POCKET-WATCH CALCULATORS

Figure 16.4: Frappant A.G. advertisement

There was a firm James Dyson Ltd, who were active near Huddersfield in about 1903 who were dyers, whether this is relevant remains to be seen.

Frappant A.G., Berlin, Germany

Another example of a little-known slide rule retailer in Germany who was selling what could be pocket-watch slide rules.

This is not likely to be a pocket-watch slide rule, but could be either a watch pocket device or a standard circular slide rule.

Figure 16.5: Heckendorf advertisement

Heckendorf, Berlin, Germany

An undated advertising leaflet for this company shows the Schacht u. Westerich (or Molter) pocket-watch slide rule in considerable detail under a part number 1959.

Nothing much is known of Heckendorf who appear to be yet another drawing and mathematical instrument retailer.

Lancashire Optical Manufacturing Co. Ltd.

The **Robinson Calculator** is extensively described in JOS Vol. 9 No. 1 spring 2000. A known example is 2 7/8″ diameter and ½″ thick. The control is via small wheels off the back of the calculator, protruding beyond the circumference of the pocket-watch case, exactly as described in the patent diagrams.

Image Courtesy of the Conrad Schure Collection
Figure 16.6: Robinson Calculator

Assuming that the device was manufactured on or shortly after the date of the original patent, this was made in 1926. The loop is not shown in the adjacent detailed photographs.

POCKET-WATCH SLIDE RULES

Ollech & Wajs GEC Slide Rule

This was discussed and illustrated on the internet during 2007, I have been unable to find the pictures subsequently. These are a variant, new old stock, made by O&W for the General Electric Company, and as such have the GEC name and logo in the top center of the dial rather than the O&W mark[33]. See also the Selectron Timer on page 115.

H. Reiss GmBH.
Liebenwerda, Germany

The Reiss 1925 catalogue shows a version of the S u.W / Molter pocket-watch slide rule with Reiss part number 5148, Figure 16.7.

Figure 16.7: Reiss 1925 catalogue

It also advertises it as being 'comfortable in the vest pocket' to illustrate the difficulty of classifying these, and there are no further clues as to source.

H. Reiss GmBH.
Liebenwerda, Germany

This is an example of the pocket-watch slide rule advertised by Reiss in their 1925 catalogue and it does look like a Schacht u. Westerich type 1400 calculator, again, possibly made by Molter.

Figure 16.8: H. Reiss (Molter) Calculator

Rechen-Max Calculex Look-alike

The picture at right has been in my papers for a considerable number of years and I have never been able to find out anything more about it!

I think it is fair to say that by my definition it is a watch-pocket calculator with a loop. It appears to have a thumb nut of some sort, and possibly a rotating bezel, though the serrations (bottom) may only be over a short portion of the circumference.

There is obviously one pair of circular scales, and the magnifying glass attached to what must be a rotating glass cover (with a cursor line engraved on it?) is an interesting addition.

Figure 16.9: Rechen-Max Calculex look-alike

I have been unable to find any relevant DRGM or German patents; we can only assume that they were imaginary!

---
33   One of these was illustrated in a talk at the International Meeting in 2010, it turns out to be a wrist watch.

I have seen other 'Rechen' labeled circular slide rules for sale, but have been unable to find out anything about the maker. Can anyone help?

Selectron (Model A)

The Selectron Timer is a rather nice combination of 60-second stop-watch and slide rule bezel made by the O.W. Company of Switzerland.

There are two models, according to the instructions, a Model A and a Model B, I have never seen an example of the Model A, the illustration in Figure 16.10 is taken from the instructions, which also appear wrong.

The instructions say that the Model A has:
1. a seconds scale to 1/5 second
2. a 30-minute totaliser
3. a units per hour scale also used for time speed calculations
4. two slide rule scales
5. two conversion scales for English decimal conversions

Figure 16.10: Selectron Timer Model A

Scale 3 is nowhere to be seen, but is a feature of the Model B, see Figure 16.11.

Just to add to the confusion, a different (with color pictures) set of instructions shows the white faced version as the Model A.

Selectron (Model B)

The Model B (Figure 16.11) is supposed to have the following additional scales to those found on the Model A:

6. a tachymeter scale to measure speed per hour of a moving object
7. a decimal scale dividing the minute into 100 parts

Note that the mechanism is quite unusual in that it is a simple rotating bezel rather than any type of special pocket-watch mechanism that is used for calculating. This and the M&P calculator are the only devices with any 'watch' capability.

Figure 16.11: Selectron Timer Model B

There are a multitude of gauge points for carrying out many conversions between different units.

Selectron slide rule watches are also known.

Unattributable Pocket-Watch Calculators

Introduction

A particularly rewarding element of the research leading to the writing of this book is that we have been able to identify (sometimes only within two or more possible families or sections of the taxonomy) the very large majority of examples of pocket-watch and watch-pocket calculators we have found.

However we have two examples, one each pocket-watch and one watch-pocket, which do not fit comfortably into any of the previous categories, and have no obvious markings to give any sort of clue. The first is definitely a pocket-watch device; the second is a watch-pocket device which offers only one clue as to possible parentage.

Unattributable Calculigraphe-like Device

The device shown in Figure 17.1 is advertised on the seller's web site[34] as a '2″ Calculigraphe Watch-Faced Circular Slide [rule]' and continues with the description:

French, 2nd quarter 20th century, unsigned. The $2^{1}/_{8}''$ diameter body is made of nickel plated brass, with domed beveled glass faces. The front face is fixed, with a moveable cursor needle; the rear face is moveable as is the cursor needle. The slide rule is in good working condition, with some scratches on the glass faces.

However all this misses the point that the main winder drives the scale at the rear (left), while the winder at the side drives both the hands as a winder and not as a clutch like a 'normal' Calculigraphe.

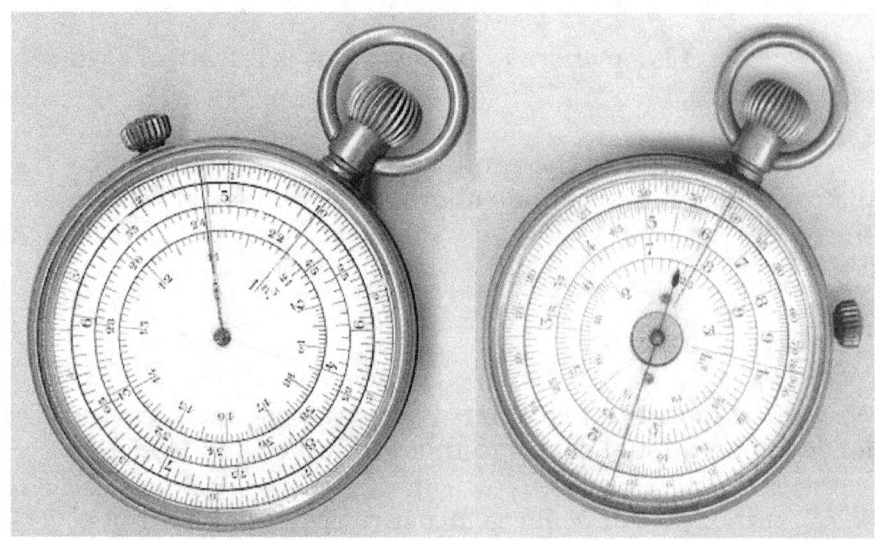

Figure 17.1: Unattributable Calculigraphe-like device

The scales are undoubtedly Calculigraphe, but the axle is very much larger and more like an early Boucher's calculator which does make this very much an 'unknown' device, and quite unusual, only two examples are known.

Likewise the side-winder is at an unusual 55 degrees to the vertical, matching only one other maker's devices, an unlikely pairing, see Appendix 2.

---

34 My thanks to Rick Blankenhorn and the Gemmary who had this intriguing device for sale in early 2010. He confirmed the actions of the two winders and he has allowed me to use the images.

Unattributable Watch-Pocket Device

The device shown in Figure 17.2 is quite unusual, it is two-sided, the 'front' having two knobs and a Perspex pointer and the 'back' is with the white scales (paper?) and a Perspex pointer. The smaller (upper) knob rotates the inner scales on the two sides, and the larger (bottom) knob rotates the pointers on both sides.

The immediately obvious similarity of the back scale with that of the S. u. W./Molter Pocket-Watch Calculator might give us a clue as to who might have made it and a possible time scale, but there is no advert known from any of the three major German makers, all of whom advertised a version of the pocket-watch calculator, but not this very unusual device.

Unattributable Calculator

A very interesting device sold on e-Bay with unknown maker, date and function.

It has a lacquered brass body some 3″ in diameter (Figure 17.3) with two sets of scales, plus a pair of slide rule scales on the body, one set '100 yards per minute', the other '88 yards per minute'. Both faces have an outer scale like the face of a clock with Roman numerals, divided into 5 minute intervals. Each side also has a rotating disc, one with 5 scales on it turned by one of the two knobs and a matching arm operated by the other knob, the second side with 4 scales and arm having different scales and with the cover having a red arrow engraved on it and a movable pointer.

Image Courtesy of the Conrad Schure Collection

Figure 17.2: Unattributable Watch-pocket device

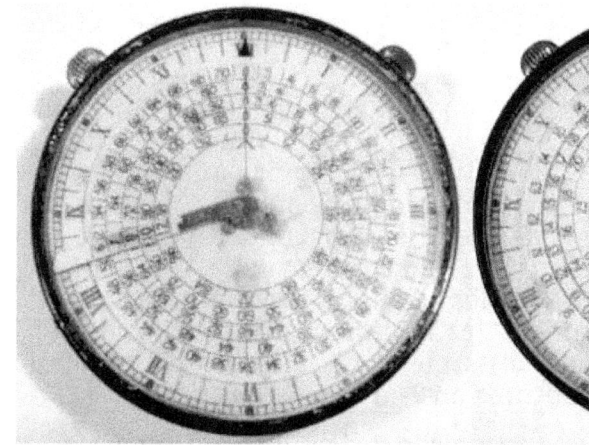

Figure 17.3: Unattributable Calculator

Undiscovered Pocket-Watch Calculators

Introduction

During the writing of this book and the attendant research, we have found a number of examples of pocket-watch slide rules where there is strong documentary evidence that it might have existed – a mention in a catalogue or such like – but no examples are known. Elsewhere we have the example of just such a device which was known from a catalogue but no examples known until some 10 years after it was first seen, when an example appeared on an internet auction site, and then a second example was found. I'm guessing that the purchaser has no idea that he has something rare and unusual – perhaps this book will catalyze more of these finds, particularly if we make a specific effort to document these undiscovered, yet to be discovered or plain 'missing' devices.

The counter proposition is equally attractive – collectors may have examples of pocket-watch slide rules in their collections which are completely unknown, and perhaps these can now be documented.

Either way, the hunt for missing (and therefore rare or unusual) examples is a very worthwhile reason to continue the search and to increase our knowledge. Not all that have been mentioned in the preceding pages are given here, and these are not variants to known devices, even though variants are in their own way just as interesting. The following six slide rule calculators are described in documents; we await actual examples being found. The seventh and eighth is a pair of examples which are informed speculation, and thus maybe a complete chimera!

Calculigraphe Type 1:

A watch type Boucher calculator with simple scales that give '... average accuracy'.

Note that there are other Calculigraphe devices which would be great finds.

> **DIFFÉRENTS MODÈLES DES CERCLES**
>
> Le premier modèle paru, a la forme d'une montre portant 2 cadrans dont les divisions permettent d'introduire dans les calculs les nombres ordinaires et les angles au moyen de leurs lignes trigonométriques, elles donnent également les décimales des logarithmes au moyen desquelles on obtient les puissances et les racines des nombres à un degré quelconque.

Figure 18.1: Snippet from 1880 Calculigraphe Instructions

Calculigraphe Type 2:

A desk type Calculigraphe with a single dial as the desk type Boucher. This broad description is similar to the desk version described in Boucher's patent (Figure 21), no examples are known. This is a strong possibility as the Type 1 above follows the watch type described in the patent.

> Le deuxième modèle paru est d'un volume plus grand que le premier, d'une forme différente, il est destiné à servir dans les bureaux. Il ne porte qu'un cadran, mais la dimension de celui-ci a permis d'y tracer des divisions au moyen desquelles on peut introduire dans les calculs, à première lecture non seulement les nombres ordinaires et les angles, mais aussi les puissances et les racines des nombres au 2e et au 3e degrès.

Figure 18.2: Snippet 2 from 1880 Calculigraphe Instructions

Desk Type Mechanical Engineer's Calculator

Advertised in the 1902 Halden catalogue this would be a splendid example of calculator, every bit as good as the other known 'desk' calculators.

| "Mechanical Engineer" Calculator in Nickel Case... | 0 | 7 | 6 |
| Ditto ditto ditto large size for desk | 0 | 12 | 6 |

Figure 18.3: Snippet 1902 Halden Catalogue

4022.	Boucher Calculator, silvered metal dials, (Calculigraph) each	$ 14 00
4022-A.	Boucher Calculator, like No 4022, but with paper dials	" 12 50
4023.	Boucher Calculator, like No. 4022-A, but with an extra hand for recording revolutions of the long hand	" 19 00
4024.	Boucher Calculator, enameled cardboard dials	" 8 50

Figure 18.4: Snippet 1903 K&E Catalogue

Keuffel & Esser Model 4023

This device 'with an extra hand for recording revolutions of the long hand' at a very expensive $19.-. is not further explained or illustrated. I do not believe that an example has ever been seen, it would be a real find and a superb addition to anyone's collection.

Thornton 1916 Catalogue

D6927 "Mechanical Engineer" Pocket Calculator (patent) with two dials. Solves multiplication, divisions, fractions, squares and square roots, cubes and cube roots, miscellaneous roots and powers, logarithms, areas of circles, sines, cosines, and tangent of angles ... nett £0 7 6

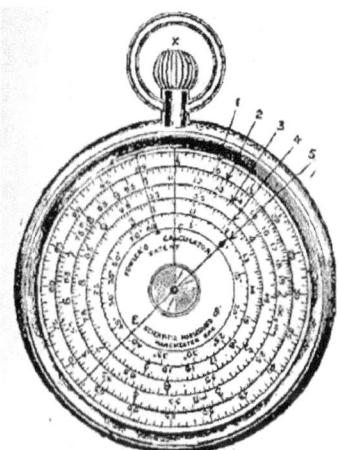

The illustration in Figure 18.5, shows a pocket-watch rule that could well be a Mechanical Engineer, but only has one crown. The description following then confuses the situation by saying two dials, which the ME did not have. It also further confuses the issue with a mention of a non-existent patent.

Figure 18.5: Snippet 1916 Thornton Catalogue

Keuffel & Esser Model 1743½ Marked K&E Co. NY.

This device, a 'Calculigraphe' but with any sort of K&E marking, either as illustrated in the catalogue, or as in Figure 4.14 for Queen, or Figure 5.4 for Fischer and others. This would be a major find and prove that the roots of the American pocket-watch slide rules definitely were in France!

Keuffel & Esser Type 4B and Type 5 Calculators

These two devices are highly speculative, and are an extrapolation from examples which are known. At left, as a reminder, is the content of the markings that would be required for them to fit the speculation.

It should be noted that I have not included the 'missing' Type 3b calculator that is mentioned in the K&E chapter, that I feel is simply a matter of time before one is found.

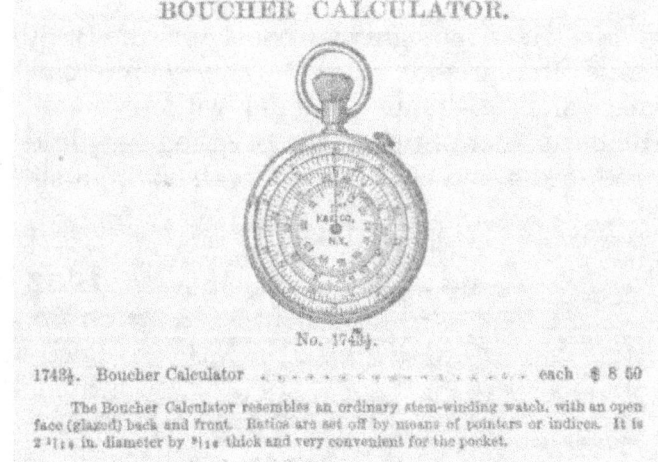

Figure 18.6: Snippet 1895 K&E Catalogue

K&E Pocket Calculator & Keuffel & Esser Co NY Pat Dec. 26 11.
Figure 18.7: Marking for a K&E Type 4B
With some reference to the last patent: 1,671,616/1927
Figure 18.8: marking for a K&E Type 5

Watch Slide Rules

Introduction

The idea of adding a rotating bezel which carries a logarithmic slide rule scale which can be rotated against another similarly graduated scale, which is either within the watch or beside the rotating bezel, does not appear to be that old. The earliest such watch has been proposed as 1923, and others suggest it is nearer to World War 2. Conrad Schure[35] originally told us that 'Breitling introduced the Chronomat – a wristwatch equipped with a logarithmic scale, – in the early 1940's and this was probably the first slide-rule wristwatch'. This has subsequently been confirmed in an excellent article available on the web[36], however it is not absolutely accurate and in the best traditions of research at least two earlier patents have been found, though indeed the Breitling Chronomat endured as the first manufactured and probably longest lived design.

Patents

We now know of a number of patents relating to watch slide rules. The following list is possibly not comprehensive. The earliest found so far is 1937 Swiss Patent No 189,447 of Oiser Szymanski of the Homis Watch Company of Bienne in Switzerland. We then have Swiss patent 204,559 to Walter Moser awarded in May 1939 for a slide rule bezel on a watch or clock. However the most significant patents appear to be Swiss patents No. 216,202 for MIMO and No. 217,012 for Breitling, both around 1940, and which actually produced significant devices with a lasting reputation. There are also two patents by Gérard Francis Wittgenstein, a Swiss national, better known as a philosopher, applied for in Switzerland in June 1943 under number 536,000, and then in the USA under USA 2,435,705 and awarded in February 1948, which are more of a curiosity than anything else. CH 680330A by Edgardo Grimm of August 1992 is for a Fuel Consumption calculator on a watch, and must be one of the last relevant patents.

The most significant design is the Breitling Chronomat chronograph watch with its famous circular slide rule. It was a commercial success, and is still manufactured today, sixty years after its creation, though without the slide rule it made famous. The slide rule element of the design continues in the Breitling Navitimer. At almost the same time the MIMO Company produced a non chronograph watch with a slide rule bezel.

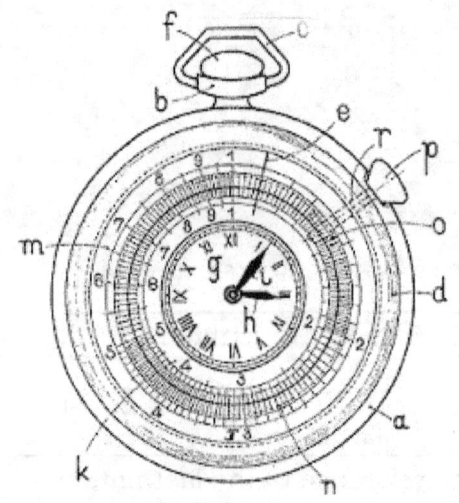

Figure 19.1: Homis Watch Co. patent

1937 Patent. CH 189,447 Oiser Szymanski, Homis Watch Co., Bienne, Switzerland.

Filed 4th June 1936, Registered 28th Feb. 1937, and published 18th May 1937, the earliest patent found. Little is known of the Homis Watch Co. except that it was active between 1920 and 1970, and produced mid-range watches. Szymanski's patent in all cases describes the combination of a circular slide rule and either a pocket-watch or a wristwatch. It does not describe explicitly the principle of the rotating bezel, but another patent No. 204,559, filed by Walter Moser in Bern, two years before the MIMO patent, describes perfectly a rotating bezel with one of the two logarithmic scales on a wristwatch.

---

35 'Slide rule wrist-watches'. By Conrad Schure, Proceedings of *'Slide Rule 98' Huttwil*, Switzerland, 1998
36 http://www.invenitetfecit.com/modeles/page-breitlingchronomat2.

Does this not look like the M&P pocket-watch slide rule produced almost 40 years previously? Is this quite the coincidence it appears to be – or is it indeed such a coincidence?

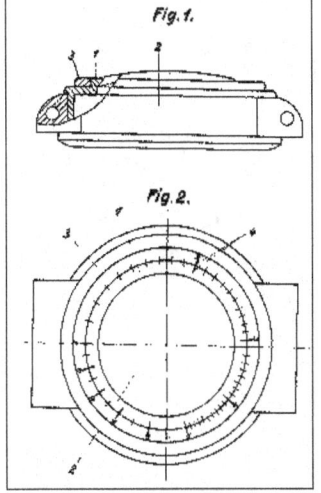

Figure 19.2: Walter Moser CH 204,559 patent

1939 Patent.CH 204,559 W. Moser

Filed on 25th April 1938, Registered 15th May 1939, and published 17th July 1939, this seems to be the earliest patent for a bezel on a watch or clock, with 'a concentric ring corresponding with the divisions of a slide rule' (Figure 19.2). The statement continues:

'Fig. 1 is a partial section by a clock according to the invention; Fig. 2 is a plan view on the clock after Fig. 1. ... that Bezel 1 the round bracelet clock 2 is a ring 3, to the hand rotatably supported concentric with divisions 4. On that Bezel 1 are likewise divisions 4. The same correspond to the divisions of a slide rule. Through Rotation of the ring 3 Multiplications and divisions performed can become' so says a lovely translation. It finishes: 'The clock can be as a bracelet or a watch formed'.

Both the MIMO-Loga and the Breitling Chronomat supposedly carry references on their dials to Swiss patents, No. 216,202 for MIMO and No. 217,012 for Breitling. In chronological order it is MIMO's patent which was filed first, just weeks before the Breitling patent, July 27, 1940 against August 26, both 1940. The principle of the Breitling Chronomat scales seems to have been first patented by MIMO. The lesser patent claims relate to the rotating bezel, a control device for rotating one scale ring and an annular magnifying glass in the periphery of the lens for ease of scale reading.

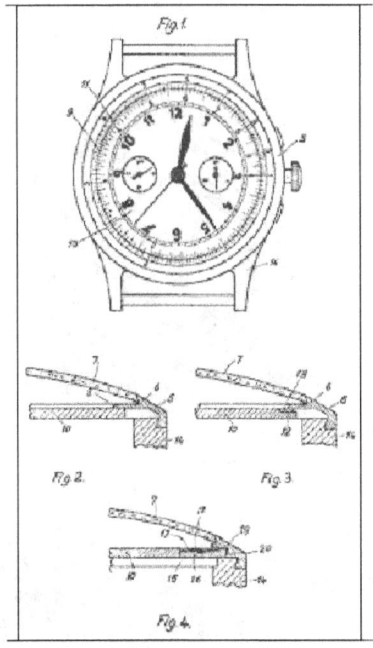

Figure 19.3: Mimo patent

1941 Patent.CH 216,202 Graff & Cie, Fabrique MIMO, La Chaux-de-Fonds

Filed on 27th July 1940, registered 15th August 1941, and published 17th November 1941.

The main claim of the MIMO patent is for a 'timepiece, characterized in that it comprises, in addition to devices and the usual chronometer chronograph, at least two logarithmic scales combined with at least one mounted on a body concentric with the rotary dial which carries the other'. There is also mention of a chronograph mechanism in the claim and the diagram accompanying the patent is that of a chronograph

1941 Patent.CH 217,012 Adrien Schweitzer, La Chaux-de-Fonds

Filed on 26th August 1940, registered 30th September 1941, and published 16th January 1942, the primary Breitling patent by Adrian Schweizer of La Chaux-de-Fonds, the same town as MIMO. Its main claim is: 'each clock [sic] for performing operations and telemetry tachometer, is characterized by two logarithmic scales, concentric and adjacent to one another and at least one of these scales is mobile and carried by a ring that can rotate around the other scale. Both scales are identical in size but progress in opposite directions from each other.

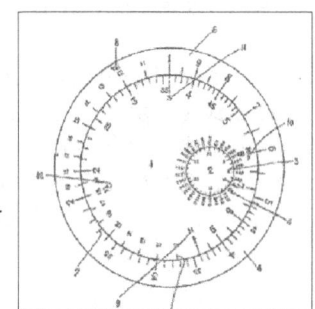

Figure 19.4: Breitling patent

POCKET-WATCH SLIDE RULES

Examination of a Chronomat dial confirms that the inner scale is graduated clockwise while the outer scale is graduated counter-clockwise. Similar designs have already been used for linear or circular slide rules, and have the advantage of facilitating some calculations, especially multiple or combined multiplication and division.

1943, CH 536,000, and
1948, USA 2,435,705 G.F. Wittgenstein

The details from this patent awarded both in Switzerland and the USA shows that it was a sophisticated patent for a rotating bezel system (Figure 19.5).

Exactly what the differences were and why it should have been awarded when there already were patents for rotating bezels with a variety of scales is hard to guess.

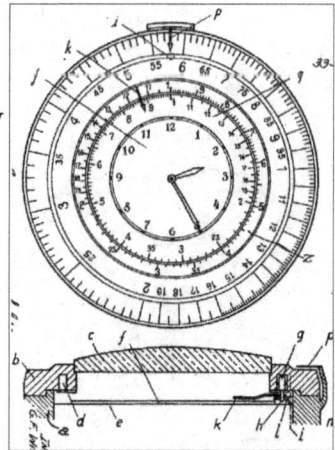

Figure 19.5: Details from Wittgenstein's patent

Early Watch Slide Rules

The dial of the first Chronomat shows the slide rule with its reversed (anti-clockwise) outer scale as described in the Swiss patent. However, the patent number shown on the face is a very early one from c1911 and has nothing to do with horology.

The original features of the Breitling Chronomat are its circular slide rule with a 'second chronograph'. The watch allowed military calculations for ballistic telemetry, athletics calculations of average speed, engineering calculations of yield or production, sales representative calculations of taxes and exchange rates.

Figure 19.6: Early Breitling Chronomat advert

The MIMO-Loga (Figure 19.7) is a very elegant wrist watch with rotating slide rule bezel but an ordinary watch (not chronograph) movement. It would make a fine addition to any slide rule watch collection. It is not obvious from this picture that it carried a Swiss patent number on the dial.

The 1946 example of a Breitling Chronomat does have the Swiss 1941 Swiss patent number (Figure 19.8).

Figure 19.7: Early MIMO Loga

The Breitling Chronomat had a very long life and was produced in many versions. In 1948 came a version with calendar and moon phases at noon, and in 1952 Breitling produced a non-chronograph version of the Chronomat without a slide rule.

Figure 19.8: Early Breitling Chronomat

In 1945 the Juvenia Arithmo, a new wrist watch design with a slide rule appeared (Figure 19.9). This advertised itself as 'The First Practical Calculating Watch'. It has three circular logarithmic scales, two of which are reversed. The watch includes a lens ring around the periphery of the glass, described in the Mimo patent and which Juvenia named their 'réfrascope'. Unfortunately they do not photograph particularly successfully.

In conjunction with the Aircraft Owners and Pilots Association (AOPA) Breitling in 1952 developed a version of chronograph watch with a slide rule bezel where the scales were all graduated clockwise so that they were suitable for calculations related to aviation. This became the Breitling Navitimer (Figure 19.10), a model, whose success eclipsed that of the Chronomat. It was made in a number of versions including a 24-hour one, the Navitimer Cosmonaut which was the first chronograph to go into space on the wrist of Scott Carpenter on the 7th Mercury program flight on 24th May 1962.

Figure 19.9: Early Juvenia Arithmo

With the development of the automatic chronograph wrist watch movement in 1969, an automatic version, the Chronomat Chrono-Matic was developed.

This was also the period when several other manufacturers of watches produced examples with a slide rule, for example Helvetia Tissot (Model Sidereal 1970), Mondia (memory model), Ollech & Wajs (models Selectron and Computer), Heuer (Model Calculator), Fortis (Easy-Math Model), and so on.

Figure 19.10: Early Breitling Navitimer

With the advent of quartz and the development of miniature electronics, the Breitling Chronomat range disappeared, in the same way that slide rules were replaced by electronic calculators. With the revival of mechanical watches the Chronomat reappeared in 1984, without the slide rule, which was now produced only on the Navitimer.

There are numerous manufacturers of slide rule wrist-watches, many of these produce replica watches, others are unashamed and unofficial copies. There are too many manufacturers to attempt to include them in this volume, suffice it to say that the internet has many excellent sites which cover this particular specialization. Here follows a few illustrations of some of the better known examples from a variety of makers in no particular order.

Watch Slide Rules

Breitling

We have already seen the early and seminal Breitling designs, the company continues to this day producing exciting designs (Figure 19.11) being exceptional in different ways.

The Breitling LED Navitimer has to be one of the most unusual watches, and beside it 'The Navitimer QP is a 'Grande Complication', a watchmaker's meister-work, made up of about 500 components, with not less than 13 pointers. These show the day of the week, date, week, month, season, leap year and the phases of the moon'. The price list then tells you why it is special and expensive: It is a Limited Edition Automatic Chronograph in an 18 carat gold body, with silver colored watch face, silver bezel and crocodile skin strap with gold buckle, price 42,000CHF, approx. £18,500 in October 2007. The cheapest Navitimer is 4,500CHF, about £2,000 – cheap!

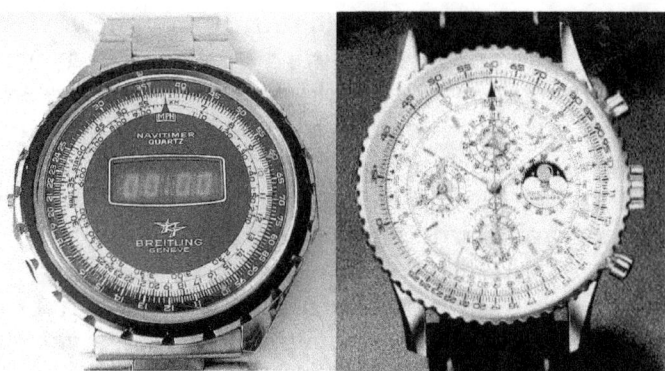

Figure 19.11: Breitling watch slide rules

Figure 19.12: Watch slide rules from Seiko (either side) and Heuer

Seiko and TAG Heuer

Seiko and Selectron

The selection of Tag Heuer, Seiko and Selectron (Figure 19.12 and 19.13) gives some idea of the variety of designs available, the Selectron are particularly interesting in comparison with the Selectron Stop watches in a previous chapter.

Figure 19.13: Seiko Slide rule watch, early and late Selectron watch slide rules

Ventura

The Ventura, sadly no longer made, is included as a most attractive designed 'modern classic', having been sold at an International Meeting of slide rule collectors in Switzerland in 1998, where the company sponsored the production of the Proceedings of that meeting.

Other companies produce slide rule watches including Casio, Pulsar, Citizen and many many other.

Figure 19.14: Ventura 'design on time' slide rule watch

Pocket Cash Registers

These devices are a new sub-category of pocket-watch - or indeed watch-pocket devices which were only first described as a genre in a presentation at an International Meeting in 2008[37]. However, these are included as representative of any of the pocket-watch style abstruse calculators or as any other device for recording, measuring or calculation. As some of these devices have already been misunderstood by myself and others (see Lafond, below) it was felt that a mention of the three devices presented at the International Meeting would alert collectors to what may be another avenue of collecting!

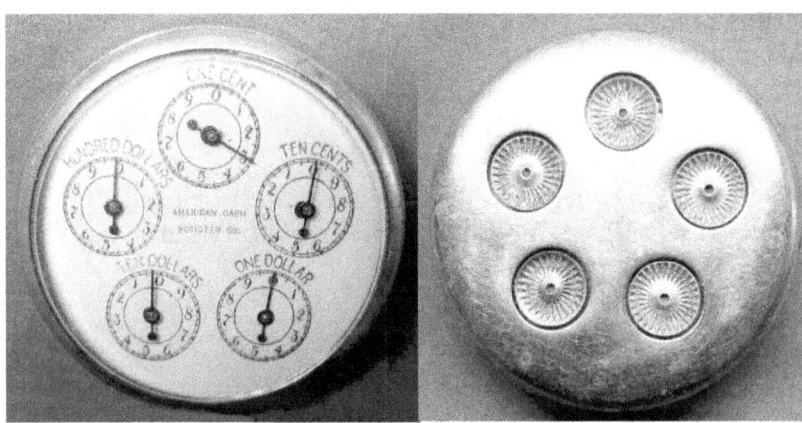

Image Courtesy of the Conrad Schure Collection
Figure 20.1: The American Pocket Cash Register

This device in Figure 20.1, was made by the American Cash Register Company. Variants are available with no name. I am not aware of a patent specifically for it. However, U.S. Patents 480,957, 528,797 and 575,476 are similar.

It is operated by five brass buttons on the back, one for each dial. When the button for a dial is turned (they can only go in a single direction), the pointer for the dial advances. When a pointer goes beyond 9, appropriate units are automatically added to the dial clockwise to it.

Clearing the machine is done by adding appropriate values to the dials. For example, if the 'one cent' dial reads 1 and all the rest are zero, 9 must be added to all dials starting with the cents and going clockwise around the unit. Clearly this can be laborious. However, it does work.

Charles Sebastian received U.S. Patent 602,918 for this device on April 26, 1898. It adds up to $10 in increments of 5 cents. It also subtracts.

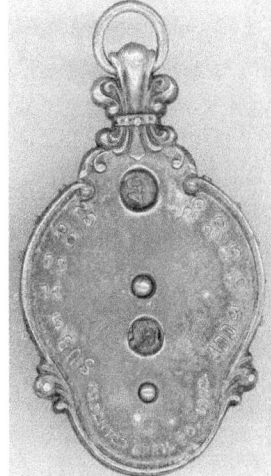

Figure 20.2: Pocket Register by C. Sebastian

The back is plain. An example in brass (illustrated) states on the back that it is a souvenir of the Louisiana Purchase Centenary (St. Louis) of 1904 (Figure 20.2).

It does not look to be very useful.

George Lafond received at least three patents for his adder: Swiss Patents 19395 of 29 avril, 1899 and 46796 of 7 janvier, 1909: also Great Britain patent 2195 of January 31, 1899.

Figure 20.3: The Lafond Cash Register

---

37   'Pocket Cash Registers', Bob Otnes in *Proceedings of IM2008*, p 178

The example shown in Figure 20.3, looks closest to Figure 4 of the 1909 Swiss patent, noting that it may be missing a face plate.

Adding is done with the stylus. Starting with the large dial at the bottom, which is in steps of five units, carries add into the small dials in a counter-clockwise direction. The top three dials are in steps of 0 to 9. Thus the largest number that may be entered is 999.95.

Clearing the device is done by the method of adding numbers until all dials read zero.

This brief chapter is completed by a 'Ken+ Add' shopping cash register, complete in its tin box with a stylus. This works in a similar fashion to the previous devices, and might just be considered a watch pocket device. (Figure 20.4)

Similar stylus driven cash registers are available in plastic.

These are another interesting variant in the watch pocket or pocket-watch calculating genre, should anyone know of any other types I would be delighted to hear about them.

Figure 20.4: Ken + Add machine

Pocket-Watch Exposure Meters

There are numerous types and variants of watch-type photographic exposure meter, a type of photographic calculator, which were a much patented subject and a number of companies – Watkins and G.F. Wynne among them – produced a large range of these devices in all languages. Representative examples and a very short explanation are included to demonstrate another watch-pocket calculator, and for completeness.

Probably the most common and the device a collector is likely to come across first is one of the Watkins 'Bee' range of exposure meters. The sales sheet on this page and the following two pages of examples is but a sample. After that we have a very small sample of Wynne's meters and some other pocket-watch actinometers.

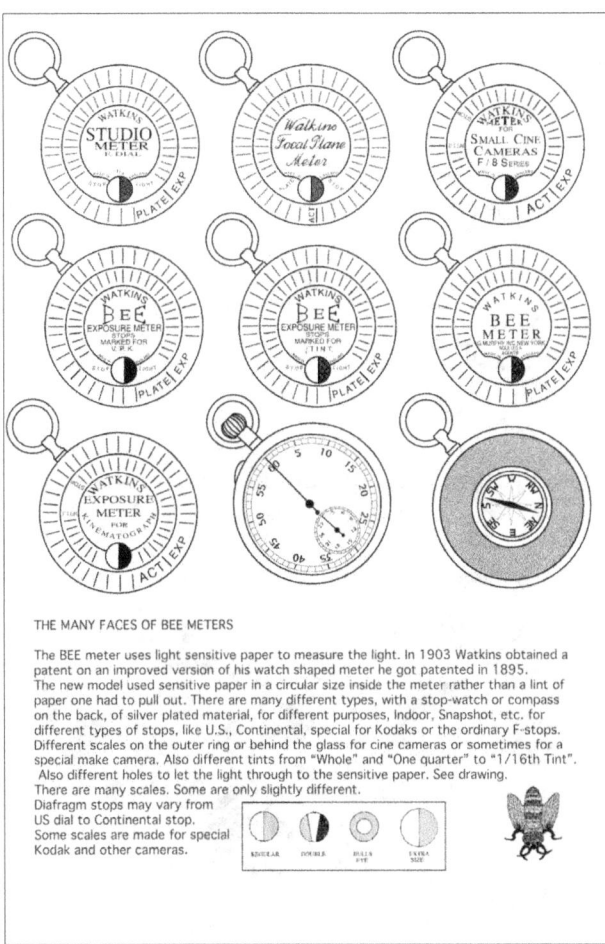

Figure 21.1: Watkins Bee Pocket-watch exposure meters

Figure 21.2: Watkins Bee Pocket-watch exposure meters 2

POCKET-WATCH SLIDE RULES

Figure 21.3: Watkins Bee Pocket-watch exposure meters 3

In Figure 21.4, is a selection of manufacturer's other than Watkins pocket-watch exposure meters, in particular from the Wynne range and a French Plaubel Peco device.

Figure 21.4: Wynne and other makers pocket-watch exposure meters

128

Watch Pocket Calculators

As mentioned right at the beginning of the book, there are a number of designs that do not meet my criteria for categorization as a pocket-watch slide rule or calculator, but would meet a much broader categorization of being a Watch Pocket device, i.e. one that would fit into a watch pocket in an old fashioned Waist-coat, also described as a Weskit pocket, or in America, a Vest Pocket.

The obvious exception that proves the rule is Halden's Calculex, which is just missing a winder to be able to be called a pocket-watch slide rule, therefore it has been included as part of the main text.

Other watch-pocket devices included in this list are thus devices such as the

- Small calculator,
- Key-chain slide rules,
- The Graphoplex Roplex (but this is really too large but is included as a Fowler Magnum is about the same size),
- The Fowler Junior (which has already been included in the Fowler section),
- The Charpentier (c1915) Cultriss's Calculating Disc, similar to Charpentier Calculator (K&E),
- The Supermathic,
- Any number of others which could almost be selected randomly, depending on the chooser's criteria.

Figure 22.1: Graphoplex Roplex

The Graphoplex Roplex

This has scales covered in plastic and is operated by 'screws', however this device is a pretty massive 5″ square (127mm x 127mm) and in no way meets any of my characteristics for either pocket-watch or watch pocket calculator.

Figure 22.2: Key-chain calculator

Key Chain Calculator

This is the opposite end of the size spectrum, a rather nice simple 25mm (1″) diameter circular slide rule on a key chain, in this case carrying a Lockheed logo on the verso, but equally available without, is also not pocket-watch.

POCKET-WATCH SLIDE RULES

There are a number of similar devices, any of which could have been featured here.

The Small Calculator
The Small calculator, patented by Roger Conant in 1900, this one says Patd. Feb 12, 1918. (Figure 22.3) This too is not a pocket-watch device, there are two versions, those interested in more information see [38]&[39].

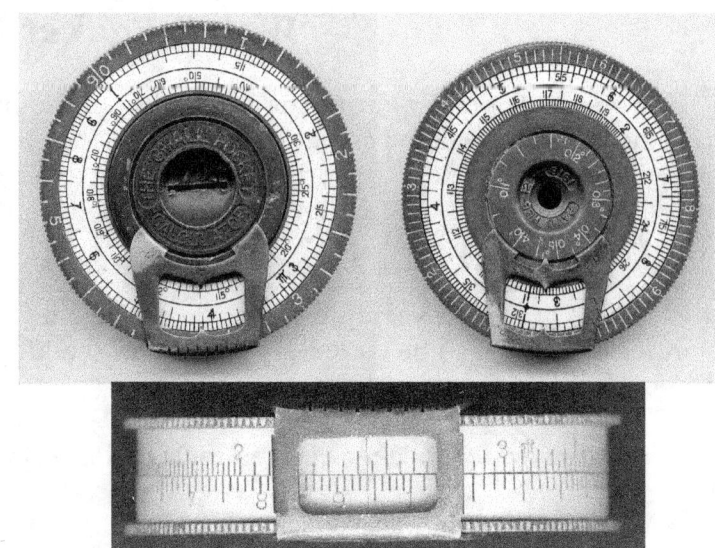

Figure 22.3: The 'Small' calculator

The Supermathic
Made in France, this is a very nice and quite unusual but quite large circular slide rule of considerable capability and charm, but once again it is not a pocket-watch calculator, but would still enhance any collection that it joined, Figure 22.4.

Figure 22.4: The Supermathic calculator

The Calculimetre
Made by Charpentier in France and possibly K&E in the USA as well as a number of other retailers such as Morin, & David, it was sold by K&E from 1893 through to 1930 under two model numbers, 1743 and 4020, for the same price - $5 - through all those years. There are a number of minor and interesting variations, it does have a loop, but is best described as an archetypal watch pocket slide rule (Figure. 22.5).

Note, Cajori says the Calculimtere was similar to Cultriss' Calculating Disc, of 1915, I have not seen one.

Figure 22.5: The Calculimetre calculator

---

38   'Small Wonder' Al Bennett in *Journal of the Oughtred Society*, Vol. 1, No 1, Feb 1992 Pg 16.
39   'The SMALL Calculator – Part II' Conrad Schure in *Journal of the Oughtred Society*. Vol. 1, No 2, Aug 1992 Pg 17.

Glossary

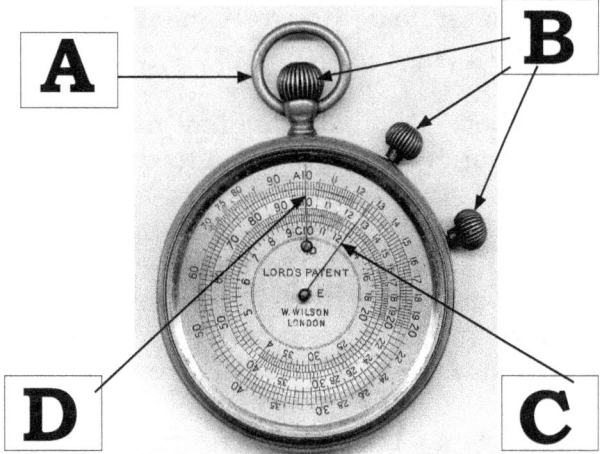

Terminology — Above we have an example of a pocket-watch slide rule with (A) a loop, (B) a crown or crowns, one central in the loop and two on the right hand side, or one central and one on the side; (C) one pointer and (D) one cursor. The disposition of the crowns is not fixed. Another example might have three crowns, one in the centre and one on either side of the central one, or else it may have two crowns, one on either side of a central loop. The scales: in this case there are four. How they operate and which of the knobs operates what is specific to a particular pocket-watch type. The device may be single sided or double sided, i.e. scales on one or both sides of the device.

German Silver — Also known as Nickel Silver, Chinese white silver, Packfong, or Electrum. This is a white alloy of approx. 60% copper, 20% zinc and 20% nickel. Some pocket-watch slide rules may actually have a sterling silver case, gold cases have also been seen advertised but I have never seen an actual example.

Brass — The brass used for a pocket-watch slide rule is a "hard" brass containing 62% copper and 38% zinc. It is then either nickel or chrome plated.

Gauge Points — Small marks adjacent to the scales in the case of a pocket-watch slide rule, marking points of a particular value, which are commonly used in calculation. Pocket-watch slide rules because of their size rarely carry many, if any, gauge points but where they do such as the bigger Fowlers, I have covered them in that particular section.

DRP/DBP — Deutsches Reichs Patent / Deutshes Bund Patent – German patents.

DRGM/DBGM — Deutsches Reichs Gebrauchsmuster / Deutshes Bund Gebrauchsmuster – German Registered designs. The English equivalent is Registered Design, and Deposé in France, though that can also mean a Registered Trade Mark. They are very useful sources of information.

POCKET-WATCH SLIDE RULES

Breveté SGDG — Breveté is the French for 'patented', not a maker's name! (SGDG: Sans Guarantie de Gouvernement). Literally, 'Without Government Guarantee'.

Crown/Key/Winder — See B above, these are different names for the basic control device of a pocket-watch slide rule, or indeed a pocket-watch.

Single / Double sided — Unlike a normal pocket-watch which is generally single sided, i.e. the back is solid metal or may have a viewing window for the 'works', pocket-watch slide rules are sometimes double sided, i.e. they have calculating elements on both sides. This is termed front and back, recto and verso or obverse and reverse.

Bow/ Crown/ Pendant — Also known as Loop, Winder and the connection to the body of a pocket-watch calculator.

Condition — For collectors, as well as dealers, it is important to have a standardized view of the condition of an example. The Oughtred Society, parent organization of slide rule collectors, and its UK counterpart, the UK Slide Rule Circle (UKSRC) uses:

1. - Very good, virtually "like new"
2. - Good
3. - Slight traces of wear, but fully functional
4. - Strong show of use, scratched and/or slight functional disorder
5. - Some defects and/or small parts missing
6. - Defective, important parts missing, bad condition

The Dutch Circle of Instrument Collectors uses a slightly different system that negates the necessity felt by some to add + and – signs to the condition number, e.g. 1 – is better than 2 +, but this is incredibly subjective:

C0 - Mint condition with all extras such as box, case and instructions, all mint, factory clean
C1 - as C0, but not all in the mint condition
C2 - Mint condition but without one or more of the extras
C3 - Very minimal signs of use
C4 - Minimal signs of use
C5 - Signs of normal use
C6 - Signs of heavy use
C7 - Small damage, but for the rest C4 or better
C8 - Damaged and well worn

It is worth recognizing that the two standards exist, know which is being used, and do not mix them.

Notes on Makers of Pocket-Watch Rules

This section on makers of pocket-watch slide rules follows the standard set by Clifton and others, and also used in my earlier books, of listing what is known of a particular maker in a common way:

Maker's name (Country where worked) dates worked, lived, or when these are not accurately known when he
  Flourished (fl)

Address: *Date: Address (note: this enables a slide rule example to be more accurately dated if an address is also quoted on a rule.)*

History: *Relevant data, who preceded and/or succeeded and any other data available. Another name in Bold will be cross-referenced elsewhere in the database.*

Made: *List of examples, including source of data. Where no source is quoted, this means it is from an actual pocket-watch slide rule seen by the author.*

Notes:

1. Unlike my earlier book, (*'Slide Rules, Their History Models and Makers'* Astragal Press, 1999) I have tried to only quote actual makers where they are believed to have made or sold a pocket-watch slide rule. This does not include relatives or other makers who may have preceded or succeeded this particular maker unless they are known to have made such slide rules.

2. I have tried to cover the vexed question of who was a true maker and who was only a retailer in the following list. I can not in any way be certain that I have got it all correct. The only manufacturer where we have 'factual' data in the shape of photographs is for Fowler, they are at the end of the Fowler section.

3. Some of the larger makers only have an abbreviated entry covering just their Pocket-Watch rules activity, and not all rules they made e.g. Stanley.

4. For further information on Wrist Watch slide rule makers I would recommend *sliderule-watches.googlepages.com* as one of many sites to look at, this book just touches on the wrist-watch side of the genre.

5. It is interesting to note that in 1921, nine of the manufacturers in the *Dictionary of Scientific Instrument Makers* claimed to make the Fuller Calculators, and seven claimed to have made the Boucher Calculator. Both designs would be deemed as expensive calculating instruments, and in all probability these companies were only retailers.

6. Sources:

Christies – Christie's Auction Catalogues	DGColl – David Green Collection	HvH – Herman van Herweijnen archive
IM2009 – Pocket-watch exhibition at that meeting	OSMan – Oughtred Society Manual	Science Mus – Science Museum Collection (Baxendall & Pugh) [8]
Toolshop Int Auc – Toolshop Auction Catalogues	Stanley – Stanley Auction Catalogue	JBColl – Jim Bready Collection
CSColl – Conrad Schure Collection	RKOColl – Bob Otnes Collection	

Makers & Retailers of Pocket-Watch Rules - Alphabetical

Army & Navy Stores (GB) c1900
Address: London, England.

History: The Army & Navy stores were well known purveyors of scientific instruments, and amongst their offerings was a Boucher calculator.

Sold: 1907 Catalogue which advertised Boucher calculators with paper scales and silvered metal dials. These are the Calculigraphe type, and are shown as made in France, they could have been the source of many of the Calculigraphes found in England.

Beaudroit Alphonse (France) 1899
Address: Seloncourt, Doubs, France.

History: Not known, but he was a watch maker (fabricant d'Horlogerie) who made the Meyrat & Perdrizet designed and patented pocket-watch calculator sometime around 1899 when the earliest versions of instruction booklet are dated.

Made: The M&P Calculator.

Berville P (France) c1900
Address: 24 Chaussee D'Antin, Paris., France.

History: Not known. Berville's was a famous French Instrument maker (known from a number of other instruments, particularly Camera Lucida) from around 1900, whose name and address was marked on a 'thin' Calculigraphe which made him probably just a retailer of the Calculigraphe, or else there is a different significance to such names and addresses being marked on pocket-watch slide rules. They do not look like advertising material.

Sold: HC 'thin' Calculigraphe

A.E.M. Boucher (France) fl 1875 - 1910
Address: A. Boucher. 5, rue du Canal. HÂVRE., France.

History: Not known, but his French and the equivalent English patent, dated 1876, was the seminal design of pocket-watch calculator The English patent was in the name of Henry Edward Newton, who was a famous patent attorney in England in the late 19th century. The name Boucher, Calcuigraphe, and Cercle à Calcul have always been used interchangeably. The very earliest designs carry the above address, later versions may have been made by **MORIN**.

Made: The Boucher Calculator. This is the seminal Pocket-Watch calculator design, usually seen in a case and has two winders that obviously has its roots in the watch-making trade. The later Calculigraphe version, supposedly an improvement by Henri Chatelain has a press button instead of the side winder. Both generally can be mistaken for a pocket-watch at a distance, certainly a stop watch.

The way they work is also pretty consistent across all the makers and versions, though that is probably a function of the excellence of the design and the patent that covers this. In general on the Boucher the crown rotates the movable scale, the side winder rotates the hands. On the Calculiraphe, the crown rotates the movable scale, and the crown plus push button pressed rotates both the hands. There is a fixed index on the reverse, which worked with the rotating scale.

Boult (GB?) 1882
Address: Not known.

History: Not known.

Made?: Charpentier calculator.

Breitling (Switzerland) 1884- 1978, and again to date.

Address: 1884: St Imier, Switzerland. Leon Breitling, founder.
1892: 3 rue Montbrillant, La Chaux-de-Fonds, Renamed 'Leon G. Breitling SA Montbrillant Watch Manufactory.'
Now: Montres Breitling Watches, P.O. Box 1132, CH-2540 Grenchen, Switzerland.

History: The Breitling Factory was established in 1884 in St Imier, Switzerland by Leon Breitling. It moved in 1892 to 3 rue Montbrillant, La Chaux-de-Fonds, and was then renamed 'Leon G. Breitling SA Montbrillant Watch Manufactory.' Like Heuer and Leonidas, Breitling was a specialist chronograph maker, and although it did not manufacture its movements, it continued to make improvements and innovations to watches it marketed. In 1915 the first wrist chronograph with pusher 'at 2 o'clock', a more natural position then at 3 or 6 o'clock for a wristwatch, and in 1933 the first 2 chronograph pushers thereby allowing a resumption of timing after stopping which was not possible with single pusher chronographs. The Breitling Chronomat appeared in 1941, it was the first slide rule watch in quantity production. In 1952 the Navitmar models appeared and also featured a circular slide rule on a bezel around the edge of the watch. In 1978 All production ceased at Breitling. The company was put up for sale and bought by Ernest Schneider. Breitling watches in general have the equivalent of a B and C scale on the watch and bezel, they also made a version of Stopwatch slide rule similar to the O&W / Selectron version.

Slide Rules:

1	2	3	4	5	6
Chronomat	W	n/a	M	n/a	B/C
Navitimer	W	n/a	M	n/a	B/C
B-1	W	n/a	M	n/a	B/C; Bezel within face, LCD display as well
Chronoslide Stopwatch calculator	SW	n/a	M	n/a	B/C; maybe model 1577, two color schemes
Stopwatch calculator (central totaliser)	SW	n/a	M	n/a	B/C

Calculigraphe (France) c1880

Address: Henri CHATELAIN,
Paris, France.

History: The name of a Boucher style pocket-watch calculator with a press button clutch rather than a second winder made by CHATELAIN amongst others possibly. It became interchangeably used with Boucher and Cercle à Calcul. In this book Calculigraphe is used for calculators with a clutch, Boucher for those with two winders, e.g. Morin and Stanley.

J. Casartelli & Son (GB) 1896-1925

Address: 1812 - 32: 37 King Street, Liverpool, England. (Lewis Casartelli)
1832 - 43: 132 King Street, Liverpool, England. (Lewis Casartelli)
1830 - 37: 133 King Street, Liverpool, England. (Lewis Casartelli)
1837 - 45: 20 Duke Street, Liverpool, England. (Lewis Casartelli)

1852 – 96: 43 Market St. Manchester. England (Joseph Lewis Casartelli)

1821 – 1900: 1&3 Duke Street, Liverpool. England

1896 – 1925: 43 Market St. Manchester. England (J. Casartelli & Son.)
1927: 18 Brown St, Manchester. England. (J. Casartelli & Son.)

1930 – 1932: 89 Old Hall Street, Liverpool, England. (J. Casartelli & Co.)

1881 – 1883: 34 Hatton Garden E.C., London (Joseph Casartelli)

History: J. Casartelli & Son, who are the company shown on a Lord's calculator, were just a small part of the Casartelli instrument making family who worked for a relatively short time. This was the name given to the partnership between Joseph Lewis Casartelli and his son Joseph Henry Casartelli who worked at 43 Market St, Manchester, during the dates given above. The father Joseph Lewis died in 1900, whereupon the business was carried on by the son till he died in 1925[40]. The Casartelli dynasty was established by Lewis Casartelli, b1784-d1860, emigrated from Italy c1787, and worked with various barometer makers in Liverpool. Some sources give him as successor to J. RONCHETTI, Manchester in 1790. It has also been stated that they were in Liverpool from 1821 to the end of the Century; this may be before Lewis married a Ronchetti and moved to Manchester, or it may be another line of the family. Joseph Casartelli took control of the business in 1845, J. Casartelli & Son were extremely well known suppliers of scientific instruments based in Manchester with offices in London. Amongst their offerings was a Lords calculator and also Boucher's calculators.

Sold: 1930? : 3⅜" (86mm) diam. Lords Calculator (made or sold?)
Boucher's calculator (sold?)
Range of Fowler's calculators (sold)

Lewis Casella & Co. (GB) 1848 - 1857
Address: Regent House, Fitzroy Square, London, England.
1858 – 1871: 23 Hatton Garden E.C., London
1873 - 1903+: 147 Holborn Bars E.C.
1872: 23 Hatton Garden E.C. & 147 Holborn Bars E.C., London

History: May have been the father of Louis Paschal Casella who traded as Casella & Co at 23 Hatton Garden, London from 1848 to 1860, then as Tagliabue & Casella at the same address from 1865 to 1870. From 1875 to 1901 they were at 147 Holborn Bars, London EC. Louis P. Casella died in 1897. May have been involved with the selection of pocket-watch calculators sold by the company.

C.F. Casella & Co. (GB) 1930 to date
Address: C.F. Casella & Co. Ltd.
1930: Regent House, Fitzroy Square, London W1. England
1951: 49-50, Parliament Street, London SW1.

Factory: Wallsey St. Works, Walworth, London SE17.

History: One of the earliest manufacturers in England, 'Casella & Co' was an extremely well known dealer of scientific instruments, and amongst their offerings was a Calculex. There was L.P Casella originally and C.F Casella later.

Sold: 1930: A6501 Fowler's watch case (No pic.) £1.-.-
1930: A6503 Calculex T3 at £1.1.- . Instructions an extra 1/3d.

Casio (Japan) 1875 - 1910
Address: Casio Calculators. Japan.

History: A watch manufacturer who produced a range of analogue and digital quartz "sports" chronometer models with a circular slide rule on a bezel round the face for many years.

Made: Many different styles of wrist watch with slide rule bezel.

---

[40] 'Barometer Makers and Retailers' 1660 – 1900' by Edwin Banfield. Barros Books, 1991. This is an excellent alternative source of makers data with lots of detail for Casartelli and Casella who were also renowned barometer makers

MAKERS & RETAILERS OF POCKET-WATCH RULES - ALPHABETICAL

Charpentier (France) 1875 - 1910
Address: Paris, France.

History: Not known

Made: The Charpentier Calculator – the Calculimetre. It has a chain loop, but that is the only "Pocket-Watch" criteria it meets. Otherwise it is a very neat and small all-metal double sided circular slide rule which could be carried in the waistcoat pocket on a watch chain. It was available with a number of 'makers' names, but who made and who sold is not certain.

Henri Chatelain (France) 1875 - 1910
Address: Paris, France.

History: Cajori shows a Calculigraphe from 1878, which is very shortly after the original Boucher patent date. The firm Henri Chatelain of Paris is now known to be the 'H.C.' shown on the surprisingly numerous versions of the Calculigraphe that have survived to date. Very little is known of Chatelain, catalogues of watch-makers show a number of watch and clock-makers of this name, but none of them bear the same initial. Whether the family firm supplied watch cases which Henri as the instrument maker filled with Boucher style innards is complete speculation, but has a nice ring to it. The Calculigraphe lasted for many years, versions with different hands, winders and so on are known. Examples of an F-C and an A-F Calculigraphe are also known. The A-F type is known from one example marked 'Swiss' and another marked 'Fabrique en France', and has 5 scales each side as compared with the 4 on the H-C version.

Despite being one of the earliest and most adventurous and prolific producers of slide rules, France only appears to have had the one pocket-watch slide rule manufacturer.

Made: An instruction manual for 1880 shows three versions of Calculigraphe:
The type 1 is a standard Boucher watch type,
the type 2 is a desk version,
and the type 3 is the 'improved' Boucher watch type with additional square and cube scales.

Citizen (Japan) To date
Address: UK Office: Citizen Watch (U.K.) Ltd.
P.O. Box 161, Wokingham, Berkshire, RG41 2FS.
Tel: 0118 989 0333; fax: 0118 977 5110

History: Many models of slide rule watch amongst which are the Model WR100 and Model 8945-087836 slide rule watches with B and C scales on watch and bezel.

Émile David (France) 1881 - 19xx
Address: A. Biévres (S.-&-O.),
5, Rue des Quatre-Fils. Paris, France

History: According to a 1901 catalogue the company was founded in 1881 specifically to make and sell instruments including Cercles à Calcul, and illustrates this capability with a Calculimtre by Charpentier. Not known when they ceased trading.

Sold: 1901: Charpentier Calculimtere

J(ohn) Davis & Son (GB) 1887 - 1907
Address: John Davis & Son (Derby) Ltd.,
All Saints Works, Derby.
also London Office at 39 Victoria Street, Westminster, SW1.
1897: 118 Newgate St E.C. London
1907: 6H Camomile Street, London.

POCKET-WATCH SLIDE RULES

History: According to various adverts produced a wide range of slide rules. Also known to have sold other manufacturers rules including the Mechanical Engineer. The firm's history can be traced back to 1779, however slide rules were first made in about 1889 when they were also importing D&P slide rules. Slide rule production increased rapidly during World War 1. They ceased manufacture c1941, may have sold other manufacturers slide rules afterward.

Sold: Mechanical Engineer calculator

Dietrich-Post Company (USA) 1937

Address: <1937: 75 New Montgomery Street, San Francisco, USA
1937: 15 First Street, San Francisco, USA
1937: Also Oakland and Los Angeles 614 Common St. New Orleans, USA

History: DIEPO(as they were also called) offered their Model 3075 Improved Halden Calculex in their 2nd edition 1937 catalogue, but not in their 1968 catalogue.
ue
Sold: 1937: 3075 Improved Halden Calculex. Mentions Amber lens.

Eugene Dietzgen (USA) 1833 - 1870

Address: Eugene Dietzgen Company
1908: 214-220 East 23rd St. New York, USA
1908: 181 Monroe St. Chicago, USA
1908: 614 Common St. New Orleans, USA
1908: 16-28 First St. San Francisco, USA
1908: 10 Shuter St. Toronto, Canada
1931: 2425 Sheffield Ave, Chicago. USA
1931: 218 E.23rd St, New York. USA
1931: 523 Market St. San Francisco. USA
1931: 318 Camp St. New Orleans. USA
1931: 805 Liberty Ave, Pittsburgh. USA
1931: 945 S. Broadway. Los Angeles. USA
1931: 1521 Sansom St. Philadelphia. USA
1931: 407 Tenth St. N.W. Washington. USA
1931: 611 N. Broadway, Milwaukee. USA
1938: 23 Market Street, San Francisco, USA

History: Dietzgen offered their Model 1797 Boucher calculator with card dials from 1902 to 1936, and a version with silvered dials from 1904 to 1931. I do not have any details. Whether they actually made these devices or if they only sold another manufacturers device is not clear. Dietzgen also sold the Calculex as United States sole agent from 1910 to 1955, their boxes and wallets for the Calculex were all well labeled with the Dietzgen name and type numbers.

Made: Boucher Type Calculators various.
Sole agent for Halden's Calculex
1910 - 55: Mod No. 1795A, Halden Calculex
1904 - 31: Mod No.1796, Charpentier Calculator
1902 - 36: Mod No. 1797, Boucher, Calculigraphe with card dials
1904 - 31: Mod No. 1797½, Boucher, Calculigraphe with silvered metal dials
1931 - Mod No. 1795A, Halden Calculex with amber colored back cursor
1938 - Improved Halden Calculex

Sold: After 1904-31 and before 1931:
1910 - Mod No. 1795A, Calculex T1, $6.25
1910 - Mod No. 1796, Charpentier, $5
1910 - Mod No. 1797_, Boucher Calc with enamelled card dials, $8.50
1910 - Mod No. 1797_, Boucher Calc with silvered metal dials, $14
1928 - Mod No. 1795A, Calculex, $9
1928 - Mod No. 1796, Charpentier, $5
1928 - Mod No. 1797_, Boucher Calc with enamelled card dials, $10
1928 - Mod No. 1797_, Boucher Calc with silvered metal dials, $11.25

J. Dinsdale (GB) c1883 - c1960
Address: James Dinsdale Limited
1960, New Station St, Leeds 1, England
also, 94, Woodhouse Lane, Leeds 2.

History: Wholesalers and retailers. Established 1883. Their shop at Woodhouse Lane, Leeds; was still open during the !960's.

Sold: In Sept 1960 sold FOWLER calculators

Dyson (GB) c1900?
Address: Not known, England.

History: Nothing is known of this firm, other than that they sold a single sided Textile pocket-watch slide rule, but whether they made it or only sold it is not known. These look very similar in style to the "Mechanical Engineer" calculators, it may thus be an early version of Textile calculator made by Scientific Publishing. It is possible that they were the firm of Dyers, James Dyson of Hudderfield, who were active during the early 1900's.

Made: Textile calculator

Elliott Bros. (GB) 1850-1939
Address: 1854 – 1855: 56 Strand, London, England

1857 – 1858: 5 Charing Cross & 56 Strand W.C., London.
1859 – 1863: 30 Strand W.C. London.
1864 – 1876: 449 Strand W.C. & 112 St. Martin's Lane W.C. London
1877: 449 Strand W.C. & 101, 102 & 112 St. Martin's Lane E.C. London
1878: 449 Strand W.C. & 112 St. Martin's Lane E.C. London
1879 – 1886: 449 Strand W.C. & 101 & 102 St.Martin's Lane E.C. London
1887 – 1899: 101 & 102 St.Martin's Lane E.C. London.
1900+ : 101 St. Martin's Lane E.C.
1900–: Central Buildings, Westminster, London.
1910–: 36 Leicester Square, London, WC.

History: Elliott Bros. of London are also known to have sold Lord's pocket-watch calculator which is sometimes also described as a textile calculator. One description gives this as a calculator on a wooden box for the textile industry; others show this as a pocket-watch with a similar suite of scales to the "Calculex".

Made: Lord's Calculator, Desk version
Lord's calculator, Pocket-Watch

F.C. (France) 18xx – 19xx
Address: Manufacture Francaise, St Etienne, Paris France

History: Some items carrying the 'FC' trade mark are also known to carry the appellation 'Manufacture Francaise St Etienne', and some opisometers also say 'Importe de Suisse'. How this becomes 'FC' is not known. There does appear to be a link to the Chatelain family company see description. The F.C. logo of a castle is almost as distinctive as the H.C. opisometer logo, and is also found on opisometers and Calculigraphe type of Boucher calculator, found in a number of different styles. Variants are known with the logo, and without, with the 'France' statement as well as without; the Calculigraphe style is very obvious. An F-C marked opisometer, complete with the castle logo, has been seen marked 'made in Switzerland', which might reflect the fact that they were only a retail organization, rather than a manufacturer.

There is information that 'FC' was also a part of the Henri CHATELAIN organisation and that the FC name resulted from confusion over an 1896 logo. This cannot be the complete explanation.

Made: Calculigraphe, various
Including selling a version of Calculigraphe to Joseph Halden prior to them making their Calculex.

Fabriques des Montres, Zénith (Switzerland) c1918
Address: Switzerland.

History: Not known other than as holders of a 1918 UK patent for a very sophisticated pocket-watch calculator.

Sold: Possibly a sophisticated patent pocket-watch calculator.

L. Fischer (France) c1900
Address: 12. B. Rue des Capucines Paris. Hotel. France.

History: Not known other than as a retailer's address on an HC marked Calculigraphe.

Sold: HC marked Calculigraphe.

Fowler (GB) 1898 - 1988
Address: Fowler and Company
1900: 53 New Bailey St, Salford, Manchester, Lancashire. (as the SCIENTIFIC PUBLISHING CO.)
1908: Sale Lodge, Sale, Manchester. (The family home where the first calculators were made).
1914: William Henry Fowler, Oakleigh, The Avenue, Sale, Cheshire.
1920: "Station Works", Sale, Cheshire.
1938: Hampson St, Sale, Cheshire.
Early 1940: West Timperley, Altringham.
1960's: Dalton Street, Rochdale Road, Manchester.
(Fowler's (Calculators) Limited), Hampson Street Works, Sale, Cheshire.

History: Founded in 1898 by William Henry Fowler (born 1853), when an article on circular calculators appeared in the 'The Mechanical Engineer', published by Scientific Publishing Co owned by Fowler. His son Harold, born in 1879, joined Scientific Publishing in 1905, also designing circular calculators. Fowler's calculators were started as the Scientific Publishing Company by William Henry Fowler in 1898 and continued to produce a wide range of pocket-watch calculators through to about 1976, and went into liquidation in 1988. Patents were issued in 1910, 1914 and 1923. CASARTELLI were the main marketing outlet apart from Fowler themselves. We know that they were exported in quantity, and that they featured in the catalogues of a large number of other manufacturers as well as retailers.

Made: The Fowler's Calculators. The earliest designs from Fowler were also in a typically pocket-watch style case, though these soon turned into the more typically pressed metal case which we see for all the later types, and there were quite a few!

If we consider a typical Fowler's Long Scale Calculator we see the following: A two sided calculator in a chrome plated pressed metal case generally under three inches in diameter. There are two winders; a central winder within a loop for a chain will generally drive a rotatable scale on the front of the calculator. The second winder, to the right of the central stem, drives a cursor on the front, and a similarly rotatable scale on the reverse.

On the front of the calculator there will be a single turn logarithmic scale which is used for the majority of calculations by moving scale and cursor to carry out multiplication and division. Working in to the center, the front will then have a long-scale where the next five, six or more scales make up the total length of the scale.

The reverse of the calculator, looked at with the second stem to the left of the main stem, has a number of standard slide rule scales; working from the outside toward the center: a short scale, reciprocals, mantissa of logarithm, square root (normally two scales), sines, tans, and further sines.

This comprehensive arrangement of scales allows most types of calculation to be performed easily, and the provision of the long-scale allows three-significant-figure accuracy easily, and four or five with a little bit of imagination! The calculators are robust, the large majority only suffering from the normal broken glass which is characteristic of the type. See the following table.

Model:	Format:	Diam:	Scales:		Dates:	Notes:
			Front:	Back:		
-	d/s cast	2 11/16"	short, 4-turn	short,3x3√		1
Type A	d/s cast	2 11/16"	short, 4-turn	short,3x3√		
Type B	s/s pres.	3 3/8"	short, 8's scale	n/a		
Type B Textile	s/s pres.	3 3/16"	short, 8's scale	n/a		
Type E1	d/s cast	2 5/8"	short,8's scale	weft, looms, reeds		
Type E1 (Textile)	s/s cast	2 11/16"	short,8's scale	constants		
Type H (early)	d/s cast	2 ¼"	log,short,√,sin	cube,3√	<1915	1
Type H	d/s cast	2 5/8"	short,CI,L,√,S	cube,3√	c1915	
Type M	d/s cast	2 5/8"	short,CI,L,√,S	cube,3√	c1915	
Type O	s/s cast	2 11/16"	short,4turn	short,3x3√	(SPC)	
Long Scale Type R	d/s pres.	2 3/8"	short,6turn	short,3x3√		
Type T (Textile)	s/s ?	2 ¼"	short	constants	(SPC)	
Textile Calculator	s/s	4 11/16"	short, weft, looms, reeds	n/a		
Textile Conversion calculator	d/s	2 ¼"?	short,8's scale?	tables	?	
Short Scale Textile	d/s pres.	2 11/16"	short,8's scale	short		
'Magnum' Textile	s/s cast	4 11/16"	short,8's,16's	n/a	1927?	
Textile Pick Finding	ds pres	3 3/8"	short,8's scale	pick tables		
Vest Pocket Calculator, Type MD	s/s ?	2 ½"	short,6turn	n/a		
Vest Pocket Calculator, Type H	s/s ?	2 ½"	short,CI,L,√,S,T,S	n/a		
Vest Pocket Calculator, TypeCSR	s/s ?	2 ½"	short/short(C/D)	n/a		
Universal Calculator	s/s pres.	3 3/8"	short,CI,L,3turn,S,T	n/a		
Universal Calculator	s/s cast	3 7/16"	short,CI,L,3turn,S,T	n/a	1950	
'Twelve-Ten' Calculator (12-10)	s/s pres.	3 3/8"	short,CI,duo-dec,S,S,T	n/a	1936	
Long Scale Textile	d/s pres.	4 5/8"	short,CI,	weft, looms, reeds		
'Magnum' Long Scale	s/s pres.	4 5/8"	short,CI,√,√,6turn,L,S,S	n/a	1927	
Jubilee 'Magnum' Extra Long scale	s/s cast	4 11/16"	short,CI,L,11turn	n/a	1948	
Nautical Calculator	s/s ?	4 ¼"	6xsine,Long	n/a	1957	
Artillery Calculator	s/s ?		'single type scales'	conversions		2
Artillery Calculator	s/s ?		short/short (C/D)	conversions		
Type RX	d/s pres.	2 3/8"	short,6turn	short,CI,L,√,LS,LT		

Long Scale	d/s pres.	2 11/16"	short,6turn	short,CI,L,√,LS,LT	c1938	
Circular Slide Rule	d/s ?		short/short (C/D)	CI,cube,3x3√		
Circular Slide Rule	s/s ?	short/short (C/D)	conversions			
'The Mechanical Engineer'	Pocket Calculator	s/s cast	2"	L,short,√,√,S,S	n/a	also 4"
Fowler's Calculator	d/s pres.	2 5/8"	short,CI,L,√,LS,LT,LS	cube,3x3√	c1935	
Junior Calculator	Circular	4 ½"	short/short (C/D),L,√,√,S,T	short,CI,L,3T,S,S,T		3
Kearns Machine Time	s/s pres.	2 5/8"?	special	n/a		
Mackay Paper & Board Calc.	?	?	?	?		

Models of Fowler's Calculators

Notes to Table showing Models of Fowler's Calculators:

1. The rear scale is worked from a center knob
2. Advertised with 'single type' dials, not known whether these were as Vest Pocket Calculator types or other.
3. This is not a true watch style calculator. Fowler took the scales used in some of their pocket-watch types and turned them into a more normal circular slide rule. Clever yes, but pocket-watch: No!

s/s   single sided
d/s   double sided
pres.   pressed metal

Frappant A.G. (Germany) 1920

Address: Frappant A.G, Landhausstrasse 37, Berlin, Wilmersdorf, Germany

History: Not known, but advertised a possible watch pocket slide rule in the 1925 VDI Nachrichten

Made: May never have made any slide rules but certainly advertised a device in c1925.

Graphoplex (France) 1950 – 1990

Address: Graphoplex,
1952 - 1963 : Graphoplex, 21 rue de Montsouris Paris 14, France
c1970 – 1975 : Graphoplex, 21 rue Paul Fort Paris 14, France
to about 1980 : Graphoplex 37260 MONTS Trade Office in Paris 21 rue Paul Fort France.

History: Not known, but made extremely high quality slide rules.

Made: The Graphoplex ROPLEX. Physical size alone does not discount this very nice device, and the scales are covered in glass. However the device is square and does not look like a pocket-watch or even a large pocket-watch. The scales are driven by a separate control mechanism, but that - in my eyes - is what discounts it from being a pocket-watch calculator - they are not stem winders.

H.C. (France) 18xx – 19xx
Address: Paris France

History: These are now known to be the initials of the firm Henri Chatelain. Chatelain, with their very unique opisometer logo, produced the Calculigraphe type of Boucher calculator, which was found in a number of different styles, for a number of years. Variants are known with the logo, and without; with the "France" statement as well as without, however the style is very obvious and there may be 'fat' and 'thin' types.

Chatelain was awarded two logos involving castles in January and April 1896. These have not been seen on slide rules.

Made: 'Fat' Calculigraphe, various.
'Thin' Calculigraphe, various

J(oseph) Halden (GB) 1877 – 1969
Address: J. Halden, Manchester, England
c1877: 8 Albert Square, Manchester.
1889: workshop at East Street, Manchester.
1900: new workshop at Lund Street, Cornbrook, Manchester. Destroyed by fire 1908.
1904: 37 Brazenose Square, Manchester. (next door to 8 Albert Square).
1908: new works at Reddish Stockport, near Manchester.
1965: Nigel Halden Limited.
By 1920 branches also at:
8&9 Chapel Street, Victoria Street, London SW,
8 Grainger St, Newcastle-on-Tyne,
65 Moor St, Birmingham,
31 Cadogan Street, Glasgow,
14 Park Row, Leeds,
and Bristol.
By 1920, they also had agencies in Berlin (Gebr WICHMANN) and Paris.

History: Established in 1877. In partnership with THORNTON at 8 Albert Square. Slide rules started manufacture in 1906? Taken over by Ozalid in 1969 when all production was stopped. We believe that he was supposed to have been granted a patent in 1910, but the Calculex is likely to have been spawned from the patent of W. Wilson in 1904, and could have been invented some time earlier. The Calculex is a delightful device and comes in various types including chrome, German silver, with Glass or plastic crystal, and with metal and paper scales. What is less well known is that they also had a desk model, which must be one of the most spectacular pocket-watch calculators. Even I agree that you would require very large pockets to carry that around!

Made: 1902 catalogue:
- Sold the FC Calculigraphe (Boucher).   12.6d
- Also a 'superior English make' version.   £1.10.-
- Mechanical Engineer   7.6d
- Desk version of Mechanical Engineer   12.6d
1908: Calculex, various versions.
1908: Desk Calculex
Calculex 2120; Glass cursors 1.5"W n/a   n/a   n/a   L,A/B,x//S,A/B,x; double sided;
Calculex 2121; Celluloid Cursors
Calculex 2122; Solid silver, Glass cursors
Calculex 2123; Solid silver, Celluloid Cursors
c1915: Desk Model Calculex, 5.25" dia
Halden Calculex (Science Mus. 161 – 1921-666)

W.H. Harling Ltd. (GB) 1851 – 1964

Address: W.H. Harling Ltd,
1851 – 1880's: Hatton Garden, London..
1874 – 1876: 9 London Place London Fields E, London
1877 – 1881: 40 Hatton Garden E.C. & London Place, London Fields, Hackney E. London
1882 – 1883: 40 Hatton Garden E.C. & Grosvenor Works Hackney E. London
1884 – 1889: 40 Hatton Garden E.C. London
1890 – 1898: 47 Finsbury Pavement E.C. London.
1899 – 1900+: 47 Finsbury Pavement E.C. & 5 Mentmore Terrace Hackney N.E. London
1899: renamed as 117 Moorgate, London
1915: 47 Finsbury Pavement, London, E.C
Sept 1930: 117 Moorgate, London EC2
c1964: Clapton London
1964: company was bought by Blundell Rules Limited (BRL) to create the Blundell-Harling (BH) Ltd Company.

Factories: 1912: Mount Pleasant Lane, Hackney. London.
Grosvenor Works, Hackney E.

History: W.H. Harling was apprenticed to W.F. Stanley. A.G. Thornton and the Threadwell Bros (who became part of Stanley) were apprenticed to Harling. An article in Vol 7 No 1 of the OSJ says they were formed in 1848, various editions of Pickworth show adverts which say Established in 1851. The OSJ article says the Finsbury Pavement address was vacated in 1899, the adverts still show this address to c1915. They were taken over by, or amalgamated with BLUNDELL in 1962, though they had ceased making slide rules in 1937/8, only intermittently continuing till 1947.
Harling were another well known firm of British Scientific Instrument makers who specialized in slide rules. Their 1930 cataloguer had a Calculex amongst the slide rule offered for sale. In 1964, they were taken over by Blundells and the firm Blundell-Harling was formed out of the joint company.

Made/Sold: 1924: 330: Calculex T1 in a catalogue at 21/-
1924: 331: Fowler calculators, 'similar to above' [sic] at 20/-
1927: 744: Calculex T1 in catalogue at 21/-
1927: 746: Fowler calculators, 'similar to above' [sic] at 25/-
1930: 744: Calculex T1/2 at 21/-
1930: 746: Fowler's at 20/-
1936: 744: Calculex T3 in catalogue at 21/-
A6503 Calculex, advertised as a T1, obviously using old copy.

Heath (GB) 1850 - 1922

Address: Heath & Co Ltd,
New Eltham Scientific Instrument Works, New Eltham, London SE9.

History: Established 1850. Absorbed into W.F. Stanley in 1926. In 1951, Heath, Hicks and Perken Ltd, formed from Perken, Son & Co, established 1852 - specialists in Thermometers. James J. Hicks and Heath & Co were also part of W.F. STANLEY. In 1922 The Dictionary of British Scientific Instruments showed that the range included Boucher's Calculating Circle.

Heckendorf (Germany) 1920?

Address: Heckendorf, Berlin, Germany.

History: Not known other than from an advertising leaflet which showed the Schacht und Westerich pocket-watch slide rule under Heckendorf part number 1958. No idea what relationships they may have had, but they look to have been a retailer of drawing and mathematical instruments.

Henry Hughes (GB) 1712 – 1946

Address: Henry Hughes & Sons,
59 Fenchurch St, London EC3.

History: Became part of KELVIN HUGHES and later part of Smiths Industries. Claim to be the longest established instrument making company in the world, able to trace their roots to 1712. This is shown as HEMLY HUGHES (wrongly – probably a miss-print) in the Dictionary .... Note also HEATH who showed a similar range of slide rules in the 1922 The Dictionary Of British Scientific Instruments. The range included a Boucher's calculating Circle:

1712: Thos Hughes (Snr.) becomes a member of the clock makers' guild.
1762: Thos Hughes (Jnr.) in business at 25 Broad Street, London.
1794: Joseph Hughes, grandson of Thos Jnr. working at 16 Queens Street, Ratcliffe.
1838: Henry Hughes, son of Joseph, born 1816, set up in business first at 120 Fenchurch St, and then at 59 Fenchurch St which continued till World War II.
1879: Henry Hughes dies, succeeded by his son Alexander.
1903: become a limited company Henry Hughes & Son. Production facility at Forest Gate.
1915 – 17: Hainault factory started and opened.
1925: Controlling interest purchased by S. SMITH & Sons Ltd.
1941: Fenchurch Street premises destroyed by bombing during WWII. Discussions with Kelvin Bottomley & Baird Ltd. resulted in the joint venture company Marine Instruments Ltd. in 1942 at 107 Fenchurch Street.
1946: H. Hughes and Kelvin Bottomley & Baird amalgamate to form Kelvin & Hughes.

Sold: Boucher's Calculating Circle

Hughes-Owens Co. Ltd. (USA) 1900 – 1945?

Address: Hughes-Owens Company Limited,
59 Fenchurch St, London EC3.

History: The Hughes Owens Company Limited 1937 edition catalogue describes a Calculex Type 1 under a model number 1775.

Sold: 1937: Mod 1775, Halden Calculex, Type 1

Heuer (Switzerland)

Address: Tag Heuer, Switzerland.

History: Produced a slide rule watch, the Calculator model, with a circular slide rule on a rotating bezel (C scale) round the edge of the watch, rotating against a fixed D scale. This has been reissued in the 1990's.

Made: Many attractive calculator watches.

Juvenia (Switzerland) 1889 - 1940

Address: Juvenia
La Chaux-de-Fonds Switzerland.

History: Juvenia was the earliest of the watch makers in La Chaux-de-Fonds, founded by Jacques Didisheim from Alsace in 1860. From 1920 they became well known as a manufacturer of wrist-watches especially elegantly decorated, and in 1945 they produced a wrist watch with a slide rule incorporated.

Made: 1945: Juvenia with slide rule.

POCKET-WATCH SLIDE RULES

Keuffel & Esser (USA) w1867 - 1982
Address: 1867: 79 Nassau Street, New York, USA.
1875: Hoboken, New Jersey, USA
1892/3: 127 Fulton Street, New York, USA.

History: Founded in 1867 by Wilhelm Keuffel and Hermann Esser, first instruments were sold in 1876 and were incorporated in February 1889. They sold their first bought-in slide rules in 1880, including Dennert & Pape rules from Germany, and probably Chatelain Calculigraphes from France. K&E made their first slide rules in 1891, and went on to become the largest manufacturer of slide rules in America. Their last slide rule, manufactured n 1976, was donated to the Smithsonian Institute. K&E are known to have manufactured the Sperry Watch Calculator and the K&E Watch Calculator, both devices covered in extremely fine detail in the OSJ Vol. 6, No 2, so that repetition in brief would not do these devices particular justice. K&E went bankrupt in 1982 and their assets were sold off after that.

Made: 1895 – 1899: Mod. 1743, Charpentier circular, 6C   MD   M   m   C/D,√,//L,T,S; Mod 1743 to 1900
1901 – 1930: Mod. 4020, Charpentier circular, 6C   MD   M   m   C/D,√,//L,T,S; Mod 1743 to 1900
1895 – 1899: Mod. 1743½ Boucher watch calculator
1901 – 1906: Mod. 4022 Boucher watch calculator
1903 – 1906: Mod. 4022-A Boucher watch calculator
1903 – 1906: Mod. 4023 Boucher watch calculator – no examples known
1901 – 1906: Mod. 4024 Boucher watch calculator
1906 – Mod. 4016, Sperry's watch calculator   W   geared differently
1906 – 1939: Mod. 4017, Sperry's watch calculator   W   geared same
1909 – 1927: Mod. 4018, K&E Circular watch calculator   W
Calculigraphe type Boucher calculator
Sperry Watch Calculator
K&E watch calculator

	Price ($) and availability of various types of pocket-watch slide rule sold by K&E (from catalogues)												
	Rule	1893	1895	1897	1899	1901	1903	1906	1909	1911	1913	1915	1916	1921
1743	Charpentier	X	5.-	5.-	5.-									
1743½	Boucher	X	8.50	8.50	8.50									
4022	Boucher					14.-	14.-	14.-						
4022-A	Boucher					X	12.50	12.50						
4023	Boucher					X	19.-	19.-						
4024	Boucher					8.50	8.50	7.-						
4016	Sperry							20.-						
4017	Sperry								18.-	15.-	15.-	15.-	15.-	22.50
4018	K&E								13.50	13.50	13.50	13.50	13.50	20.25
4020	Charpentier					5.-	5.-	5.-	5.-	X	5.-	X	5.-	

	Rule	1922	1925	1927	1928	1930	1931	1932	1933	1934	1936	1937	1939	1941
4016	Sperry													
4017	Sperry	22.50	22.50	22.50	22.50	22.50	22.50	22.50	22.50	22.50	22.50	22.50	22.50	
4018	K&E	20.25	20.25	20.25										
4020	Charpentier	X	5.-	5.-	5.-	5.-								

X	Not listed in catalogue
	Not available as identified

Lancashire Optical Manufacturing Company Limited (GB) c1926

Address: Manchester, England

History: The Lancashire Optical Manufacturing Company Limited was the probable manufacturer of the pocket-watch slide rule from Frederick Robinson's Patent No 256,903 of 1926.

Made: c1926: Pocket-Watch slide rule to Robinson's patent

Lawes Rabjohns (GB)

Address: Lawes Rabjohns Ltd
Abbey House, Victoria Street, Westminster, London SW1.
also at (1952):91 Cornwall St, Birmingham;
Faraday House, Todd Street, Manchester;

Factory: Dacre Works, Brooklands Road, Weybridge, Surrey.

History: 1952: Major distributor of Mathematical instruments with a large range of slide rules, including Fowler.

A. Leitz (USA)

Address: A. Leitz Company.
San Francisco, USA.

History: Adolph Lietz was born in Leubeck, Germany in 1860. and immigrated to San Francisco in 1879 where he worked in several scientific instrument shops before opening his own business. Lietz purchased the business of Carl Rahsskopff in 1880 and began his own business in 1882. Lietz originally joint ventured with another maker, Gottlieb A. Mauerhan, to form 'Lietz and Mauerhan,' a relationship that lasted for about a year. When Mauerhan departed, Lietz teamed up with Conrad J. Weinmann who had previously worked for Carl Rahsskopff. The company was renamed 'A. Lietz & Co.' and produced surveying instruments and related tools. The firm incorporated in 1892 under the name 'The A. Lietz Company' and Weinmann possibly left at about that time. In 1910 they added a complete line of drafting materials and engineering equipment. In 1947, after 65 years of production, the firm discontinued the manufacturing of surveying instruments. Their business changed to being an importer and distributor. In 1960 the company started handling the Umeco brand of surveying instruments and then added instruments from Japan made by Sokkisha. The Frank Paxton Company purchased the business in 1965 and moved its headquarters to Kansas City, Missouri. The company name was also changed to 'The Lietz Company.' and then in the early 1990's the firm name was again changed, this time to 'Sokkia.'

Sold/made: c1920: Molter's watch pocket slide rule.

Lord (GB)

Address: Lawrence Lord, Mill Manager.
66 Devonshire Road, Burnley, Lancaster, England.

History: Not known. Lord's calculator was made by Elliott Bros, Waddington, Wilson and others. See Patent 22,210 of 1892 which covers a large wooden desk type and the watch types.

Sold/made: c1910:Lord's calculator with metal C/D scales, plus others. Variations exist with different sizes and different numbers and dispositions of knobs.

Manloves (GB) 1892 and later

Address: Nottingham, England
Rouen, France

POCKET-WATCH SLIDE RULES

History: See Manlove, Alliott & Fryer (below)

Made: Boucher calculator, later version - Manloves

Manlove, Alliott & Fryer (GB) 1867 – 1892 and later
Address: Nottingham, England
Rouen, France

History: Edward Manlove and Alexander Alliott were drapers by trade. With J.G. Seyrig they set up a bleaching company and developed a centrifugal drying machine as the Centrifugal Company in Nottingham. This versatile firm also made steam trams, laundry machinery, vacuum pumps and centrifuges for purifying palm oil , and also the Atkinson engine, a patented adventurous design of engine built by them from 1889 to 1892.
1837: This evolved into the firm of Manlove, Alliott & Co. Ltd., based in Lenton, Nottingham but when expansion was necessary they opened their Blomsgrove Works on Ilkeston Road in Radford, Nottingham. The company won an award at the Great Exhibition in 1851 for its centrifugal Washing and Drying Machine. In 1874 the company developed the first incinerators for the destruction of waste. It was designed and patented by Albert Fryer in 1876 and originally called a Destructor, it was engineered by Manlove & Alliott. They became Manlove, Alliott & Fryer and in 1886 it was incorporated as a Limited Company. The Rouen address was in place by 1887. By 1891 they were supplying equipment for the cotton industry. The company was awarded a royal warrant by King Edward VII. In 1914 the company described itself as Engineers, Colonial and General Specialties: Engines, Boilers, Sugar Machinery, Oil Mill Plant, Power Laundry Plant, Centrifugal Machines, Refuse Destructors. Employees: 400. They were still going in 1949, and the company existed till 1959 when it was taken over by the Melbray Group. Manufacturing continued in Ilkeston until 1969. Why they chose to make or, more likely, to retail a pocket-watch slide rule is anyone's guess!
Also seen as 'Manloves, London'; agents for Boucher in the UK.

Made: Boucher type calculator – early, but not the earliest (Manlove, Alliott & Fryer)
Boucher calculator, later Stanley version – Manloves

Manlove Alliott & Co Limited (GB) c 1886
Address: London, England

History: See Manloves (page 147) and, Manlove Alliott & Fryer (above)

Made: Boucher calculator, middle version – Manlove Alliott & Co Limited

Matsku (USSR) 1950?
Address: USSR

History: Not sure whether this is a company name or just a logo. Made or sold a very simple 2" dia. pocket-watch calculator in a plastic box. Small 2" diameter pocket-watch calculator, the same as 'Sunrise'; this retailer has the logo 'Matsku'.

Made: Pocket-watch calculator with C/D,L scales.

(M&P) Meyrat & Perdrizet (France) 1880?
Address: Seloncourt, Doubs. France

History: In 1880 Meyrat et Perdrizet were awarded French patent number 139,898 under the title 'Règle à calcul circulaire'. Nothing further is known of M&P, and it is not known whether they patented their device elsewhere. The device was made by watchmaker Alphonse Beaudroit also in Seloncourt. Examples are known with instructions dated 1899 which imply that they made these unique slide rules for almost 20 years.

Made:
Type 1: 2¼" dia pocket-watch type calculator with a watch movement incorporated
Type 2: 2¼" dia similar calculator but without a watch movement
Possible Type 3: There were versions of the Type 1 with and without a second hand, whether this made a 3rd type is a moot point.

MIMO (Switzerland) 1889 - 1940
Address: Graef et Cie, Fabrique Mimo (Manufacture Internationale de Montres en Or)
La Chaux-de-Fonds Switzerland.

History: Graef et Cie, Fabrique Mimo was established in 1889 in La Chaux-de-Fonds by Otto Graef. They preceded by a few weeks the Breitling patent for an effective watch slide rule which was built onto a non-chronograph watch, the MIMO Loga. MIMO was an innovative manufacturer of wristwatches and produced, for example in 1930 the first watch with date window at '3 o'clock' in the MIO-MOmètre, also an elegant rectangular chronograph in 1936, the MIMOlympic. In 1940 the founder, who was then over eighty years, entrusted the company to his son Willy and Paul and the company approached and joined Girard-Perregaux, where the MIMO Loga is also listed as a product.

Made: MIMO Loga non chronograph watch with slide rule bezel.

Moko (Germany) 1900?
Address: Not known, Germany

History: Not known.

Made: Moko Lightning pocket-watch calculator

Wilhelm Molter (Germany) 1921 - ?
Address: Techniches Büro Ingenieur Wilhelm Molter
Karolinenstrasse 51
Nürnberg. Germany

History: Formed 1921, c1923 produced a circular slide rule which may also have been exported to the USA via a relative of Molter in about 1925. They also apparently made a DRGM and DRP Patented pocket-watch type sold by Schacht U. Westerich, Reiss and Wichmann as well as by themselves.

Made: Nr. 8406 Circular slide rule (Pocket-watch) 65 mm dia, 6 mm thick, for commercial and technical calculations.
Pocket-Watch Calculex sold by Wichmann.
Unknown number pocket-watch slide rule 2-sided with crown and loop.

Mondia (Switzerland) Not known
Address: Mondia, Switzerland.

History: Produced a slide rule watch, the 'Automatic 'Memory' Model with an in-built circular slide rule. This one is more unusual as it has the two scales within the watch crystal, the scales being driven from external buttons which give the initial impression that the watch has stop-watch functions. The two knobs rotate both scales, there is a hair line engraved on the crystal.

Morin H (France)[41] 1880 – 1954+
Address: 1880 founded by Henri Morin.
1886 association with Genesse to create a current workshop.
c1905 links to Georges Boyelle, with a patent for metal harness testing.
1880-1910: 3 Rue Boursault, Paris, France.
c1910-1954 & present?: 11 Rue Dulong, Paris 17, France.

c1930, Boyelle-Morin joined by Paul Beau, with interests in planimeters.

---
[41] My grateful thanks to David Rance who made me aware of the article *Morin – Not strictly a slide rule maker* by Willy Robbrecht in the Dutch Kring newsletter MIR35 of February 2004.

c1964 bought Secretan.
post 1964, joined with Serpi, and then themselves might have joined or been bought by Vion and ceased in business

Workshop: 1880 – 1909: 203, rue de Vaugirard, Paris

Atteliers (Makers) 1886 - H. Morin & Gensse à Paris (seen with both addresses) from an undated catalogue: " Pour cause d'Agrandissements la maison H. MORIN".

Catalogues (1914 and 1930 seen with the names Boyelle-Morin (A. & M.) and Paul Beau (E.P.) not sure of significance.

History: Morin were known as a firm of precision instrument makers, similar to W.F. Stanley in the UK, with a particular emphasis on engineering design, tachometry (stadia & surveying) and artillery tools as well as slide rules. Various catalogues are known, some have indeterminate dates. In these are shown an interesting variety of pocket-watch slide rules, including some particularly fascinating possible prototypes, Calculigraphes, as well as more normal devices such as Charpentier Calculimetre, Halden Calculex. There is some difficulty in interpretation, the devices are called Calculig raphe, yet the pictures show something more akin to a Boucher calculator complete with "AB" and "Cercle à Calcul" markings as on early Boucher calculators. The dates are difficult to rationalise, the earliest confirmed dates on the catalogues are some 35 years after Boucher's invention, and 30 years after the earliest HC Calculigraphe known. Even so, Morin had the capability to make Boucher's devices. Bought Secretan c1964. Post 1964 bought Serpi and then possibly been taken over by Vion.

Made: 1911: 8188 "Nouveau Calculigraphe" 20FFr.
1911: 8664 Calculimetre 10FFr (buckskin case 10FFr75; hinged case/box 12FFr)
1911: 9116 Cercle Halden 15FFr (with the interesting comment: "These are delivered by us as we receive them from the factory. So we deliver them without any warranty. We remind you that the replacement of each glass is charged 3 francs, a price imposed by the factory".)

1914: 9903 New Calculigraphe for the Stock Market 20FFr

1925/6: 8188 "Calculigraphe Boucher" 45FFr
1925/6: Cercle Halden (the comment this time is : "Circle Halden, made in England, can be delivered any day but the difficulty of replacing glasses has meant that we are almost abandoning the type".)

1925/6: 8664 Calculimetre 44FFr.40
1925/6: 9974 Calculimetre with cursor 54FFr (it seems unusual to sell the cursor separately)

1940: 12190 "Calculigraphe Boucher" nickel case, card scale
1940: 12191 "Calculigraphe Boucher" nickel case, engraved metal scale
1940: 12192 Instruction leaflet for the calculator

J.V. Navlakhi (India) c1950
Address: J.V. Navlakhi & Co
533 Kalbadevi Road, Bombay, India.

History: Not known, but they were obviously importers and retailers of various instruments including the Fowler range of calculators. It is nice to know that even members of the British Empire had a hand in selling pocket-watch slide rules, and that it was the ubiquitous Fowler range is even better.

Sold: c1950: The full range of Fowlers calculators..

Negretti & Zambra (GB) 1851- 1980
Address: 1851 – 1857: 11 Hatton Garden, London
1858: 11 Hatton Garden, 59 & 68 Cornhill E.C. London
1859: 1 & 11 Hatton Garden, 59 & 68 Cornhill & 107 Holborn Hill, London

1860 – 1861:1 Hatton Garden E.C., 59 Cornhill E.C. & 107 Holborn Hill W.C.
1862 – 1864: 1 Hatton Garden E.C., 59 Cornhill E.C. & 122 Regent St. W. London.
1865 – 1869: 1 Hatton Garden E.C., 59 Cornhill E.C. & 153 Fleet St. London
1870 – 1872: Holborn Circus, Holborn Viaduct E.C., Charterhouse St. E.C., 59 Cornhill E.C., 122 Regent St. W. & 153 Fleet St. E.C. London   1873: Holborn Viaduct E.C. Charterhouse St., 45 Cornhill E.C., 122 Regent St. W. & 153 Fleet St. London
1874 – 1885: Holborn Viaduct E.C., Charterhouse E.C., 45 Cornhill E.C. & 122 Regent St. London.
1886 – 1890: Holborn Viaduct E.C., 45 Cornhill E.C. & 122 Regent St. London.
1891 – 1900+: 38 Holborn Viaduct, 45 Cornhill E.C. & 122 Regent St. London.

History: Established 1850, still making slide rules in the 1920's. Extremely well known firm of London instrument makers with an extremely wide product range. Also retailed other maker's equipment.

Made: Advertised Boucher's Calculating Circle, also known from a 1998 ToolShop Auction entry for a Boucher's Calculator. The minuscule illustration shows a Calculigraphe type device, i.e. it looks to have the push-button rather than second crown, and from the catalogue we assume it was marked Negretti & Zambra.

Ollech & Wajs (Switzerland) 1956 – 1980's
Address: Zurich, Switzerland

History: Also known as O&W; Ollech & Wajs started business in the 1950's when Albert Wajs began making and supplying stainless steel bracelets for wristwatches. In 1956, a partnership was formed with Mr Ollech, and they soon began manufacturing wristwatches. In the 1960's they were selling a high quality professional divers wristwatches for US $12. These watches became very popular with US soldiers who bought them privately, as they were the best quality watch and value for money they could find, and they were a vast improvement on their inferior quality government issued disposable watches. Towards the late 1970's, Mr. Wajs bought up much of the Breitling stock for the aviation models such as the Navitimer. They began producing their own label watches with the Breitling cases and the same caliber's used in Breitling watches. These watches were branded "Aviation" and are now highly prized amongst collectors. By the early 1990's O&W subsequently began production again, this time under a new company, formed by Albert Wajs. The company is called A. I. Wajs, who proudly present A. I. Wajs Army Watches. They still use the logo and the brand name Ollech & Wajs or O&W, as these brand names are owned by Albert Wajs.

Made: made/sold the Selectron Timer 2⅜" (60mm) in diameter.
Also various slide rule watches.

Pedos S.A. (Switzerland) Not known
Address: Renan - J-B. Switzerland

History: A catalogue with brief instructions (undated) shows that they made a Calculigraphe A-F. This is a two sided pocket-watch calculator. The catalogue shows other pocket-watch style counting and measuring equipments.

Made: An advertising leaflet and instructions for the 4" dia. A-F Calculigraphe with 5 scales per side, was produced by Pedos S.A., a Swiss firm. This is a very different device of much higher quality, marked 'Fabrique en France'. The known example (see earlier section) is marked 'A. Fischer', presumably the A-F in the title.

Frederick Post Company (USA) 1937
Address: Frederick Post Co.
Chicago, Illinois, USA.
New York, USA.

History: Established c1890; sold various manufactures rules as well as their own slide rules. Various associations with other companies:
c1936, Post-Hemmi; c1959, Dietrich-Post, originally a branch office of POST; c1970, Post-Teledyne. What the nature of the early associations was is not known, however Teledyne bought out Post c1970. Also have had known slide rules "made in Occupied Japan". Better known for a range of Hemmi like rectilinear rules, the 14th edition, 1925 catalogue also offered:

POCKET-WATCH SLIDE RULES

Sold:
- 1925: 1492 Boucher calculator (Calculigraphe) with enameled card dials
- 1925: 1492A Boucher calculator (Calculigraphe) with silvered dials
- 1925: 1493 The improved Halden Calculex (T1 variety)

Queen (USA) 1860 - 1912

Address: James W. Queen,
1888: 924 Chestnut Street, Philadelphia, USA
The Union, 91 Walnut Street, Philadelphia, USA.

History: "James W. Queen was born in Philadelphia in 1815. He is first listed in 1839 Philadelphia directory as an optician. In 1860 he became associated with Samuel L. Fox and the firm became James W. Queen & Co. For a number of years there was a branch office in New York City. James Queen retired in 1870 and died in 1890. The business was continued as James W. Queen & Co. until 1893, when it was incorporated as Queen & Co. Queen & Co., Inc. existed until 1912 at which time it was reorganized as the Queen-Gray Co. by John G. Gray and continued as such until Mr. Gray's death in 1925[42]." . Known to have sold Faber slide rules c 1902 and also a version of the Calculigraphe with their name on it.

Made: Sold a named version of the 'Calculigraphe' Pocket-watch calculator.

Reiss (Germany) 1882 to date.

Address: R. Reiss GmbH Fabrik technischer Artikel Liebenwerda, Germany
Reiss, Bad Liebenwerda, Germany.
Reiss, Bad Liebenwerda, DDR
Reiss, Zeichentechnik GmbH, Bad Liebenwerda, Germany.
Reisszeugfabrik
Nürnberg. Germany

History: Founded in 1882 by Robert Reiss as a mail order specialist for office and drawing supplies. 1899 started making slide rule like instruments, which were sold from about 1902. First made and sold their own slide rule designs in 1912. In 1928 became a subsidiary of Gebr. Wichmann due to getting into financial difficulties. Having survived WW2, they were broken up and reformed as a State Owned Enterprise in East Germany in 1947. Joined Meissner to become V.E.B. Mantissa in 1972 until 1984 They continue to date as part of the Wichmann organization. 1923 patent for a rectilinear slide rule. Still making a range of slide rules as late as 1970, the later identified slide rules are from the Concise Encyclopaedia of Mathematics from Van Nostrand Rheinhold c1971. See also Eichmuller and Bayerische Reisszeugfabrik A.G. who preceded this company name but had no links.

Made: Made and / or sold a version of the S u. W / Molter calculator.

Renan – J – B. (Switzerland) 1850?

Address: Switzerland.

History: This is actually a municipality in the district of Courtelary in the canton of Bern in Switzerland, but I have seen it wrongly described as a maker.

Made: Where the firm of Pedos who made and / or sold the Calculigraphe A.F. were based.

Secretan (France) 1789 - 1924+

Address: 1924: 151 Boulevard Auguste-Blanqui, Paris XIII
c1960: 44 rue Etienne Dolet, 94230 Cachan, France.

Workshop 1924: 12-20 Boulevard St Jacques, Paris

---

[42] Smart, Charles E. *The Makers Of Surveying Instruments In America Since 1700* Troy, New York: Regal Art Press. 1962

History:	Morin bought Secretan c1964, and the final (?) manifestation of Morin and Lerebours et Secrétan, founded in 1789, now known as Secretan Ch. Épry & Jaquelin, succrs.
Made:	The 1924 Catalogue has:
	3742 Calculigraphe Boucher double cadran papier. 32Fr.
	3743 Calculigraphe Boucher double cadran métal. 34Fr.
	3744 Calculimetre Charpentier tout en métal. 40Fr.
	3745 Calculimetre Charpentier en écrin.(case). 45Fr.

Schacht und Westerich (Germany) 1826 to date

Address:	1846: Schacht u. Weterich formed.
	1907: Großen Bäckerstrasse, Hamburg, Germany.
	1923: 16 - 24Großen Bäckerstrasse, Hamburg, Germany.
	1925: Hamburg 1, Germany
	Schacht & Westerich, Technischer Zeichenbedarf,
	Hamburg, Germany.
History:	Founded in 1826 by Conrad Schacht, joined with Adolph Westerich in 1835. A pocket-watch calculator was covered in some detail in the Journal of the Oughtred Society Volume 4, No 1, and I will not repeat the information. It is not certain whether they actually manufactured the device, however the chances are quite high that they were only the retailer, as the device was also found for sale by Wichmann and it is likely to have been made by Molter. This is not a Boucher style calculator; it is a circular slide rule in pocket-watch form.
Made:	2.25" diam. Pocket-watch calculator, two sided, C/D//4 scales. The center knob turns the inner of a standard circular C/D scale, the side stem turns the pointers, which in the case of some models is a wedge with a hairline scribed on it. Lord's calculator is similar but does not appear to have hands or any sort of pointer. Still in business today making drawing instruments and selling writing materials.
	1923: System 'Thomas' Rechenuhr (not a real pocket-watch slide rule
	1925: 8406 Kreisrechenschieber (possibly the Molter / Calculex device)

Scientific Publishing Co. (GB) 1898 - 1915

Address:	1898: Corporation St. Manchester, England
	1901 - c1915: 53 New Bailey Street, Manchester,
	1908: Workshop in the Family home, Sale Lodge, Sale, Cheshire.
	<1914: Oakleigh, the Avenue, Sale, Cheshire.
	c1915: Fowlers & Co. 53 New Bailey Street, Manchester.
History:	Established in 1898 (When Fowlers Calculators were set up) and best known for the publication of technical pocket books. The 1904 Mechanical Engineers Pocket Book shows a watch type calculator. Owned by Fowler. The Scientific Publishing Co. were the predecessors of Fowler & Co and were set up to make and sell Pocket-Watch slide rules starting with the Mechanical Engineer pocket-watch slide rule in its various manifestations and then via a limited range of other pocket-watch calculators which ultimately became Fowler calculators of various types. Calculators carrying the Scientific Publications Company name were available for a short time, from about 1907 to 1914. Scientific Publishing continued as a publisher for many years after, the slide rules being made by Fowlers afterward.
Made:	1898 – 1910: 1¾" Mechanical Engineer marked 'Scientific Publishing'
	1898 – 1910: 2" Mechanical Engineer
	1898 – 1910; 2½" Mechanical Engineer
	1898 – 1910: 2½" Mechanical Engineer – marked 'Price 6d. weekly'
	1898 – 1910: Mechanical Engineer – 'Swiss Made'
	1910 – 1914: Fowler's Patent Pocket Calculator (center button) (later Fowler Type 'O' with 2 crowns)
	1914 – Type 'O' Calculator, (2 crowns) (was Patent Pocket Calculator)
	1911 – Fowler's Textile Calculator (later Type 'T')
	1914– Type 'T' Textile calculator

POCKET-WATCH SLIDE RULES

Selectron (Switzerland)
Address: Selectron, see O&W.

History: This was a brand name of O&W, who made a slide rule watch as well as a stop-watch with slide rule, similar to other models from more expensive makers such as Breitling.

G. Small (USA) c1900 – 1920?
Address: Small & Co. Waltham. Mass.
G. Small, Boston, Mass..

History: SMALL circular calculator, beautifully made in cast aluminum, approx 2" dia with scales on edge and faces and an ingenious mechanism for allowing the two halves to work together.

Made: The SMALL Calculator. There are two models which are definitely small enough to fit into a vest pocket, but the physical layout is such that it could never be called a pocket-watch type, and therefore it is more likely classified as a vest pocket calculator.
1900: "Small" Pocket Calculator - as patented   2"U u M m C/D on edge only.
'Small' Pocket Calculator 2"U u M m C/D on edge,S,T,"//A,S1,T1,L.

W.F. Stanley & Co Ltd. (GB) 1853–1999
Address: W.F. Stanley & Co Ltd.
1853: 4 & 5, Great Turnstile, Holborn, London
1927: 286 High Holborn, London W.C.1.
Head Showrooms: 79–80 High Holborn, London WC1.

Also at:
13 Railway Approach, London SE1,
8 Hatton Gardens, London EC1, (from 1951 – Heath, Hicks & Perken)
52 Bothwell St, Glasgow.

1967: New Eltham, London SE9. (Head Office and Main Works).
Glasgow: 52 Bothwell St. C2.

Factory: 1951–1999: Head Office and Main Works: New Eltham. London. Possibly ex Heath Factory. Also later.

History: W.F. Stanley was born 1829, started the business in 1853. One of the oldest firms in the mathematical instrument making business, see C.J.A. Allen's History of Stanley, 1953. They made and sold a large variety of pocket-watch slide rules of the Boucher type for a number of years as described in the section devoted to them.

Made: Stanley–Boucher Type calculator with and without 'rev counter' in various materials and with a variety of scale materials as well
For example in the 1898 Catalogue 2 versions of Boucher are described:
- D553, Boucher's Pocket Calculator ... latest improvements ... and as ... my own make, but whether this means 'I made it' or 'made exclusively for me' we can only speculate.
- D553A, Stanley-Boucher Calculator ... gives also the number of revolutions of the log hand on center of dial.
Note that they also advertised the availability of Nickel Silver, Silver and Gold cases, no examples of which are known.

In the 1912 Catalogue various Boucher's calculators are described:
- K3622 – in Nickel at 12/6d
- K3623 – in Silver at £1.5.-
- K3624 – Stanley Boucher's in Nickel at 17/6d
- K3625 – Stanley Boucher's in Silver at £1.10.-

In the 1924 Catalogue only the one version of Boucher's calculator is described:
- M3622 - without the revolution counter. Note the change of identity number, the alpha character preceding the number identifies the catalogue, in this case an 'M' catalogue.

In the 1931 Catalogue there are two versions shown under 4 part numbers, these are:
- P3622, Boucher's Pocket Calculator,
- P3623, as 3622 but a presentation model in a silver case,

- P3630, Patent Stanley-Boucher Calculator, with the additional rev-counter scale,
- P3631, as 3630 but also a presentation model in a silver case.

In the 1958 Catalogue there are no Boucher calculators, however three Fowler types are offered, these are:
- A8931 Fowler's Universal calculator
- A8932 Fowler's 'Magnum' Long Scale calculator
- A8933, Fowler's Jubilee 'Magnum' Extra Long Scale calculator

Boucher Calc (Science Mus 160 1908-138)

J.H. Steward (GB) 1852 - 1919

Address: The Strand, London, England.
1861: 206 Strand W.C. London
1862 – 1865: 406 Strand W.C. London.
1866: 406 Strand W.C. & 54 Cornhill E.C. London
1867 – 1868: 67 & 406 Strand W.C., 54 Cornhill E.C. & 63 St. Paul's Churchyard E.C. London.
1869 – 1871: 66 & 406 Strand W.C., 54 Cornhill E.C. & 63 St. Paul's Churchyard E.C. London
1872 – 1873: 66 & 406 Strand W.C. & 54 Cornhill E.C. London
1874 – 1878: 66 & 406 Strand W.C. & 54 Cornhill & 63 St. Paul's Churchyard E.C. London.
1879 – 1880: 66, 406 & 456 Strand, 54 Cornhill &   63 St Paul's Churchyard E.C. London.
1881 – 1885: 66, 406 & 456 Strand W.C., & 54 Cornhill E.C. London.
1886 – 1888: 66, 406, 456 & 457 Strand W.C. London
1889 – 1892: 406 & 457 Strand W.C.2 & 54 Cornhill E.C. London
1893 – 1900: 406 & 457 Strand W.C. & 7 Gracechurch St. E.C. London.
1895: 406 & 408 Strand, London
1945: 406 Strand, London WC2.

History: Established 1852. Well known and respected slide rule maker, who specialized in sporting and military instruments. They appear to have made the 'RHS' spiral slide rule and some military rectilinear specialist slide rules, but it is not known whether they made or just retailed the 'Boucher' type Pocket-Watch calculator they advertised. It is more likely that they only sold rules they had bought in.

Made: 1878, Boucher calculator.
1910, Cajori mentions Steward selling a Boucher's calculator.

Sunrise (USSR) 1950?

Address: Leningrad, USSR.

History: The situation with Russian makers of pocket-watch calculators is somewhat confused to say the least. It is known that there were at least three retailers of two types. Another type by my definition does not classify as a pocket-watch slide rule, rather it is a very nice circular slide rule which has glass covered faces. It featured on the Internet some while ago.
Sunrise was based in Leningrad and made a small 2" diameter metal/plastic pocket-watch calculator in a Bakelite case, several examples of which have come out of Russia. It is a two sided device which has hands driven by separate winders. Some types are marked with KL-1, which may be a model number. This has a "circular arrows" logo. The third is I believe earlier and cruder and has no logo.

Made: KL-1; 2" diameter pocket-watch calculator

Technical Supply Company (USA) c1913

Address: Scranton PA USA.

History: Not known other than from a catalogue selling Boucher's calculator.

POCKET-WATCH SLIDE RULES

Sold: Their 1913 catalogue describes a Boucher calculator that is clearly marked 'Calculigraphe' on its face.

A.G. Thornton (GB) 1878 – 1995

Address: A.G. Thornton Ltd.,
1878: 39 Great Cheetham St, Manchester. In partnership with Halden.
1879: 109 Deansgate, Manchester. Enlarged 1890.
1895: South King Street, Manchester.
1897: 11 St. Marys Street, Manchester.
1904: Paragon Works, 2 King St. West, Manchester.
Main office and warehouse, destroyed by fire in WWII.
1949: Langley Lane, Northenden.
A new purpose built factory, except slide rules made at Derby St. Openshaw.
2005 to date: British Thornton ESF Ltd., Factory in Keighley, Yorkshire, England[43]

History: Originally set up in 1878 by Alexander George Thornton, became a limited company in 1940, and became British Thornton in 1967. Thornton was originally in partnership with Joseph Halden, though this only lasted from 1878 to 1880. Started to manufacture slide rules after 1900. 1902, patented a new design of slide rule, presumably after already making them. Final slide rules manufactured c1975, and the company name finally changed to Education and Science Furniture in 1992. Closed in 1995, renamed as ESF, and then re-opened with the British Thornton name and exist to date. Advertised and sold both Calculex (from 1905?) and Boucher's Calculating Circle, no named examples known.

Factories:
>1880: Workshop at John Dalton Street, Manchester.
1897: Workshop at Bridge Street, Manchester.
1907: Minerva Works, Sydney Street, Salford, Manchester.
1912: Cross Street, off Lloyd St, Hulme.
1920s: 41 King Street West, Manchester.
2005: Keithley, Yorkshire England

Sold: Their 1916 catalogue includes a section on Pocket Calculators watch type
D6927: Mechanical Engineer with two dials and single winder. 7/6d.
D6927½: Boucher (Calculigraphe) card dials. 12/6d
D6927¾: Boucher (Calculigraphe) metal dials. 15/-
D8622: Fowler's Patent Calculator.

US Blueprint (USA) Not known

Address: Not known.

History: In all probability US Blueprint, New York; and Chicago Blueprint and American Blueprint can be assumed to be related in some way, with virtually identical catalogues.

Sold: 1916 New York Blueprint lists 'Improved' Calculex 2¼" diameter by ¼" thick, as well as Charpentier and Boucher calculators.
1939 US Blueprint selling slide rules from a number of manufacturers including Halden slide rules

Waddington (GB) Not known

Address: W. Waddington,
Coventry, England.
also:
R. Waddington
Coventry, England.

History: The Waddington family of Coventry were well known watch makers but can not be dated, William and Richard are known, both on Lord's calculators.

---

[43] www.british-thornton.co.uk/about.htm

MAKERS & RETAILERS OF POCKET-WATCH RULES - ALPHABETICAL

Made: 2.75" dia Lord's Calculator with D/C/B/A; A is a strange scale, 2 knobs, no cursors (R. Waddington)
2.75" dia Lord's Calculator with D/C/B/A; A is a strange scale, 2 knobs, no cursors (W. Waddington)

Watts (GB) 1887 – 1927 +

Address: Messrs E.R. Watts & Son,
123 Camberwell Rd, London SE5.
1927: 104 Victoria Street, Westminster, London, England. Works at Camberwell.

History: Established 1887 (according to their 1927 catalogue at which point they were not selling slide rules). Makers of surveying and other precision instruments.

Made: Boucher's Calculating Circle

F. Weber Co. Inc (USA) 1851 - 1870

Address: 1931: F. Weber Company (currently Weber Art)
Philadelphia, Pennsylvania
Also Baltimore.

History: Weber were a well known company founded in 1953 and becoming F. Weber & Company in 1887 selling artist and drawing materials as well as a wide range of their own and other makers slide rules, including the Calculex.

Sold: 1931: 4294, Calculex T1, $7.50

J.H. Weil & Co. Inc. (USA) Unknown

Address: c1930: J.H. Weil & Co
Philadelphia, Pennsylvania

History: known as 'Weilco' and c1930 published their 10th catalogue covering surveying instruments, drawing and blue-print materials, artists and stationary materials

Sold: No 1167: Boucher's calculator (Calculigraphe illustrated) for $10
No 1172: Halden's Calculex (T2) for $7.50

A. West & Partners (GB) 1888 - 1950

Address: 36 Broadway, Westminster, London. SW1 England

History: Established 1888 (1930 catalogue) and still existed in 1953, history not known..

Made: 1930: Calculex, nickel and silver versions, both with glass and Perspex cursors.
1930: Desk Calculex
1930: Fowler Long Scale (double sided) and Magnum calculators.
1953: Mod 2620 Calculex Type 3
1953: Boucher's Calculating Circle

Gebr. Wichman (Germany) 1873 to date

Address: Gebr. Wichmann mbH,
c1900/10, Karl-Strasse 13, Berlin NW.6, Germany.
c1938, Karl-Strasse 13-14, and
Marienstraße 19-20, Berlin NW. 7, Germany.

History: Established 1873, sold other manufacturers rules, though they may also have made their own simple slide rules. In 1970 in the USA they were selling their own as well as Halden, and Schacht U. Westerich and other slide rules as well. It has been strongly asserted that Wichmann never made any slide rules, whether this is true of standard rectilinear and normal circular rules is a separate argument. It is certainly true that they only sold other manufacturers pocket-watch calculators. Around 1910 Halden's Calculex featured in their catalogue, and immediately prior to World War II they sold the Schacht u. Westerich calculator.

Made:	1910 Catalogue: No 1399, Halden's Calculex
c1938 Catalogue: No 1400, pocket-watch type
Sold Calculex – see the Calculex section
Sold Schacht u. Westerich calculator

Edward Wilson (GB) c1900

Address:	Exeter, Devon, England
History:	Not known.
Made:	June 1903 - Produced the original patent for what was sold for many years after as the Halden Calculex.
An example that follows the patent carrying Edward Wilson's name is known, it is not known who made it.

W. Wilson (GB) 1920?

Address:	1 Belmont St., London. S.W (though another record shows this address as London NW)
History:	Not known whether the above address is relevant to the maker of Lord's calculators, and it is not known if there was any relation to Edward Wilson, above, but this seems doubtful.
Made:	Made / sold a 2" dia. version of Lord's calculator (Types 2, 3 and 4) with A/B/C//L,A,deg scales on one side, and A/B=C/D on the other. 3 knobs and 2 cursors.
Also a Type 2 version single sided with A/B=C/D scales and 3 knobs.
Lord's Calculator (Science Mus 506 1960-25)

Zénith (Switzerland) c1918

Address:	Switzerland.
History:	Not known, but see Fabriques des Montres. Zenith were makers of a pocket chronograph, sold by W. Watts and others.
Made:	Patent for pocket-watch calculator

Unknown Makers / Retailers / Devices

1. Unknown Calculigraphe-like device - 2⅛" diameter double sided calculator with Calculigraphe like scales but a side winder rather than clutch.
2. Unknown maker of a Type 2 Lords calculator, examples in nickel plate and silver are known.
3. Type 1 Calculigraphe – described in an 1880 instruction leaflet in French.
4. Type 2 Calculigraphe, a desk model – described in an 1880 instruction leaflet in French.
5. Single scale FC Calculigraphe.
6. Calculigraphe pour la Bourse.
7. Desk model of a Mechanical Engineer, listed in a Halden's 1902 catalogue.
8. Keuffel & Esser Model 4023 ; listed in a K&E 1903 catalogue.
9. Rechen-Max Halden look-alike, unknown maker.
10. Calculator, unknown function, unknown maker, unknown date.

APPENDIX 1

Appendix 1 – Calculating with Pocket-Watch Type Slide Rules

Instructions for the Calculigraphe

For those who have used either rectilinear or circular slide rules, the translation into 'pocket-watch' is neither difficult nor time consuming, particularly if you are looking at a Lord's calculator with its movable scales like a slide and stock. On the other hand for a pocket-watch slide rule that has movable hands and pointers it is a bit more difficult, and to enable you to see how to calculate with such an example, and to understand what your fore-bears had to contend, with the following is an OCR of pages 29 and 30, i.e. the relevant Appendix from *Slide Rules and How to Use Them* by Thos. Jackson, [7] published in about 1900. It contains all the idiosyncratic spelling and punctuation; I have only made one correction in the seventh line where 'match' has been corrected to 'watch'. See how you get on with it. There then follows a translation from the Russian instructions for a KL-1, and finally a translation from the French instructions for the A-F Calculigraphe.

APPENDIX.

THE "BOUCHER" WATCH-FORM CALCULATOR, OR "CALCULIGRAPHE

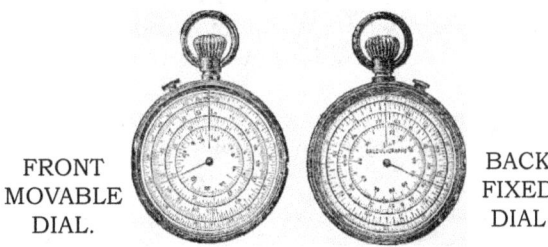

FRONT MOVABLE DIAL.   BACK FIXED DIAL

FIG. 16.

This elegant little instrument is, of course, logarithmic in principle, and if, for convenience, we regard it as almost equivalent to a 12½–cm. (or 5–inch) Slide Rule reduced to circular form, then the explanations already given for the Slide Rule (see pages 4 to 18), together with some additional remarks as to the manipulation of the mechanism, etc., should make the manner of using it both simple and clear.

The front dial (Fig 16) is capable of being rotated, in either direction, by turning the milled knob, precisely as when winding or adjusting a keyless watch ; the back dial is a fixture. There is a pointer-needle, or " hand," to each dial ; these correspond to the cursor of the Slide Rule and are rotated (simultaneously) by first pressing down the " stop button " and then turning the key-knob, or " winding."* At the front of the Calculator, fixed to its metal casing and lying close to the movable dial, is a short pointer or needle which we may call the " index line."

Of the four divided circles on the front (or movable) dial the two smaller ones together form the " roots " scale ; the next one is the " calculating circle," and the outer circle is the sine scale, corresponding to scale S of the Slide Rule. The three inner circles of the back (or fixed) dial constitute the " cube roots " scale, and the fourth or largest circle is the " log scale." All values are read by reference to the " calculating circle." using the rotative " hands " as projectors. Thus, if we set the " hand " to 4000 on the " calculating circle, " on the sine scale we have the angle in degrees (=23° 35')

* It should be carefully noted that it is essential that the stop-button should be pressed well down, as otherwise the instrument is apt to suffer serious damage in the winding process.

29

of which ·4 is the sine ; also, on the smallest circle of the dial we read one set of the figures for the square root of 4000 (= 2000, for √4, √400, √0·04, etc.), and on the next circle we read the other set (= 632, for √0·04, √40,

POCKET-WATCH SLIDE RULES

√4000, etc.). Further, if before setting the " hand " to 4000 we had *taken care to see that the 1 of the calculating circle was exactly at the fixed* " index-line " (but not otherwise, of course), on turning the Calculator over we should find that the " hand " on the fixed dial would be indicating the logarithm of 4 (= ·602) on the largest circle, and that the readings under the " hand " on the other three circles would be the three possible values of the cube root (as explained on pages 12 and 13), namely: —159 on the smallest circle (3√4 =1·59, 3√4000=15·9) ; 342 on the next circle (for cube root of 40 or of 0·04) ; and 736 on the third scale (for cube root of 400, or of 0·4, etc.).

When *multiplying*, say in solving a x b=x, as the " calculating circle " consists of one scale only, we need to make use of the fixed " index line " and the " hand " to mark off a portion of its circumference corresponding to log. a ; then we add to this a portion corresponding to log. b by suitably revolving the dial, and thus obtain x under the " index line " for the " sum of the logs " reading, or product of a x b. For example, say a = 1·5 and b = 3 ; bring 15 under the " index line " and set the " hand " to 1 ; then bring 3 under the " hand " and read the answer (= 4·5) under the "index line."

In *dividing*, as in solving a ÷ b = x, it is important to notice that we still commence by setting a under the " index line " ; instead, however, of setting the " hand " to 1 and bringing b under the " hand " (as in multiplication) we do *exactly the reverse, i.e.,* set the hand to b (the divisor), then bring 1 under the hand, and read the result, x, under the index line.

The solving of such expressions as $\frac{12 \times 14 \times 2\cdot2}{4\cdot2 \times 20}$ = x, by alternately multiplying and dividing, is a very simple matter if we note that each separate operation leaves the result up to that stage *under the " index line " ready for further treatment* ; thus, when we have multiplied 12 by 14 the product is at the " index line " ready to be divided by 4·2, so we may proceed by setting the " hand " to the divisor (4·2) and bringing 1 under the " hand " ; the result to date is then at the " index line," ready either to be divided by 20 or multiplied by 2·2. The " hand " is also ready set at 1 (after the operation of division) so if we take the multiplying first we have nothing to do but to bring 2·2 under the " hand," and the product, to date, will be under the " index line " ready for the final operation of dividing by 20.

30

Instructions for Russian Pocket-Watch Slide Rules

A more up-to-date set of instructions-for-use for a pocket-watch slide rule is the following translation for the Russian KL-1 series. The main items in the diagrams are numbered as follows:
- 1 – is a thick jet-black painted circumferential band of metal
- 2 & 3 – are the two stem winders which go through this band – the one moving the scale is numbered 2, is black tipped, the one numbered 3 is red tipped and moves the pointers simultaneously
- 5 – is the short 5mm fixed cursor line directly under the black stem winder
- 8 – are the two red 'hands' and the central pivot points

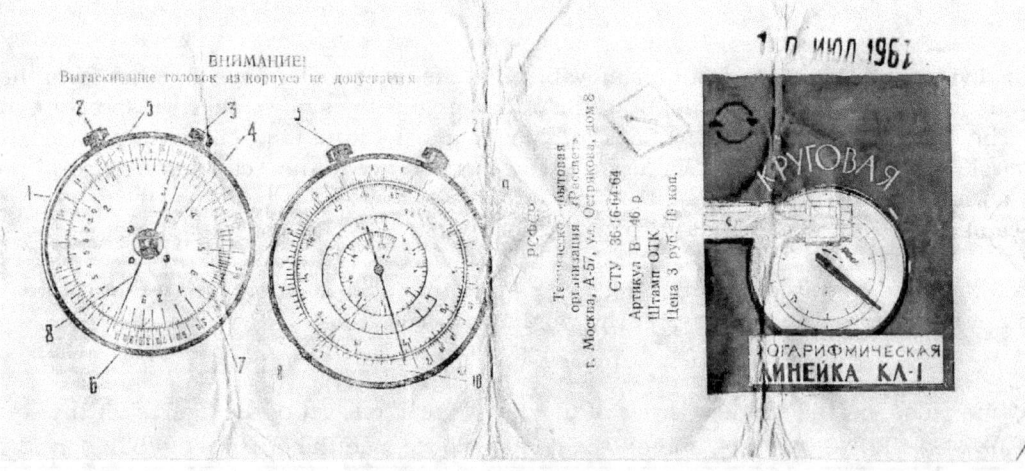

APPENDIX 1

This SLIDE RULE (model KL-1) is approximately 2″ in diameter. It is intended for performance of trigonometric and mathematical operations, such as:

1. Multiplication
2. Division
3. Squaring
4. Extraction of a square root
5. Finding of trigonometric functions of a sine
6. Finding of trigonometric functions of a tangent
7. Finding inverse trigonometric functions (of sines and tangents)
8. Calculation of the area of a circle.

The slide rule consists of chrome metal housing with two knobs, 2 dials (one of which revolves with the aid of the black knob), 2 pointers (which revolve in unison with the aid of the red knob), and a fixed indicator. The fixed indicator is on side 2, directly aligned with the black knob.

There are 3 scales on the fixed dial on side 1: The outer scale- for basic calculating. It is the inverse of the inner moveable scale on side 1 (equivalent to a DI scale); the middle scale S - for calculating the sines of angles; the inner scale T- for calculating the tangents of angles.

There are 2 scales on the moveable dial on side 2: The outer scale - the scale of the squares (equivalent to an A scale); the inner scale -for basic calculating (equivalent to a C scale).

Mathematical calculations on the KL-1 slide rule are performed as follows:

MULTIPLICATION (using the moveable internal scale, fixed indicator, and moveable pointer on side 2). Rotate the black knob (2) to position the index (of the inner moveable scale) under the fixed indicator (5). Rotate the red knob (3) to position the moveable pointer over the first cofactor (on the inner moveable scale). Rotate the black knob to position the second cofactor (on the inner moveable scale) under the fixed indicator. Read the product under the moveable pointer (on the inner moveable scale).

DIVISION (using the moveable inner scale, fixed indicator, and moveable pointer on side 2). Rotate the black knob to position the dividend (on the inner moveable scale) under the fixed indicator. Rotate the red knob to position the moveable pointer over the divisor/denominator (on the inner moveable scale). Rotate the black knob to position the index (on the inner moveable scale) under the moveable pointer. Read the quotient under the fixed indicator (on the inner moveable scale).

SQUARING (using both the inner and outer moveable scales, the fixed indicator, and the moveable pointer on side 2). Rotate the black knob to position the root number (on the inner moveable scale) under the fixed indicator. Under the same indicator, read the square of the root number on the external moveable scale.

THE EXTRACTION OF SQUARE ROOT (using the inner and outer moveable scales, the fixed indicator, and the moveable pointer on side 2). Rotate the black knob to position the radicand (the squared number) (on the external moveable scale) under the fixed indicator. Under the same fixed indicator, read the square root of the radicand on the internal moveable scale.

POCKET-WATCH SLIDE RULES

FINDING TRIGONOMETRIC FUNCTIONS OF ANGLE (using the fixed scales and the moveable pointer on side 1). Rotate the red knob to position the pointer over the angle in question. Use the inner spiral 'T' scale for tangents or the middle 'S' scale for sines. Under the same pointer, read the function of the angle on the fixed outer scale.

FINDING INVERSE TRIGONOMETRY FUNCTIONS (using the fixed scales and the moveable pointer on side 1). Rotate the red knob to position the pointer over the value of the trig function (on the outer fixed scale. Under the same pointer, read the angle (on the T or S scale) corresponding to the function.

CALCULATION OF THE AREA OF CIRCLE (using the inner and outer moveable scales, moveable pointer, and fixed indicator on side 2). Rotate the black knob to position the "C" on the inner moveable scale under the fixed pointer. Rotate the red knob to position the moveable pointer over the diameter (on the inner moveable scale) of the circle in question. Rotate the black knob to position the index of the outer moveable dial under the fixed indicator. Under the moveable pointer, read the area of the circle on the outer moveable scale.

Calculigraphe A-F Summarized Instructions
Translated from the French leaflet by Pedos

Instructions Summarized for the use of the Calculigraphe A.F.

Multiplication: To Multiply 2.4 by 3, = 7.2
Place the '1'on **D** against 2.4 on **C**, place the pointer on 3 of **D** and read the product 7.2 against the pointer on **C**.

Division: To Divide 8.4 by 1.5, = 5.6
Place the pointer upon 8.4 on **C**, bring 1.5 on **D** under the pointer, place the pointer to 1 on D, and read the quotient 5.6 indicated by the pointer on **C**.

Inverse Proportion: To transform 1/25 into a decimal fraction, 1/25 = 0.04 Place the pointer to 25 on **B** and read 0.04 under the pointer on **C**.

Fractions: To transform the fraction 3/25 into a decimal fraction. Place the pointer to 25 on **B**; bring the 1 on of **D** under the pointer, place the pointer to 3 on **D** and read the result 0.12 under the pointer on **C**.

Squares: To square 3, 3^2 = 9
Place the pointer on 3 on **E, F**, and read the square 9 on **D**.

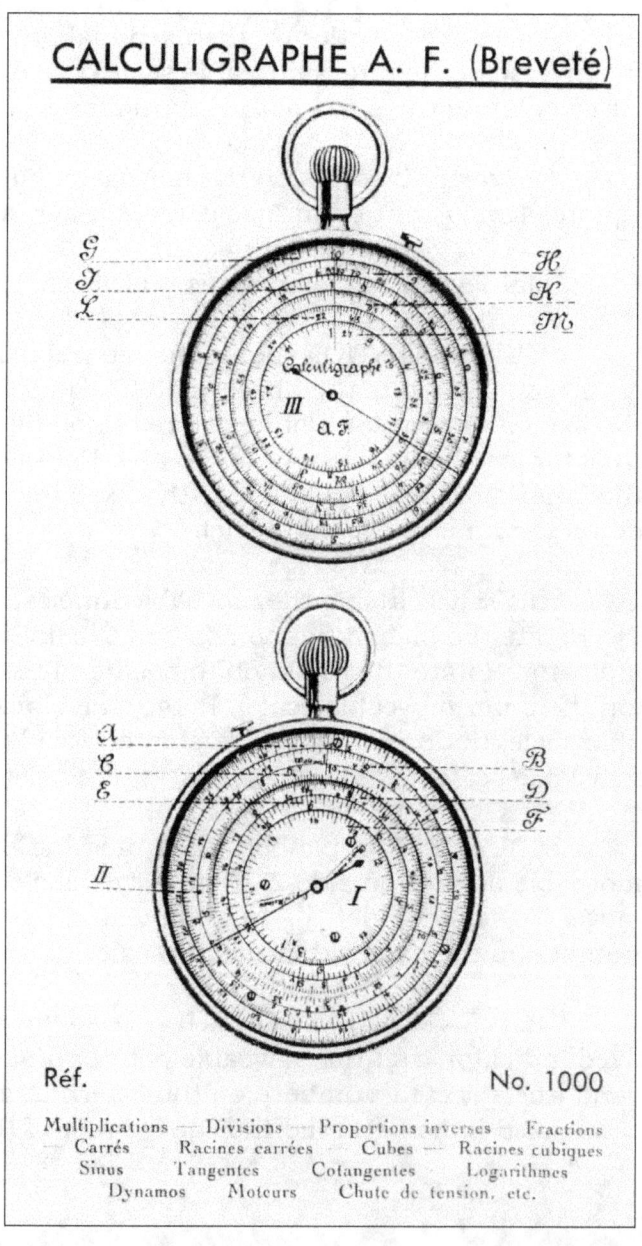

APPENDIX 1

Square Roots: Examples:
$$\sqrt{9} = 3; \quad \sqrt{49} = 7; \quad \sqrt{0.16} = 0.4; \quad \sqrt{0.09} = 0.3;$$
Place the pointer to the number whose root you wish to extract on **D** and read the root on **E, F**. If the number which we want to extract the root of is greater than 1, divide the number into segments of two digits from the decimal point, from right to left. If the last segment left two figures we read the result on **E**, if there is no figure, read the result on **F**.
If the number is smaller than 1, divide it into segments of 2 digits after the decimal point, but going from left to right. If the first segment of significant figures that we encounter has two figures read the root on **E**, if there is one figure the answer is on **F**.

Cube Roots: Examples
$$\sqrt[3]{8} = 2; \quad \sqrt[3]{27} = 3; \quad \sqrt[3]{125} = 5; \quad \sqrt[3]{0.08} = 0.2; \quad \sqrt[3]{0.027} = 0.3; \quad \sqrt[3]{0.125} = 0.05;$$
Place the pointer to the number whose root you wish to extract on **J** and read the roots on **K, L, M**. For numbers much greater than or much smaller than 1, proceed as for square roots except one divides the numbers in segments of 3 digits. If the section considered has one digit, read the root on **M**, if it has two digits, read the root on **L**, and if it has 3 digits read the root on **K**.

Sines: To find the value of Sine 32°.
Place the pointer on 32 on **II** and read the result 0.53 on **J**.

Tangents: For angles between 6° and 45°, tan 7°20' = 0.1286.
Place the pointer on 7°20' on **A** and read the result 0.1286 on **C**.

Cotangents: For angles between 6° and 45°, cotan 7°20' = 7.776.
Place the pointer on 7°20' on **A** and read the result 7.776 on **B**.

Logarithms: The logarithm of 1.35 = 0.1303
Place the pointer on 1.35 on **J** and read the result 0.1303 on **G**.

Voltage drop: To find the volt-drop in a line where the section is 70 mm², the current is 60 amperes and the distance between 2 stations is 80 meters.
Place the pointer on 60 on **C**, bring 70 on **D** under the pointer, place the pointer on 80 on **D**, bring the 1 on **D** under the pointer, place the pointer on the radial mark "**Ch. De Tension**" and read the result 2.38 on **C**.

Translation from the French "Pedos" instruction sheet – June 2010

Appendix 2 – Identifying Pocket-Watch Slide Rule Makers

One of my possibly more stupid ideas came as a result of trying to find some distinguishing feature that would allow us to differentiate between different makers of the same pocket-watch slide rule, initially between the various known and unknown makers of Type 2 and Type 3 Lords'. The simple idea was to measure the angle between the side-winders or clutch and the main key. This followed on from the opinion that any manufacturer who had set up a production line to make a particular calculator, inherent in which were the drawings, jigs and/or any other fitments that would be used to drill the holes in the watch case, and also in any armature inside the case, that were needed to fit the side winders or clutches, would need a very good reason to change the angle that the designers had chosen. Changing this angle would involve expense in re-drawing and re-tooling, and therefore would not be a popular exercise. Hence the angle might be a constant for each maker – why change something that was not broken?

Extending this idea to its logical conclusion and measuring the angles of both winders and clutches on all non-Fowler pocket-watch calculators produced a surprising result! See the table on the following page.

The perhaps surprising result was that no two calculators – other than those that truly did have the same parentage and were made in the same time frame – had the same angle from the vertical on their winders and clutches!

If we look at this in more detail, we can see a number of case were we can draw or confirm conclusions:

- Early Boucher calculators and those with the Manlove, Alliott & Fryer appellation have the same angle to their winders, and when the rest of the calculator is considered, it can be seen that they were made at the same time and most probably by the same maker..
- HC Calculigraphes as well as Fisher examples are pretty likely to have the same maker as they have the same angle to their clutch buttons. Incidentally, it makes perfect sense that the clutch button is nearly vertical for ease of operation; a winder at the same angle could be awkward (see Lords Type 4.) Queen are different.
- FC Calculigraphes, on the other hand have a different angle to their HC brethren, even though they carry identical scales. This must be taken slightly on-trust, as the number of FC Calculigraphes which have been measured is very limited.
- The difference in angle between Mechanical Engineer calculators and the later SP Types illustrates that they were a different design, albeit both from Scientific Publishing. The ME used a pocket-watch case; the later designs used the cast or sintered aluminum alloy case.
- That HC and AF Calculigraphes use the same angle despite being obviously by different makers (or are they?) and is perhaps the exception that proves the rule.
- The 'Unknown' maker of the Calculigraphe Type calculator with a winder rather than a clutch is not immediately obvious as one of the makers of either Boucher (e.g. Stanley) or indeed Calculigraphe, but is different to both.

There is a caveat to all this. The majority of measurements have been taken from images of the calculators, if the image is not exactly flat and centered on the axle of the device, and then there is a certain amount of parallax which can make the angle of the winder/clutch appear slightly different.

Does this make a foolproof method of identifying a maker of these devices? Yes, I think so, until proved otherwise!

APPENDIX 2

Pocket-Watch Slide Rules
Winder & Clutch, Angles from the Vertical for Various Makes

Maker	Calculator	Winder	Clutch	Notes
Boucher	Very early	40°		
	Early	60°		
	Manlove, Alliott & Fryer	60°		As early Boucher
	Manloves	65°		As Stanley's Boucher?
Stanley	Boucher	65°		
	Stanley Boucher	70°		
Dyson	Dyson	85°		Maybe made by SP?
Casartelli	Lords T1	30°		
Elliott	Lords T1	30°		
R&W Waddington	Lords T1	30°		
Unknown 1	Lords T2	35° & 75°		
Unknown 2	Lords T2	35° & 70°		
W. Wilson	Lords T2	35° & 70°		
W. Wilson	Lords T3	35° & 70°		Double sided calc.
W. Wilson	Lords T4	±25°		One winder each side
Scientific Publishing	Mech Eng	75°		All sizes. Early design
Scientific Publishing	Single Scale ME	75°		
Scientific Publishing	Type O	45°		Later
Scientific Publishing	Type T	45°		Later
Scientific Publishing	Type M	45°		Later
Schacht u.Westerich	Pocket Calc	50°		
Meyrat & Perdrizet	Type 1	±35°		One winder each side
Meyrat & Perdrizet	Type 2	35°		Only one winder
Molter	Pocket-Watch	55°		Various examples
HC	Calculigraphe		30°	(thin & fat)
FC	Calculigraphe		25°	(thin?)
AF	Calculigraphe		30°	
Queen	(Boucher)		27°	Calculigraphe
L. Fischer	Calculigraphe (thin)		30°	Says HC on it.
K&E	Early Sperry		±25°	Two clutches
'Unknown'	Calculigraphe Type	55°		

Bibliography

[1] *Slide Rules, their History Models and Makers.* Peter Hopp: Astragal Press 1999

[2] *Patent Applied For – A Century of Fantastic Inventions.* Coppersmith, Fred, Lynx J.J.: Co-ordination Press, 1949. Pages 14 and 17 deal with this particular device

[3] *A History of the Logarithmic Slide Rule and associated instruments.* Cajori, Florian: Astragal Press reprint, 1994

[4] *The Use and Working of the Watch Calculator and the Slide Rule.* Anon.
Scientific Publishing. 1st edn. c1900?
The Preface states: '…or Watch Form of Calculator, which was introduced by the proprietors of the *'Mechanical Engineer'* a few years ago …'
Chapter 1 paragraph three states 'The instrument made by the proprietors of *'The Mechanical Engineer'* is shown in Figure 1, Plate 1, full size". (Plate 1 shows two sizes of ME with 1¾" and 2½" dials). The advert is very similar to Figure 9.4 in here.

An undated Second Edition has a different advert and Figure 1, where only the 2" dial is mentioned in the text and shown in Figure 1 of Plate 1. The advert is very similar to Figure 9.5 in here.

[5] *The Slide Rule*; C.N. Pickworth; Various editions, especially edition 6, 1900.
This has an advert for SPC with the same ME diagram as [4], priced at 7/9d. or 12/9d. for 2½" dial. See also Figure 9.4 in here.

[6] *Newnes Slide Rule Manual*; F.J. Camm; Various editions, from 1, 1944 to 6, 1963. Published by George Newnes Limited, London. This carries a description of how to use a Calculex and Fowler Calculator, various pagination.

[7] *Slide Rules and How to Use Them* by Thos. Jackson, Chapman & Hall, Limited, London; published in about 1900.

[8] *Calculating Machines and Instruments: Catalogue of the Collections in the Science Museum* by D. Baxendahll & Jane Pugh, Science Museum; London 1975.

Late Additions

Manlove Alliott & Co Limited

A recently seen Boucher's calculator carrying the label of Manlove & Alliott & Co Limited allows us to more accurately date this as being before the formation of Manlove Alliott & Fryer Limited in 1886. The style follows that of the Manlove Alliott & Fryer example (Figure 1b) including size, the scales and font. However the name and other labelling is more akin to that of the Manloves example (Figure 1a) being circular in format. It does not seem to carry an 'AB' signature, but it does have the large axle that seems to be a feature of the early Boucher devices. Interestingly and surprisingly, the second winder looks to be perpendicular to the crown, this 90° angle being unique to this design and not the same as the earlier and later ones which mirror their closest relation, Manlove Alliott &Fryer after the Boucher itself,and Manloves like the Stanley Boucher.

Figure 1a: Manloves

Figure 1b: Manlove Alliott & Fryer

NOTES

www.ingramcontent.com/pod-product-compliance
Lightning Source LLC
Chambersburg PA
CBHW081721100526
44591CB00016B/2453